FAMOUS

THE
WORLD FORGOT

Also by Jason Lucky Morrow

The DC Dead Girls Club:
A Vintage True Crime Story of Four Unsolved Murders in Washington
D.C.

Deadly Hero:
The High Society Murder that Created Hysteria in the Heartland
(Coming Soon)

FAMOUS CRIMES
THE
WORLD FORGOT

Ten Vintage True Crime Stories
Rescued from Obscurity

JASON LUCKY MORROW

Historical Crime Detective Books
Tulsa, 2014

Published by: Historical Crime Detective Books, Tulsa, OK
Editor: Gloria F Boyer, gfboyer.com
Additional Editing: Judith and Clint Richmond
Cover Design: Jason Morrow

ISBN-13: 978-0692352427
ISBN-10: 0692352422
First Edition, 2014
10 9 8 7 6 5 4 3 2 1
.

for Alina, the love of my life

Additional photos related to the cases presented in this book
can be found at:
http://www.HistoricalCrimeDetective.com/forgotten/

Contents

A Special Note on Historical Accuracy

As a former journalist, my style of writing is to make the story entertaining, but to also stick to the facts. I go where the research leads me and in the end, the story is the story. All of the dialogue, quotes, and events in this book are how they appeared in the original source material. To help make the characters come to life, I relied on clues and statements within the research material to guide me with how I portrayed their body language, facial expressions, mannerisms, gestures, and voice inflections. These character traits are used to enhance the scene and set the mood without altering the facts.

The stories in this book were assembled together like a jigsaw puzzle from more than 400 newspapers, magazines, books, maps, census reports, and other resources. In any work of nonfiction, it is inevitable that some facts will be incorrect. In the rush to meet deadlines, newspaper reporters often got primary and secondary facts wrong. Readers who explore these cases on their own may find newspaper accounts with conflicting information. This is not uncommon, especially when it comes to dates, the spelling of names, and other minor details. When confronted with those issues, I did my best to verify the information I have included for accuracy.

Introduction

ALTHOUGH MANY ESSAYS have been written that attempt to analyze the true crime genre, the contribution that newspapers have made to the field often goes unexplained.

During the latter half of the 1800s, three important variables came together that increased the public's fascination with crimes stories: improved methods of manufacturing paper, cheaper printing presses, and compulsory public education which led to higher literacy rates. When these items were in place, newspapers across the country multiplied. By the turn of the century, the market had become over saturated.

Born from this glut was a fierce competition for survival in which circulation wars broke out between rival newspapers. To gain the most readers, editors needed to provide them with content that would drive sales. Invariably, lurid stories of murder and other crimes accomplished that goal by appealing to a universal fascination with the dark side of the human mind.

To win the war, daily battles were fought and won by getting to a story first and scooping the competition. Editors could no longer sit back and wait for stories to come to them; reporters had to be sent into the field to sniff them out. One such war, between New York City publishers William Randolph Hearst and Joseph Pulitzer, led to the creation of tabloid journalism. This produced a new breed of writers and editors who introduced aggressive tactics in both the gathering, and presentation of news, with a special emphasis on crime. These men were smart enough to understand that once readers became invested in a particular case from its inception, they were committed to following the story to the very end. This produced a naturally occurring serialization, of sorts, that left readers with a drive to learn, *what happens next?*

By the early Twentieth Century, news agencies like Associated Press and United Press were able to flourish on the back of an emerging new technology that produced telex machines capable of transmitting entire stories over telegraph wires. This eventually included photographs by the 1920s, with improved and more efficient methods by 1934. With market demand for scandal driven murders, police shootouts, brazen robberies, and melodramatic court cases thoroughly established, crime stories were able to breakout of their immediate geographic area and spread nationally. Several notable examples from this time period include the cases of Harry Thaw, Sacco and Vanzetti, Leopold and Loeb, Ruth Snyder and Judd Gray, and the Lindbergh kidnapping.

But these cases, as well as those of noted gangsters and depression-era bank robbers, are the ones that history remembers most. As I state on my blog, HistoricalCrimeDetective.com, they are the crime stories that have been told by movie and television producers, magazines, and book publishers, "*ad infinitum* to *ad nauseam.*"

My purpose for writing this book was to salvage obscure true crime stories and repackage them in an entertaining fashion to appeal to a wide audience that shares my appreciation for their educational and historical value. I wanted to go beyond the same, tired old stories and discover 'new' old stories. Although a long line of researchers and authors better than me have also taken on this same mission, I wanted to embark on my own explorations and make a humble contribution to the true crime genre.

The selection process for the ten stories in this book had to meet a simple criterion—that they were once very famous crimes, nationally publicized, that have not been adequately explored or written about in decades. Additionally, I wanted this book to feature a cross-section of cases that covered different locations, time periods, and types of killers.

From there, the decisions of which stories to include were completely arbitrary. I relied on my "reporter's instinct," to tell me if a certain case was worthy of further examination. Because of that, I make no assertion that the stories presented here are the *most* famous and forgotten, or that these ten are *better* than any others.

As enjoyable as it was to dig into these cases and write about them, I look forward to exploring more famous crimes the world forgot and presenting them in future volumes. Thank you for purchasing this book and I sincerely hope you enjoy it.

If you did enjoy this book, I would be grateful if you could post a short review on Amazon and/or GoodReads.com. Your support really does make a difference. As an independent researcher and writer, reviews and word of mouth to family and friends are my only sources of advertising. By telling others, these stories can reach more people who find them just as fascinating as you do.

Chapter One: Denver's "Capitol Hill Thug," 1900-1901

"Silent, stealthy, mysterious, the Thing goes out into the night and back again to its lair, like a beast of the jungle that prowls and preys by night, and, gorged and hidden, bears naught and cares naught for the hue and cry by day. The terror of the invisible, the tragic, baffling secrecy of a scourge, are about the Thing, and it is the diabolical master and the deadly hunter of the hill. . . . It is a mystery of mysteries." – *The Boston Globe*, February 24, 1901.

IN THE WINTER of 1900, Denver police had a big problem and local newspapers had big headlines. Women walking alone in the Capitol Hill area were getting their heads bashed in with a wooden club or iron pipe by a "deranged fiend." By Christmas, five women had been attacked and one of them was dead. Unlike the common footpads that stalked the poorly lit streets, the head-basher never robbed any of the women or sexually assaulted them. Instead, his singular motive didn't make sense to police: to hunt down women walking alone after dark and crack open their skulls.

Newspapers christened the woman-hating attacker with several monikers, from the most popular—"The Capitol Hill Thug," and "The Capitol Hill Slugger," as well as "The Sandbagger,"—to the least popular but more ominous "The Thing." More than one newspaper reporter would remind his readers of the "Jack the Ripper" slayings not too long ago in faraway London. It was a good comparison, but these women were not prostitutes. They were normal women going about the daily business of living. Many of them were just trying to get home after attending church services. In every documented case, a dark shadow crept up behind the victim as she walked in the late evening hours and laid her out with one or two blows. Then he just disappeared.

At first, Denver police didn't even connect the crimes. It would take them a few months to realize they had a madman hunting women. Muggings were a common occurrence, but those were robberies. This was something else—something they didn't immediately understand.

According to the best-known facts of the day, the Capitol Hill Thug[1] made his debut on Friday, August 24, when he struck twice in one night. Just after eight o'clock, twenty-eight-year-old Elva Jessup was walking home from the corner of 16th Avenue and Pearl Street where she had attended synagogue services at Temple Emanuel. It was a short walk south to her home at 1421 Pearl, and her mind was on the service of Rabbi Friedman. She could have attended the following day but her husband Alvin had other plans. He was a successful insurance agent for the German-American Alliance Insurance Company.

Because she was looking toward the pavement ahead of her, Elva never saw the figure emerge like a phantom from a dark enclosure at 1545 Pearl, take two quick steps behind her, and swing his club with everything he had. The blow knocked her forward, sending her crashing into the sidewalk with a large gash on the back of her skull. Eventually she recovered, but she turned out to be the lucky one that night.

Lillian Bell, who also went by the name Lillian Martin, was less fortunate. Although described by newspapers as a "half-witted girl," she was no girl. She was forty-five years old. The Capitol Hill Thug found her alone around 11:00 p.m. in an alley

---

[1] The "Thuggee" or Thugs of India were an organized group of professional killers and highwaymen who were known to operate from the 13th century until about 1840 when they were eradicated. Stories of their deeds were popular at the turn of the century.

between 16th Avenue and Washington Street—a two-minute walk from where Elva Jessup went down. Lillian died from her injuries eleven days later without providing any information to police.

Exactly one month later, on September 24, Emma Carlson was walking home from church around eight o'clock in the evening when the Thug caught up with her at the intersection of 16th Avenue and Emerson Street. The twenty-three-year-old live-in maid for the Edward Seerie family heard something behind her, turned, and was struck on the forehead. Despite a blow that almost knocked her unconscious, Carlson was able to get a look at her assailant. She staggered to the door of a neighbor's house, rang the bell, and was let in, where she fell bleeding and disoriented in the foyer. Before she was taken to the hospital, Emma described her assailant as a small man with a very white complexion.

Although three victims in one month should have alerted authorities to a pattern, Denver at that time was experiencing an abnormally large number of women who were mugged by footpads and ruffians. A critical op-ed piece from the *Colorado Springs Gazette* declared that the problem was so bad, Denver women could "no longer dare complain to police." The editorial scorched the Denver Police Department, whom they claimed were more interested in rounding up drunks and indigents to cast votes favorable to the whims of the local Democratic Party.

"Last night's record [of muggings and burglaries] was but a fitting climax to the devilment that has run riot in Denver from the time the police department transferred from police duties to herding up dive keepers and inmates who will vote next November [1901] for carving out the wishes of the present state and city administration."

Even if the political charges were unwarranted, it was apparent that Denver had a street-crime problem during this period and a more proactive police initiative was needed. With the cover of darkness and a prevalence of similar crimes to shield him, the Capitol Hill Thug was able to operate without detection until the night of Friday, October 5, when he clobbered Annie McAtee near her home at 3130 Humboldt Street—twenty-three blocks north of his previous hunting grounds.

More than two weeks after the attack, one of Annie's brothers reported to the *Denver Post* that her condition was slowly improving. "Since she has been at her home, there has been a change for the better," George McAtee conveyed. "She does not yet remember the incidents on the evening she was struck down. There is but a dim recollection of having been hit, but nothing distinct to time and place, nor anything about her assailant."

As a target of the Thug's apparent hatred for women, twenty-six-year-old Annie was a bad choice. Her brother George was a successful Denver merchant who had the money and connections to make a lot of noise. She got more newspaper coverage than the other women, and the family offered a $200[2] reward for information that would lead to her attacker.

The McAtee family made such a fuss in the newspapers that it apparently sent the head-whacker underground for more than two months. For seventy-eight days the women of Denver went unmolested by the Thug—until he struck again three days before Christmas. This time, he found Mrs. Dewart E. Young near her home at 938 Corona Street. She was fortunate to survive despite a bad head injury that required medical treatment. Like McAtee and Jessup, she was caught off-guard and did not get a look at her attacker.

That Christmas, the people of Denver wished for an end to the assaults. But 1901 brought no relief, and it was going to get worse before it got better. The Thug returned to his grisly business on Sunday, January 6, by bashing forty-six-year-old Julia Dohr near 16th Avenue and Ogden Street. She was knocked down while walking to a house on Ogden where she

---

[2] The equivalent of about $5,500 in 2014.

was employed as a housekeeper. After she was hit, the Thug shoved her into a hole being dug for a new cellar.

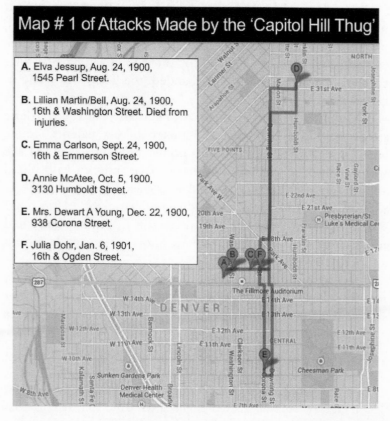

Map # 1 of Attacks Made by the 'Capitol Hill Thug'

A. Elva Jessup, Aug. 24, 1900, 1545 Pearl Street.

B. Lillian Martin/Bell, Aug. 24, 1900, 16th & Washington Street. Died from injuries.

C. Emma Carlson, Sept. 24, 1900, 16th & Emmerson Street.

D. Annie McAtee, Oct. 5, 1900, 3130 Humboldt Street.

E. Mrs. Dewart A Young, Dec. 22, 1900, 938 Corona Street.

F. Julia Dohr, Jan. 6, 1901, 16th & Ogden Street.

The assault on Dohr was the third attack to take place along 16th Avenue and the fourth within a tight cluster. The Annie McAtee slugging occurred nearly two miles to the north, and the Young attack was three miles to the south of the cluster. Examined together, the attacks ran in a north-to-south line along Downing Street. In spite of the pattern they formed, the locations also revealed that the Thug was being more careful. He was reading the newspapers and planning his hunting trips to strike where police least expected. He was also striking women when they least expected it. The first four women were hit between eight and eleven o'clock at night. For the last two,

Young and Dohr, the Thug changed his pattern by hitting them sometime after six o'clock.

After the Dohr attack, the good husbands of Denver had had enough. A vigilante crew was formed to patrol the streets, with some of the men dressed up as women. They were successful in deterring attacks for one month, but when their enthusiasm waned and they disbanded, the Thug was ready to strike again.

Around 7:15 on the night of February 16, young Marie Frazer stumbled back to the doorstep of her parents' home, where she collapsed. When her mother brought her inside she was horrified to find her daughter's "face smeared with blood and dirt and her clothes covered with weeds and splinters." As she drifted in and out of consciousness that night, Marie could only remember leaving the hairdresser at 6:30 p.m., but could recall nothing else. She didn't even know where she had been knocked down.

There might have been two victims that night if it weren't for the diligence one young woman took in observing her surroundings as she made her way home, a Denver correspondent reported:

> Probably the best description of the Capitol Hill Thug is given by Miss Everest, a pretty little girl of sixteen years. She is employed at a dressmaking establishment and last Saturday night [February 16] she started home after dark. She has to pass several dark streets and two of them have no houses. Here, she observed a man following her.
>
> She stopped to give him an opportunity to pass, but he stopped also. She walked fast but he walked faster and was gaining on her. She ran and he pursued her. She darted into the first house she came to and the man ran down an alley, doubtless thinking he would catch her as she came out the other side of the block. A couple of ladies took the frightened girl home.
>
> Monday morning she met the same man again and he looked at her and her sister who was with her closely. She saw him

distinctly. He was of medium height, with very light skin and a large drooping black mustache. His nose was quite prominent. His eyes were blue and wild. He wore a long gray Ulster and a crush hat.[3]

If this was the Capitol Hill Thug, instead of one of the many other ruffians lurking in the streets of Denver, his published description didn't necessarily need to concern him. Since the McAtee attack, Denver police had rounded up scores of suspects and held them without charge until satisfied of their innocence, or until another attack occurred. These arrests became something of a joke throughout Colorado since Police Captain Hamilton Armstrong, then chief of detectives, would often boldly proclaim they had got their man—and their man was always crazy.

In October, the Capitol Hill Thug was supposedly Joseph Shaklee, who was arrested in Greely, Colorado. No facts were given as to why he was arrested, but police suspected he was the Thug and told reporters, "Shaklee is mentally unbalanced." On November 22, Captain Armstrong was confident that David Pace was the "scoundrel who has been guilty of numerous attacks on women." However, when Armstrong was pressed for reasons or evidence on why Pace was their man, it was reported that "he will not give his reasons for his conviction, but he seems very sure of his ground."

On January 8, Armstrong was certain the slugger was a man named Maryuissen. A few days later, the Capitol Hill Thug was ruffian George Turner, who was caught in the act of trying to rob a woman. Like all the others, Turner was "undoubtedly crazy," declared the chief of detectives. In their desperation to make an arrest, Armstrong's madman theory slipped into the narrative of the investigation and chipped away at police credibility. But the police weren't the only ones to follow this line of thinking. After consulting with an expert, the *Denver Post*

---

[3] A type of hat that can be folded or collapsed.

declared the Thug "a pervert." How they came to that conclusion is unclear since no sexual violations had occurred.

After several more innocent men were arrested, proclaimed to be the Thug, described as lunatics, and later released, the *Aspen Tribune* offered their opinion. "The Denver police have again captured the thug of Capitol Hill. Every arrest they make they are dead sure he is the fellow they are looking for so many weary days. We do not wish to discourage them but we have a presentiment that this man [name not given] is not the one. He belongs to that great army of men who cannot tell where he was on a certain night and therefore falls under suspicion."

While the *Tribune* mocked police with sarcasm, they also ridiculed them with exaggeration. "It is not safe to walk the streets [of Denver] unless one has a bowie knife in one hand, a revolver in the other hand, and a Gatling gun pointed to the rear under each arm. Several times the police have declared that they have at great expense secured some valuable clues. The clues were all they ever secured. They have chased phantoms and pursued shadows and allowed the real criminal to escape with exasperating regularity."

So far, only Lillian Bell had died, but that changed on the hellish night of Friday, February 22, when the Capitol Hill Thug attacked three women in one hour. If Armstrong needed motivation to recalibrate his investigation, there was never going to be a better time than now. With three attacks in a short period, and all within a few blocks of each other, there was bound to be a witness. But when one came forward and told police what he saw, it was something they simply didn't want to hear—or accept. It was too outrageous to believe.

The first to go down that night was forty-year-old Mary Short, a black woman who was found in a vacant lot near 16th Avenue and Clarkson Street. She was unconscious when found and never recovered. She died from a skull fracture one day later.

Shortly after 8 p.m., Emma Johnson, 30, was walking home from the Swedish Methodist Church when she was waylaid near 19th Avenue and Pennsylvania Street. After she regained consciousness, she staggered back to the home of Dr. Frank Waxham at 1901 East Colfax, where she was employed as a servant. She had a deep cut behind her right ear and a skull fracture. Although she was listed in critical condition, she survived.

Thirty-six-year-old Josephine Unternahrer received a devastating blow in an alley behind 1950 Pennsylvania Street, close to where Emma Johnson was struck. The blunt instrument the Thug used cut a five-inch-long gash behind her right ear. At first, doctors at St. Joseph's Hospital expected her to live. Before she was placed under anesthesia, she described a man much like Miss Everest did: medium-sized build, large black mustache, and wearing a black crush hat pushed far back on his head. The Thug had chased her, and when he caught up to her he reportedly said, "I'll get you now."

He did. She died a few days after she was operated on.

The trio of brazen attacks in one night brought the Thug's death count to three, and women stopped going out at night. The story of what happened in Denver on February 22 was picked up by newspapers from San Francisco to Boston, where one writer waxed eloquent with an Edgar Allen Poe-style characterization of "The Thing:"

> Silent, stealthy, mysterious, the Thing goes out into the night and back again to its lair, like a beast of the jungle that prowls and preys by night, and, gorged and hidden, bears naught and cares naught for the hue and cry by day. The terror of the invisible, the tragic, baffling secrecy of a scourge, are about the Thing, and it is the diabolical master and the deadly hunter of the hill…. It is a mystery of mysteries.

By now, the reward had climbed to $400, including $100 from the *Denver Post*, where another writer, unencumbered by any poetic style, gave a more practical account of the situation: "The affair has now become so serious that the public can no longer hesitate in the duty which it owes itself to get rid of the murderous terror, who, if less spectacular, is little less fatal than Jack the Ripper, whose fiendish crimes in the Whitechapel district of London startled and horrified the people of the civilized world."

There it was. Denver had its own "Jack the Slugger." The pressure on police became so great that their mandate now was to crack the case by whatever means necessary. When a feasible suspect emerged a few days later, their desperation led them to confidently decree, once again, that the Thug had been captured. Like all the other times before, this confidence came without a thorough investigation.

A series of events that began on Monday, February 25, seemingly blew the case wide open for the next six weeks, only to have it shut again and put Denver police back to square one.

Over the weekend, Armstrong announced a bold new initiative to sweep the Capitol Hill area and "leave it to every person on the hill to appear and satisfy police that they have had nothing to do with the outrages." Instead of refocusing his manhunt with detective work, his great plan was to throw scores of men in jail and hope that the Thug would be sifted out somehow.

"Every person" was a purposely broad characterization of the people they were actually going to target. The police had no intention of harassing the merchants and respectable men of Capitol Hill. They were after a different sort of man. On Monday, police took to the streets and boarding houses to round up men like Al Cowan, a dirt-poor laborer with few friends and few belongings. Like the fourteen others picked up that day, he was a man on the edge of society looking for work. Although these men fit a certain economic class that Armstrong wanted his men to target, the chief of detectives selectively ignored what the one witness to hell-night had to report—the one they didn't want to listen to. "The only person who saw him added a new phase to the mystery by declaring that he thought the thug was a man in a policeman's uniform," reported a Denver dispatch to the *Eagle County Blade* the morning after the three attacks.

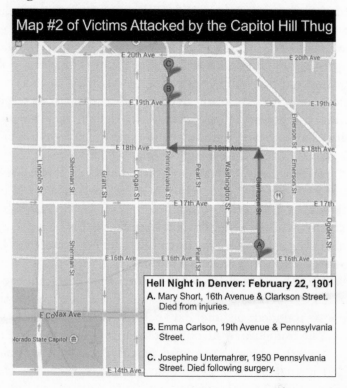

Map #2 of Victims Attacked by the Capitol Hill Thug

Hell Night in Denver: February 22, 1901

A. Mary Short, 16th Avenue & Clarkson Street. Died from injuries.

B. Emma Carlson, 19th Avenue & Pennsylvania Street.

C. Josephine Unternahrer, 1950 Pennsylvania Street. Died following surgery.

At the time of Cowan's arrest, there was nothing to single him out to detectives and he had attracted no special attention. Along with others picked up that day, they were held without charges and their worn-out clothing did not resemble a policeman's uniform.

On Tuesday, Albert James Frederick, a fifty-eight-year-old army barber and veteran of two campaigns, limped into the medical office of the police department surgeon to have the dressings on a leg wound changed.[4] As he set his cane to the side and climbed up on a wooden exam table, another patient in

---

[4] No sources could be found to explain how he received his leg wound.

the doctor's office was reading aloud a newspaper story about the attacks. The story also carried the news that the city's Fire and Police Board was putting up an additional $500 reward "for the capture of the Capitol Hill Thug who has been assaulting and murdered women." When Frederick heard this, he boldly proclaimed that on Friday night he got a close-up view of the Thug. He was so confident in his declaration that the police surgeon persuaded him to talk to Captain Armstrong.

According to his story given to police and then eagerly relayed to reporters, Frederick was walking in the vicinity of where Mary Short was attacked and had passed by her a short time before he heard a woman cry out, "Oh!"

"The man [her attacker] then turned and ran down toward him and passed him so closely that he brushed his coat against Frederick," a Denver correspondent reported. "He had a good look at him and says he will always remember his face. He then became alarmed as he realized that it would not be safe for him to be found nearby and he hastened away."

When police heard Frederick's story, they escorted him to general lock-up where they were holding the fifteen men they had just rounded up the day before. After Frederick saw Cowan, he immediately identified him as the man who had run past him after Mary Short was attacked. Grilled by police, Frederick stuck to his story. Cowan was the man he saw. He is the Capitol Hill Thug, he said.

As soon as Cowan's name was attached to the case, a narrative formed around him that ostensibly came from Captain Armstrong and then made its way into newspapers friendly to the chief detective. At the same time, other newspapers were naturally skeptical and more cautious in their reporting. Police were sure they had arrested the Thug in the past, only to release him for one reason or another. Why believe them now?

On both sides of the debate, doubts about Frederick quickly surfaced throughout Colorado. These misgivings were based on his reputation as "an unreliable sort," and his eagerness to claim the combined reward which had reached $900. The other problem the public had with Armstrong's star witness leaned toward racism—his and theirs. Frederick steadfastly maintained that his dark skin came to him from Arabian parents born in Mecca. Those who challenged him directly, saying he was actually black or mulatto, discovered this was the quickest route to his explosive temper.

"Frederick gives his testimony with a great abundance of detail but, despite all this, his story is not given entire credence," reported one of the more cautious newspapers the following day. "Persons in the city who have known Frederick since he has lived here say that he is unreliable and that his only motive in giving testimony against Cowan is to secure a part, at least, of the reward offered for the slugger. There is none but circumstantial evidence against Cowan, except that given by Frederick. It is not at all improbable that Al Cowan, suspected of being the Capitol Hill Thug, is innocent of the crimes which he is charged."

With this and other reports expressing doubts, police were quick to try to overcome them. The story they gave about evidence found and bizarre statements attributed to Cowan quickly branded the forty-two-year-old ranch hand as the Thug. According to Captain Armstrong, who questioned Cowan alone, he was picked up on the streets toting a revolver, some cartridges, and more importantly, "an iron bar about a foot in length."

If the iron bar didn't convict him in the nation's eyes, then it was the rest of what Armstrong reported that sealed Cowan's guilt: "He answers the meager descriptions that had been obtained of the man who has been terrorizing the women of this city."

Questioned by Captain Armstrong in jail, Cowan said he "had been persecuted by women."

"Why were you persecuted by women?" Armstrong asked.

"I was. I hate them, but I'll not tell you anymore. I don't trust anyone!"

Unsurprisingly, Captain Armstrong advanced his personal opinion that, like so many of the other Thugs who were arrested, Cowan was undoubtedly insane. "He does not talk coherently and appears to be mentally unbalanced," the chief of detectives reported.

This version of Cowan and his alleged anti-women statements seemed certain to convict him. Under the bold-faced headline, "**Hates All of Womankind**," Captain Armstrong's two-hundred-word account made its way into large and small newspapers throughout the United States.

But Armstrong's story conflicted with another newspaper report that appears to have come from multiple sources within the police department. That account claimed Cowan was arrested while in his room at a boardinghouse on Arapahoe Street, at an address that would have put him nearly one mile from the scene of the attacks on the 22nd. The story did confirm that a revolver, a shaving razor, and cartridges were found in his room, but "nothing incriminating was found there nor on his person when searched." No iron bar was ever mentioned in the February 26 story that appeared one day before Armstrong's.

The earlier story also reported on Cowan's appearance and the one suit of clothes he owned did not meet the descriptions given by victims and witnesses. "He has been working on a ranch near Denver for a couple of years. He had but one suit of clothes. He had a soiled black hat, wore black shoes and corduroy pants. His shirt was soft cotton and had not been washed for some time."

Even with these inconsistencies, "Chief Armstrong is sure he is the guilty man."

Despite his conviction in the press, Cowan's friends argued for his innocence. People at the boardinghouse where he lived reported he was in his room during the night of the February 22nd attacks—except for a fifteen-minute period when he went out and came right back.

Al Cowan

A day or two after Armstrong questioned Cowan, Frederick's reputation received a further blow when the Colorado adjutant general revealed that the army barber was a morphine addict and had the letters to prove it. An enraged Frederick explained that those letters to the administrative officer came from his ex-wife eight years ago, but he had since conquered his addiction while serving in the army.

Even with their chief suspect in custody, the police arrested more men on suspicion of being suspicious. Calvin Brown, a black man, was arrested and held for several days after Cowan's story went public. It was no coincidence that Brown and the others were crazy too. Denver's apparent epidemic of lunatics running loose led the *Aspen Tribune* to sarcastically remark, "When the crazy men of Denver are used up, the Denver Police will get a railroad pass and go down to Pueblo after a fresh supply." Pueblo was home to the Colorado Insane Asylum.

But instead of going to Pueblo, Armstrong's detectives could have gone to Kansas City, where Dr. C.W. Palmer, a professor of telepathic sciences, announced he was going to use "soul-force" to extract the secrets from Al Cowan's mind.

"Dr. Palmer's method," an Iowa newspaper wryly reported, "is to choose a subject in Kansas City who will be placed in the fifth-stage of hypnotism. The subject in Kansas City is supposed to be in sub-conscious communication with the Denver criminal, can read his inner-most thoughts, and reveal them to his controller, Dr. Palmer."

Apparently, the Denver police cooperated with Dr. Palmer, because telegrams were sent to him describing Cowan's condition as "a slight increase in his nervousness" but he gave no sign of breaking down. If there was nervousness on his part, it may have come from the detectives standing around waiting for Dr. Palmer's "soul force" to take effect.

Afterward, Cowan was locked up in solitary confinement, and Armstrong gave orders that no one was to talk to him except the jailer and Armstrong himself.

The pendulum of Cowan's apparent guilt seemed to swing back and forth with each newspaper article. A swing toward innocence came after William Howe of Raton, New Mexico, wrote Denver police that he knew Cowan in 1887 as "Bug House Davis"[5] when he worked as an ice peddler at the local hot springs. Davis, he said, "raved like a mad man against women and said he proposed to kill them all off."

Armed with the letter, Armstrong went to Cowan's cell, convinced he finally had the one piece of evidence that could break his suspect. The *Aspen Daily Times* was there to witness the exchange.

Cowan replied that he had never been in New Mexico and denied all knowledge of a man by the name of Howe. He said that he had never worked anywhere in the South and seemed to be ignorant of what the captain was talking about.

He admitted that he had worked in Gilpin County, Colorado in 1897 for a few months. Then he grew sullen and morose again and relapsed into silence. No effort of the captain could induce him to open his lips and he remained thus until the baffled

---

[5] "Bug house" is period slang for an insane asylum.

police officer retired in disgust. Armstrong says that he can see no signs of any confession and he has more doubt than ever that Cowan is the man at all.

The pendulum swung to guilt when Mrs. E. J. Grove came forward to say that Cowan was the man she saw near the Short murder scene and "that he acted very suspiciously," a newspaper reported.

> Her story is this: One night she was with her little girl and had been to visit friends. On their way home she had crossed a vacant lot and as she approached a telegraph pole she noticed something move. She was frightened and started to run. Then, she decided it would be better to face it out and if necessary to make a struggle. She steadily advanced and soon saw Cowan. She described him minutely. She says he had a club which was white and looked like hickory to her.
>
> She said he tried to slide around the post and hide, evidently intending to take her unawares, but she was possessed of considerable nerve and she walked up to him and faced him. He dodged back against the post and skulked away while she stood there ready to fight him. It would have been impossible to run away with the child in her arms and she thought her action cowed the brute.

If she was able to describe Cowan "minutely," it didn't hurt that his picture had been published before she came forward. Her story also contained another important clue—the white club that looked like hickory. Immediately after Frederick's story went public, a young hardware store employee came forward to say that on the Monday before the Friday night attacks, a man who resembled Al Cowan had purchased two hickory pickax handles from his store. Newspapers reminded their readers that a hickory pickax handle was found not far from where Annie McAtee was attacked. This circumstantial evidence would have contributed to his guilt except for one small fact: Armstrong had already told reporters that they had found him in possession of an iron bar.

Ever since Armstrong's "Hates All of Womankind" story appeared in newspapers across the country, Cowan was careful to keep his mouth shut. One month of interrogation by the captain and his detectives had uncovered nothing. Armstrong admitted Cowan's refusal to talk was infuriating, but also indicative of his mental instability.

As his preliminary hearing date of March 25 grew closer, Cowan was blessed by a fortunate turn of events. David Rees, one of the city's most aggressive attorneys, took pity on Cowan and agreed to defend him. Then, Judge William Rice granted Rees a twenty-four-hour delay to allow the other boarders from the rooming house on Arapahoe Street to be assembled and vouch for his client's whereabouts on the night of February 22.

When the courthouse doors opened on Tuesday morning, March 26, the spectator gallery filled up in less than thirty minutes. A large throng of curious men and women lined the walls and the space between the bench rows, blocked the courtroom doors that were left open, and spilled out into the corridor and down the hallway. There was no courtroom drama that first day, but Rees did succeed in having much of the prosecution's evidence thrown out. In spite of the fact that his client was charged with killing Mary Short, the evidence brought forward pertained to Josephine Unternahrer and was ruled inadmissible. Although the newspapers never mentioned it, the hardware store employee and Mrs. E. J. Grove were not called to testify by the prosecution.

Cowan was now on a lucky streak—and it was about to get better.

The fireworks came the next day when Albert Frederick, the star witness for the prosecution, took the stand and sat there helplessly as his testimony was "torn to pieces by Rees." Like most courtroom confrontations, it began simply, with no indication of the dark turn it was about to take.

Sensitive to his being labeled by newspapers as a black man, Frederick denied these scandalous rumors and answered the prosecutor's background questions that he was born in London from Arabian parents who had emigrated from Mecca. On the night of Mary Short's murder, he was crossing a vacant lot near 16th and Carlson when he saw a woman pass him. A short time later, he heard her scream, looked behind him, and saw a man standing over her with his arm raised and "something shiny in his hand."

Instead of helping the poor woman, he hurriedly walked away as he "didn't want to get mixed up in any fight." After the deed was done, Mary Short's attacker turned and ran past Frederick, who was able to get a good look at him.

"THAT," he exclaimed dramatically from the witness chair as he pointed at Cowan, "is the man!"

From that moment on, everything went downhill for Frederick and the prosecutor. Understanding his sensitivity to being called black, Rees knew just what to say to provoke the witness on cross-examination.

"Are you not a Negro?" Rees asked him.

"No! I am not," Frederick replied emphatically. "My parents were born in Mecca."

"If you have lived in colored boardinghouses and worked in colored barber shops, it must be that you are a colored man," Rees declared.

Frederick grew irritated and stated he was not colored. Rees smiled and continued to press him with variations of the same question. Unaware that the attorney was baiting him, Frederick's anger boiled over, giving Rees the opening he wanted. For the crafty defense attorney, he didn't care if Rees was black, Arabian, or Indian; he just wanted the witness to lose his composure.

"Frederick raved over it and finally [grabbed] a revolver and said that Rees was a dirty skunk and that he would kill him. Rees was not disturbed in the least and a constable disarmed Frederick and forced him to sit down," the *Aspen Daily Times* reported.

"Do you not use morphine?" Rees asked when Frederick had been made to take his seat.

He admitted that he had in the past but then switched to a very dramatic voice to proclaim, "That by God's help, I am through with it forever!"

"It made you imagine things, didn't it?" Frederick refused to answer that question or anything more about his morphine use.

Rees continued his attack with a series of questions designed to test Frederick's memory about places he'd worked and people he knew. "The witness," the *Aspen Tribune* reported, "showed a lack of memory that was surprising."

"What was the weapon the defendant used to strike the woman?" Rees inquired.

Frederick rose again from his chair, pointed to the revolver police confiscated when they arrested Cowan, the same one he had grabbed a moment earlier, and said: "As God is my judge, that was the weapon."

"How do you know that that is the weapon?" Rees asked.

"Well, I know it is, that is all."

Frederick saw his mistake and tried to recover, but it was too late. He stammered on about how he *knew* it was the revolver used to beat Mary Short around 8:00 p.m., in the dark, with no street lights to aid his vision. It didn't seem plausible to most observers. Why would the Thug use a revolver, instead of a wooden club or iron pipe as the head wounds had indicated? The iron pipe Armstrong said they found in Cowan's room was only mentioned that one time, and was never introduced into evidence. The lone weapon they found in Cowan's room was his revolver. If Frederick wanted the reward, he had to testify that the "something shiny" he saw used to strike and kill Mary Short, was in fact, Cowan's revolver.

It was time for the lion to go in for the kill. The defense attorney's final line of questioning was to all but insinuate that Frederick had killed Mary Short, a black woman, because he was an intimate friend of hers, and that he had escorted her to the vacant lot where she was mortally wounded.

"Rees succeeded in driving him with rage," the *Aspen Daily Times* correspondent wrote. Cowan's attorney paused his brutal cross-examination on that note and Judge Rice adjourned for the day.

But the drama didn't stop there. "As they left the courtroom, Frederick followed Rees, calling him a liar and a coward," the *Daily Times* continued. "Now, keep cool, Frederick," Rees said as he turned around to look at him. "You know that the reason you recognized that revolver was that it was yours. You killed that woman, and you know it! You struck her with your wooden crutch—didn't you!?"

This time, Frederick could say nothing and he melted into the crowd and disappeared. Rees didn't care if his revolver comment made no sense—since it was clearly his client's—he wanted to continue his vicious attack on Frederick's character to steer public opinion away from his client.

His strategy seemed to have worked. "It is possible that he may be arrested," the *Aspen* reporter speculated for his readers, "but police will say nothing about it."

After the disastrous testimony of the prosecution's star witness, an editorial in the *Aspen Weekly Times* criticized the Denver police department:

> The police of Denver have a new suspect for the Capitol Hill Thug. This time it is not a crazy man but the witness against Al Cowan. The poor police, when they once catch a man hang onto him with great tenacity. They find that it saves them the trouble of hunting up another victim. Crazy men seem to be the favorite marks of the police officers. It is a safe bet that the man who has committed these outrages is too smart for the Denver policemen.

The next day, March 28, Judge Rice considered Rees's motion to dismiss the charges. After a daylong debate, the judge eventually ruled against him. Rees used this minor setback to step up his attacks. His first target was the Denver police who he claimed were keeping Cowan in jail until after the election so they could keep their jobs. Rees said the mood of the city was that the police would not do the right thing by liberating his poor client, who was maligned in the press, falsely accused by the real killer, and held without charges for one month.

"Who said it?" the prosecutor demanded to know.

"I can bring you fifty, yes, one hundred men in as many minutes who have said it," Rees fired back. "It was said before three times that number last night in a meeting of the chamber of commerce."

The chamber of commerce was a Republican stronghold.

"If the chief of police would do his duty, he would, without a moment of delay, arrest Frederick," Rees continued. He had the attention of the crowded courtroom and he wasn't about to let up. "Cowan was thrown in jail and kept there for a month and no charge was made against him and no complaint made out. When he went in he weighed 155 pounds. Now he weighs less than 135."

When a policeman heard this, he laughed a little too loud and Rees turned on him. "Oh sneer if you will, but I would like to see your impervious soul go through what this man has had to!"

Rees then thundered at Frederick "and gave him a scorching that made him shrink into his seat visibly." But this time, Frederick wasn't taking the bait and he was more subdued and cautious in his testimony. "He weighs his words before he gives them an utterance," an *Aspen Tribune* reporter observed.

The defense attorney then catalogued Frederick's contradictions. Mary Short wasn't struck on the right side of the head, as Frederick claimed, it was the left. When he asked Frederick about a clock that was near the scene, Frederick said yes, he saw it. But there was no clock. Never was. And then there was the weapon, the revolver he so confidently claimed was the murder weapon just the day before. Now, he wasn't so sure.

Turning to the gallery as if he were giving a closing argument, Rees branded Frederick every type of evil he could spit out:

> Frederick has been a soldier, he says he served in the army. Yet he saw a woman murdered by a man and did not go to her rescue. He is a cowardly dog and a scoundrel and he is either a liar or the murderer by his own evidence! This man who goes on crutches part of the time and part of the time is sound on his feet, this cowardly dog has contradicted himself again and again and his evidence is worthless!

The prosecution put up a weak argument for Frederick's testimony, and the case against Cowan was continued to Friday, March 30. As he adjourned for the day, Judge Rice made it a point to state that this was not about politics or improper influence, but about justice, and it was necessary to continue the trial.

Rees fired back that he could not put Cowan on the stand against a man "as low as Frederick" who would have him convicted just to collect a reward for a woman he probably killed himself.

When Friday came, a very reluctant Frederick took the stand. The day before, the police surgeon told reporters that a "wild-eyed" Frederick came to him begging for help. Angry mobs had chased him through the city trying to kill him, he claimed. Men on the streets spat on him and called him names. He swore he would not use the morphine, the doctor reported, but it was clear to the physician that he already had, and the alleged persecution Frederick suffered was likely all in his mind.

"When did you first hear of the reward?" Rees asked him.

He heard about it on Monday, three days after the three women were brutally attacked, he answered. A man read it to him out of the newspaper. Frederick told him that he could identify the killer, but he was advised to "keep his mouth shut." Instead, he went to the police surgeon who dressed his injured leg and told the story to him. The doctor advised him to speak with Captain Alexander.[6] Attorney Rees then emphasized the fact that Frederick had done nothing to expose a murderer until he heard that a combined $900 reward[7] was being offered.

The defense then called two men from Cowan's boardinghouse who testified that he was in his room on February 22 between the hours of 6:30 and 8:30 p.m.—except for a fifteen-minute period when he went out and then returned. Since the attacks occurred between 7 and 8 p.m., it damaged Frederick's testimony, which by then was proclaimed "all but worthless."

Two soldiers, named Lipman and Johnson, testified that Frederick could not have been out the night of February 22, because he was in the barracks between 7:00 and 7:30 p.m.

Cowan himself was called to the stand later that afternoon. He proved himself to be a strong witness who came across as believable, and with a far better memory than his accuser. He was, newspapers reported, nothing like the "unbalanced" man the police had described just a month before.

"He made a very good witness for himself," the *Aspen Daily Times* reported. "He was very cool and told his story in a straightforward manner. His memory for dates and places was much better than expected."

When asked if he hated all women, Cowan said it was not true. Asked about the alleged statement he had made to Captain Armstrong about hating women, Cowan asserted he had never said anything like that. When the prosecutor took a shot at Cowan, trying to confuse and muddle him, Cowan just shook his head and responded calmly that he "did not hate women in particular."

Cowan made such a good witness on his own behalf that public opinion began to sway in his favor, and another newspaper reported that "he did not seem half as crazy as

---

[6] This version of how he heard the story is slightly different from previous accounts.

[7] The equivalent of about $25,000 in 2014.

Frederick in whom the police seemed to have pinned so much faith."

Court reconvened on Monday, April 2, with two army captains who gave testimony that further chipped away at Frederick's story and reputation. Frederick, it appears, was not telling the truth when he said his morphine addiction was behind him, they told the court. They described several circumstances which gave them doubt.

After the morphine revelation, the prosecutor asked the judge for a one-day continuance. The request surprised Rees since there were still several good hours of testimony left in the day. He protested, saying his client's freedom was at stake, and he indignantly proclaimed Cowan did not deserve to be in jail one day longer.

Rees need not have worried. The case was so dismal for the prosecutor that he wanted time to consider whether to press on or to abandon it completely. Judge Rice granted his request for a continuance, extending it an additional day to Wednesday, April 4.

That morning, the prosecutor surprised everyone when he announced he was going to drop the charges since "he had learned that Cowan was to be arrested on a charge of lunacy and tried in the county court."

Rees jumped to his feet and demanded Cowan be released at once. Judge Rice granted his motion, but before Cowan could make it out of the building he was rearrested and taken to the county courthouse, where the lunacy charge was read to him.

Despite the fact that an immediate victory had just been snatched from him, Rees told reporters he vowed to stick with his client whom he felt was being persecuted by a politically motivated police force. Rees pressured Denver County Judge Ben Lindsey[8] for a speedy hearing, which was granted for Monday, April 9, at 7:30 p.m. Cowan was moved out of the city

---

[8] Judge Benjamin Barr Lindsey, later recognized as the founder of the U.S. juvenile court system. The Lindsey-Flanigan Courthouse in Denver is, in part, named after him.

jail and confined in the newly built insanity ward of the county hospital.

At the sanity hearing, three doctors who had briefly examined Cowan proclaimed he was insane. Then, Cowan himself testified, followed by three of his close friends. Cowan presented himself well and his pals described him as a normal man with no long-seething hatred toward women.

"When placed on the stand himself he made such an admirable witness that neither the opposing counsel or judge could baffle him," the *Colorado Springs Gazette* reported. "When placed on the stand he explained to the judge in detail the cause of the rumor which had gone out."

It was the experts versus the laymen, and Judge Lindsey sided with Cowan and his friends. After six weeks and two days of incarceration, Al Cowan was finally a free man. During this time in jail, the real Capitol Hill Thug kept a low profile. No attacks on women were reported while Cowan was in jail. This may have raised some suspicions that Cowan was actually the Thug, but fate would once again intervene on his behalf.

Ten days later, whether he was anxious to get back to work or wished to make it appear that Cowan *was* guilty, the Thug attacked thirty-five-year-old Eliza Monroe[9] near the corner of 25th Avenue and Downing Street. When the police heard this, they immediately ran to Cowan's boardinghouse, where they found him asleep in his room.

The Capitol Hill Thug was still loose in the city of Denver and it wasn't Al Cowan. Exhausted with police incompetence, the *Aspen Democrat* reported on this story under the blazing headline: "**Denver's Stupid Police Force**."

Two men who heard Monroe scream came running to her aid as the Thug was trying to drag her into an alley. When they approached, they scared off her attacker, later describing him as a "short, thick man," the *Democrat* reported. He was later seen boarding a trolley car before he disappeared.

---

[9] Her name was also reported as Elizabeth Munroe.

Cowan stayed in Denver looking for employment but after two weeks he announced he was giving up and would travel to Central City, Colorado, to look for work in the mines. If he couldn't find a job there, he would go to Cripple Creek. He also told reporters he was recognized throughout the city and didn't like the notoriety.

"In speaking of the trial, he said that Frederick was the man who caused all his trouble," recounted the *Aspen Daily Times*. "He did not believe Frederick was a Negro for no Negro would have been so unrelenting in following an innocent man."

Epilogue

Al Cowan was never heard from again after he left the Mile High city. A few more attacks by the Capitol Hill Thug were committed that summer, and then he, too, was never heard from again.

Captain Armstrong was later promoted to Chief of Police. With train fare provided by the Denver prosecutor, Albert Frederick traveled as far east as he could go, to New York City, to escape the angry citizens of Colorado.

Al Cowan after his trial.

Chapter Two: The Murder of Father Kaspar Vartarian, 1907

ON THE SUNDAY afternoon of May 26, 1907, there was a bad smell coming from somewhere inside the New York City apartment of Mr. and Mrs. Henry Scherrer. To the middle-aged German couple, it smelled like a dead cat. They inspected the furniture, corners, and cabinets in five of their six rooms before moving on to the parlor that was recently converted into a boarding room. Their new Armenian tenants hadn't been seen in nearly a week, but the smell had to be coming from in there.

Nearly three weeks before, John Mouradian and Paul Sarkasian paid Mrs. Scherrer $3 for two weeks' rent. When the payment for the next two weeks came due on Wednesday, May 22, the two men explained to Annie Scherrer that they had to go out of town for a few days and were unable to pay the rent until they returned. The three then came to an agreement that a large wooden trunk, which had arrived earlier that day for Paul, could be used as collateral. Mrs. Scherrer would hold onto the trunk, and when they got back, they would have her $3.

Four days went by without Mrs. Scherrer's giving her tenants much thought until the reeking smell of a dead cat permeated the apartment. Without hesitation, the Scherrers entered their tenants' room, sniffed around, and noticed that the rancid odor was centered on the trunk tucked far back against the corner. Henry Scherrer carefully opened the lid and saw three black robes, two pairs of shoes, a clerical collar, and a small, round, soft hat. It was the kind of hat that an Orthodox priest might wear.

Underneath those items was the crumpled, half-naked body of a dead man.

Henry screamed, dropped the lid and fled to a nearby police station where he notified the watch commander. Soon, a half-dozen policemen, the coroner, and several newspaper reporters converged on the Scherrer's second-story apartment at 333 West 37th Street. When the city detectives arrived, they saw that the dead man was in a fetal position with "the head bound against the knees with a heavy strap that had been passed over the back of the neck and buckled at the shins."

It was worse than a dead cat.

At the city morgue, Dr. Timothy Lehane removed the body of a 160-pound man who was about forty-five years old, and five-foot four-inches in height. Judging by the broken neck and other shattered bones, the coroner concluded the victim was "crushed into the trunk" while he was still alive by at least two men. With no other signs of violence, Dr. Lehane hypothesized that the victim was drugged with knock-out drops, crammed inside the cheap, wooden trunk that measured 42 inches long, 18 inches wide, and 24 inches high, and died a slow death from asphyxiation. To fit him inside the small space, his killers had to snap his neck and break some bones. Although no identification was found, his long, black beard, streaked with gray hair, indicated that he may have been an Orthodox priest—a belief supported by the clothing found in the trunk.

News that an Orthodox priest was found murdered in a trunk spread fast through New York City. By nightfall, a throng of nosy people lined up at the city morgue, hoping to get a look. One of the curious was John Karanfilian, a trustee of the Armenian branch of the Greek Church in Hoboken, New Jersey. One look at the pallid, half-naked corpse was enough, and he gave everyone in the room the name of the dead priest: Father Kaspar Vartarian.[1]

---

[1] American newspaper reporters found it nearly impossible to spell any

KASPAR VARTARIAN OF THE Armenian Apostolic Church was a priest without a congregation. He came to the United States in 1899 from Muş, Turkey, after he was banished by Turkish authorities. Like many of his fellow priests from Turkey, Father Kaspar fled to the safety of Armenian-settled enclaves in America. His son soon joined him, and instead of moving to Chicago where his brother lived, Father Kaspar chose to live on the East Coast, where he eventually settled down in New Jersey.

"He was what is known among us as a 'free priest,'" Bishop Horsep Sarjin later explained to a newspaper reporter. "That is, he was subject to no orders from anyone, but roamed about begging contributions from wealthy Armenians and occasionally holding services in one of our churches."

A reporter from Joseph Pulitzer's *New York World* gleaned from Father Kaspar's friends that, in addition to carrying around the donations he collected, he always wore a small silk bag around his neck said to hold precious jewels and gold he had smuggled out of Armenia eight years prior. He never displayed his wealth and was always careful with the bag, which was tucked inside his shirt. Even though he kept it hidden, many of his fellow Armenians knew about it. It was no secret.

When Father Kaspar's son died in 1905, he sank into a deep melancholy from which he never recovered, friends reported. Not long after he lost his son, his wealthy brother in Chicago died.

By the time he was murdered, Father Kaspar was afflicted with what doctors then called, melancholy.

Less than twenty-four hours after his body was discovered, the murder of Father Kaspar was front-page news from New

---

of the Armenian names correctly or consistently. Father Vartarian appeared in some newspapers as Father Vartanian. A thorough check of census records and a city directory could not yield the correct spelling, so the author chose the most frequently published version of his name.

York to San Francisco and Los Angeles. Although rare, trunk murders were not unheard of, and the very words seemed to excite the populace to what they hoped would be an intriguing murder mystery. Even the tiny newspaper in Red Cloud, Nebraska, childhood home to future Pulitzer Prize-winning author Willa Cather, carried the news.

As New York City reporters were piecing together a victim profile, detectives were working fast to identify their chief suspects. Inside the trunk, they discovered the name "Sarkis" engraved under the lid, and on the outside, "Ermoyian." Police also found a meal ticket for "S. Ermoyian Brothers" restaurant in Chicago, and the silk bag Father Kaspar was rumored to keep his jewels in. If "Sarkis Ermoyian" owned the trunk, then police wanted to talk to him.

They were now looking for three men and, although the last names of John and Paul would often change between newspapers, along with whatever alias witnesses knew them as, they were essentially the same two men who had rented the room from Annie and Henry Scherrer: John Mouradian and Paul Sarkasian.

But it was Sarkis Ermoyian who police were most interested in, and his description was distributed throughout the five boroughs: five feet tall, a pointy face with pockmarked skin, and greasy black hair. One of his acquaintances told reporters Sarkis looked like a weasel.

It wasn't much to go on, and five-foot-tall men tended to disappear in large crowds—even if they did look like weasels.

From evidence found inside the trunk, and by questioning those in the tight-knit Armenian community, detectives were able to put together a timeline of Sarkis Ermoyian's life up to the day Father Kaspar was murdered. Four or five months before, Ermoyian had moved to New York from Chicago, where he owned a restaurant named "S. Ermoyian Brothers" that had gone out of business. After he arrived, Sarkis began charming his way into the good graces of Charles Holopigian, the owner of a successful neighborhood restaurant in Hell's Kitchen. Charles's nephew, Simeon Perkirian, also became influenced by the little man's braggadocio and stories of his culinary success in Chicago. But alas, poor Sarkis was robbed, and he needed a good place to live quietly as he rebuilt his fortune with his superb cooking skills that would remind all their Turkish, Greek, and Armenian customers of home.

No problem, Simeon said, Sarkis could rent a room from him and pay rent when he got back on his feet. Simeon's generosity didn't stop there. He also loaned Sarkis $140 to buy a share in his Uncle Charles's restaurant. It was a lot of money and it had taken years of working at the wire factory to save it. Sarkis Ermoyian, the nephew was fooled into believing, was a good investment.

Everyone was captivated by this new arrival and saw a bright future with Sarkis Ermoyian. Everyone, that is, except Charles Holopigian's Irish-borne wife. She saw through the charming mask Sarkis wore, past his pock-marked face, and into his black soul. Like many women, she had a capacity for intuition that men lacked. She had a sixth sense, an ability to detect the malingering, malcontent type—and that's exactly what she saw in Sarkis Ermoyian.

As soon as he started cooking in Holopigian's kitchen, Sarkis brought in his acquaintances, John [who may have been related to Sarkis] and Paul to work in the restaurant, and "the three became fast friends," the *World* recorded.

However, within just a few days, it became obvious to nearly everyone in the Armenian neighborhood what Mrs. Holopigian could have told them from the beginning: "that Ermoyian was not a man not passionately enamored with hard work," the *New York Tribune* reported. "For the short time he was in the restaurant business with the Holopigians, most of his time was employed in quarrelling with the patrons of the restaurant."

"My poor husband, he believes anybody," Mrs. Holopigian told a reporter, with a trace of the *I told you so* in her voice. "This man, Ermoyian, came here from Chicago after Christmas and put $140 into the business. His friend, Mouradian, came in as a dishwasher and Paul Sarkasian came too, to see the others. They became friends.

"Ermoyian began to get nasty with the customers. If a man bought cigarettes, he would swear at him and tell him he ought to buy cigars, and if he wanted soup, he would try to make him order steak."

One of the few customers Sarkis *was* pleasant with was Father Kaspar, who frequented the restaurant often and became friendly with Sarkis, John, and Paul.

"Then, the Armenian priest," Mrs. Holopigian continued, "they called him priest, came in here all the time to see them. Ermoyian said to me one day after the priest left: 'That priest has got a lot of money. He buried a brother in Chicago and the brother left him a lot. I knew him in Chicago.'"

It became something of a well-known secret within the tight-knit Armenian community that Father Kaspar didn't trust banks. They knew about his silk bag and they also knew he wore a money belt to hold the money he inherited from his brother. He was peculiar that way.

It only took one month for the partnership with Sarkis to disintegrate, and the small man was pressured to sell out his share to Charles's brother for $100. Bitter over losing $40, borrowed money that wasn't even his, Sarkis stole fifty meal tickets worth $3 each from the Holopigians, sold them around the community for a discounted price, and pocketed the money.

"He was a bad lot," Mrs. Holopigian said with disgust. "If I could get my hands into his greasy hair, the police wouldn't have to do anything to him. Why, after he sold out to my husband's brother for $100, he told a Turk that he was going to get even with him for the loss of $40. The Turk came and told my husband about this threat."

His exact words were "he would fix Charlie for life."

Sarkis's quarrel over money and death threats toward his former business partner spilled over to his landlord, Simeon

Perkirian, whom he still owed $140, plus $20 for rent. Eleven weeks before the discovery of Father Kaspar's body, Sarkis was kicked out. He kept a key to the apartment, and left his trunk behind.

He would come back for it later.

Sarkis brooded over his bad luck. He'd always had rotten luck even though he worked hard and tried to make the best of it. If he was ever going to get a piece of good luck, he'd have to make it or take it himself, and he knew just where to find it.

As he had done with the Holopigians, Sarkis ingratiated himself with Father Kaspar, and the two were often seen together with John and Paul not far behind. As an itinerant preacher who traveled from one Armenian neighborhood to the next collecting money for the church, Father Kaspar depended on the generosity of others to lodge him as a guest in their home, and to provide him with meals. Although he had the donation money, it wasn't his money to spend. He did have his brother's inheritance, but for some reason, he held on to it and never spent any.

After he was kicked out of Simeon's apartment, Sarkis moved into a two-room apartment on 10th Avenue. On May 8th, John and Paul rented a room with Henry and Annie Scherrer, who recalled a man that fit Sarkis's description as a frequent visitor of their tenants. To her, the little Armenian weasel was unforgettable. She also remembered the priest.

"The priest who was murdered slept at my house three times," Mrs. Scherrer told reporters with a thick German accent. "Once, he was here two nights in succession. He slept on a lounge in a room adjoining that occupied by Paul and John.

"The last time he came to the flat to spend the night was a week ago Wednesday on May 15. I did not see Father Kaspar again until last Wednesday morning [May 22] about 8 o'clock when he came to look for the Armenians. They had gone and he waited for them only a few minutes. As he went out he said he would return later. I saw him go out and looked at the clock, it was about 9 o'clock."

Both detectives and intrepid reporters spoke to more witnesses and were able to trace the movements of Father Kaspar for the rest of the day. After he left the Scherrer home at nine in the morning, he was next seen around noon, by a woman who knew him, buying a pound of coffee in a small Armenian grocery store.

He was never seen alive after that.

Around 2:30 in the afternoon, Annie Scherrer said Sarkis Ermoyian and a blond-haired deliveryman arrived at her home with the trunk which they lugged into the room rented by John and Paul. Although she had seen the pock-marked man before, she couldn't remember his name. "This is Paul's trunk," he told her.

Three hours later, John and Paul returned from work. Paul went into the kitchen and asked Mrs. Scherrer if the trunk had arrived.

"Yes it did," she replied.

"That is good as I had owed you for a week's board. I can leave it as security for we have to go away for a few days," Paul reportedly told her.

Pleased that Mrs. Scherrer had agreed to the arrangement, the two men went into their room but after examining the trunk, Paul returned to the kitchen with a troubled look on his face—as if he'd just discovered something horrible.

"They came back to me in a few minutes and said that a mistake had been made in the trunk, that they had got the wrong one. They asked me if I would allow them to take it away. I said 'no,' they would have to pay their board first."

Mrs. Scherrer didn't know it then, but she had just agreed to keep a murdered priest in her home. It was also the moment when John and Paul learned what kind of man Sarkis Ermoyian really was—someone who could murder a priest.

Not knowing what to do, the two men returned to their room, where Mrs. Scherrer could hear them whispering. An hour or so later, they asked her for some paper and ink to write a letter to their mother back in Armenia. The two men continued talking in whispered tones as they wrote a letter in the Scherrer's kitchen. She wondered why they didn't want to write the letter in their room and chose the kitchen instead. When they were finished, they returned to their room, where they remained until they were heard leaving sometime after midnight. Mrs. Scherrer never saw them again.

For the next four days, the body of Father Kaspar Vartarian began the slow process of decay until the smell led to the discovery on Sunday afternoon.

LITTLE SARKIS ERMOYIAN COULDN'T RESIST showing off his newly acquired wealth to the people who had scorned him the most: the Holopigians. Two days after he murdered Father Kaspar, Sarkis walked into their restaurant wearing rich man clothes.

"He was very properly dressed," Mrs. Holopigian remembered, "and seemed to be flush with money. He had on a new blue serge suit, and a fine black hat, new shoes and a scarf. I asked him the reason for all his apparent elegance and he said he had a good job with a wall-paper concern at 10th Avenue and 37th Street. He was working for a Mr. Thibault, he said. I did not believe this and in order to satisfy my curiosity, called there. It was as I thought. They did not know him."

Newspaper reports also stated that he went around with a beautiful young woman on his arm. Like his new suit, she was purchased with the money taken from the dead priest.

Forty-eight hours after Father Vartarian was discovered in Sarkis Ermoyian's trunk, Captain James McCafferty and his detective bureau had pieced together all the major elements of the crime with the exception of where the murder took place. Now, he needed to place a blockade of undercover detectives and policeman around the city to contain his suspects.

More than twenty detectives were assigned to watch the piers for all outgoing steamships. More of them descended on Grand Central Station to scrutinize passengers boarding outbound trains. Detectives in Chicago monitored all inbound trains from New York City in case Sarkis tried to return to his old haunts. Even police in Fresno, California, were alerted when it was learned that Sarkis had a brother there and had recently inquired about moving in with him. The brother discouraged this, and told him not to come. He didn't like Sarkis either.

The net was tightening. Dozens of short, unsuspecting men were rounded up because they "looked suspicious," but were later released. In Chicago, twenty men were arrested at the old address of the Ermoyian Restaurant. They remembered Sarkis and told detectives what they knew about his departure five months before—and the trunk he took with him.

McCafferty and his detectives were optimistic. The men they were hunting were careless and stupid. They left behind a trail of clues and plenty of witnesses. It was as if Sarkis Ermoyian were so blinded by his greed that he was incapable of giving much thought to how he was going to escape with Father Kaspar's money and jewels.

Even though the three men lacked criminal intelligence, they made up for it with dumb luck. On May 29, Sarkis and John Mouradian left New York City undetected on a New York Central train bound for Montreal, Canada. Two days later, they boarded the steamship *Ionian* bound for England. They reached Liverpool on June 9, took a train to London where they stayed for a few days, then made their way to the south of France where there was a large Armenian community. Even though their names and a detailed description had been cabled to English and French police, Sarkis and John checked into the Hotel de Gazar in Marseilles under their own names on June 19.

Whether he was the designated patsy or not, Paul Sarkasian was the odd man out. He stuck around New York City for a few days before the body was discovered. He then followed the same escape route taken by Sarkis and John. From Montreal, he boarded the *Virginian* which left for Europe on June 7. Paul also made his way to Marseilles, where French police were more alert in his case and, in late June, he was arrested and held for extradition back to New York.

Captain McCafferty could barely contain his joy when interviewed by reporters from the *Tribune, Evening-World,* and, less popular, *New York Times.* He was possessed with a new confidence for bringing all three men to justice and made a bold prediction for the arrest of the other two.

"The police of the whole world are working together to bring the murderers of the Armenian priest to justice," Capt. McCafferty boldly told a *Times* reporter. "Never was there such a thorough canvas of the civilized globe made to catch a murderer. Circulars with the printed description of the men, together with a statement of the nature of the crime, have been sent to almost every city of prominence in the world with a request that the police arrest the men in the circular and communicate at once with the New York Detective Bureau. As soon as the state department arranges for the requisition, we will send a man to Marseilles to bring the prisoner over here."

But the state department wasn't going to do anything because assistant district attorney Charles Nott didn't want to do anything, citing a lack of evidence against Paul Sarkasian. Even though his detectives may have gotten a confession out of him, Nott didn't even want to try, McCafferty complained.

Paul's luck saved him again.

Put on the defensive, Nott told a *Tribune* reporter the following day that there was insufficient evidence against Father Kaspar's killers. "The evidence was not sufficient to bring them back. Unless the police furnish us with better evidence than what we have now, Father Kaspar's murderers may never be brought to justice."

Nott had a point. Although there was plenty of evidence against Sarkis Ermoyian, he didn't have much on Paul Sarkasian.

Charles Nott

Frustrated over the loss of his suspect, Capt. McCafferty sent a telegram to the American consulate in Marseilles pleading with them to interrogate Sarkasian—with harsh methods if necessary. "Tell Sarkasian he stopped at 161 Antoine Street, Montreal, with the others. Make him tell about the murder. Tell him it will be best for him. We know more than he thinks," reported the *New York Sun*.

Detective McCafferty was wrong in his assumption that the three had escaped across the Atlantic together, and in his estimation of the level of Paul's involvement in the murder, but that didn't seem to matter. With no experience in performing interrogations or investigations, Consul John Skinner turned Paul Sarkasian loose. The district attorney's refusal to push for Sarkasian's extradition zeroed out all of McCafferty's enthusiasm for bringing Father Kaspar's killers to justice, and he simply gave up. There was nothing more he could do.

A few days before Paul was arrested and held for extradition, an Armenian-American vacationing in Marseilles met two other Armenian men from New York City. One of them was short, with pockmarked skin and greasy hair. The other Armenian was taller and seemed more cordial. George Kurkjian would later tell the *New York World* that, at the time, he was unaware of the murder of Father Kaspar, and he did not recognize Sarkis Ermoyian and John Mouradian from their detailed descriptions published in the newspapers.

The two travelers told him they had just arrived from Egypt, but one look at the perfect condition of their fancy American clothes told Kurkjian differently. He grew suspicious, and when he visited the American consulate and read the New York newspapers, he decided to investigate these two strange men a little more. By visiting the same Armenian restaurants they frequented, and by asking around, Kurkjian met a man named Boghos who told him the two had thousands of dollars and were on their way to Varna, Bulgaria, to start a business. Boghos reported that they told him he wouldn't succeed in America in a few short years unless he knew a "trick." They knew the "trick," but they weren't sharing it with him. But what they did share with him was their address in Bulgaria, which Boghos then passed on to Kurkjian. When Kurkjian returned to New York City in August, he gave the address to the *New York World*, which published it under the following announcement:

> To Commissioner Bingham, Chief of Detectives McCafferty, District Jerome, et al
>
> The present address of Sarkis Ermoyian, John Mouradian and Paul Sarkasian wanted for the murder of Father Kaspar Vartarian is 523 Balik Bazaar, Varna, Bulgaria.
>
> - The World

Believing they had just made a major break in the case, the *World* was more than disappointed in the reaction of the New York Detective Bureau, who clearly had given up the hunt for Sarkis Ermoyian and John Mouradian. It was a surrender that included a barely contained disgust for the district attorney's office. When pressed for an official response to the *World's* publication of the Bulgarian address where the suspects could be found, Deputy Police Commissioner Arthur Woods replied, "The Police Department won't do anything in view of the district attorney's attitude in refusing to extradite the suspect [Paul Sarkasian] arrested some time ago in Marseilles."

"Then, you mean nothing will be done?" a reporter challenged.

"The police department won't do anything in view of the district attorney's attitude," Woods repeated. "If the *World* will furnish us with any other evidence it has, we will proceed."

"Do you mean you will wait until the *World* digs up all the evidence?" he was asked.

But Woods never answered the question directly and instead, the *World* reporter wrote, "The Deputy Commissioner of Police, who is introducing Scotland Yard methods into detecting, fell back on the line of defense, instead putting the matter up to the district attorney. There was no eagerness to arrest and bring back the three Armenians last seen with Father Kaspar."

After consulting with the United States Consulate in Marseilles where he was being held, Paul Sarkasian returned to New York City in December 1907 to proclaim his innocence and clear his name. After his arrest on December 20, which was arranged through a fellow Armenian acting as an intermediary, Sarkasian told police everything he knew, including how he discovered the priest's body, his own escape to France, and his reason for returning.

On the day the trunk was delivered to his boarding room at the Scherrer residence, Sarkasian reported he came home from work and found the trunk in his room tied shut with ropes. Curious, and with the key resting on top of the lid, Sarkasian untied the ropes and unlocked the trunk. He told police he was shocked to find the priest's body, and when he felt it, it was still warm.

"The next day I could not find a steamer on which I could sail before four or five days, and so I took a train to Montreal. There I took a ship to Marseilles where I was arrested. I stayed there after my release, but have always wanted to return to this country and assure my sister and brother-in-law who live in Providence, Rhode Island, that I was innocent of the murder, for I knew they must have heard that suspicion had been directed against me."

Sarkasian found passage to America working as a coal passer on the steamer *Peruvia*. He later told investigators he had not seen John Mouradian or Sarkis Ermoyian since May. Since Paul Sarkasian was known to be at work during the daytime hours when Father Vartarian was likely murdered by Ermoyian, he was not indicted.

Epilogue

Because of Assistant District Attorney Charles Nott's unwillingness to extradite Sarkis from Bulgaria, Father Kaspar Vartarian's killer was never brought to justice. Six years later, Nott was promoted to serve as a judge of the New York General Sessions Court.

Chapter Three: The Carver Family Hatchet Murders, 1930

ON THE AFTERNOON of April 2, 1930, Lottie Alsmeyer was resting on her bed, ready to drift off into a peaceful nap. It was a beautiful Wednesday with temperature-perfect weather near Sebring, Florida. The orange trees were in full bloom, proudly displaying their five-starred blossoms. Their scent blended with the breeze that flowed through an open window into Lottie's room.

The twenty-six-year-old housewife had just closed her eyes when she heard two loud bangs coming from her neighbor's house. Pulled back from the edge of sleep, she rolled over to face the window and opened her eyes. The eerie silence was broken by two soul-piercing screams. That got her out of bed and as she stood by the window, looking over at the Spanish-style bungalow the Carver family had recently moved into, she heard four more gunshots that instinctively made her jerk back.

Whatever was going on over there, she knew it was really bad. Anxious and afraid, she tried to calm her one-year-old son, Richard, who had just started crying in his crib. She was stroking his forehead when her mother-in-law walked into the bedroom to check on Lottie and her grandson. As the two women debated whether they should call the police or go next door, their telephone rang: it was the neighbor, William Carver.

There's been a terrible accident with his wife and son, he said, and he wanted her to come over. He had already telephoned police and called for a doctor, but it would be a little while for word to reach them.

Down the street in the opposite direction of the Alsmeyer home, Neal Cash had just finished changing a tire on his truck when he heard four gunshots. He stopped to look in the direction of the home the Carvers were renting from his friend, Tom Mitchell. Just as he turned his attention back to putting his tools away, he heard three loud screams followed by a short pause, and then two more gunshots.

The thirty-eight-year-old started his truck and drove one hundred and fifty yards to the house, where he stopped, jumped out, looked through the living room window, and then ran inside through the front door without bothering to knock or call out. After crossing the living room to the dining room, Cash found Ben Whitehead, the Carver's black chore man, lying on his back near the bathroom door. There was a bullet hole just above his right eye and, judging by his empty stare at the ceiling, Cash knew he was dead.

Alerted by the agony-tempered groans of a woman in the room to his right, Cash slowly pushed open the bedroom door and saw William's wife, Ruth, on the floor in front of the bed. Her head was covered in blood and she was thrashing from side to side, moaning in pain. Her young son, lying next to her, was also covered in blood and wasn't moving. From the quick scan he gave the room, he understood two things: Mrs. Carver's injuries were too severe for him to be of much help, and there was an alarming amount of blood covering both the woman and her son.

As Cash hopped in his truck and drove away to get help, Lottie Alsmeyer had finished getting dressed and ran toward the Carver's patio door on the opposite side of the house. Mr. Carver was standing there waiting for her. In an almost hysterical voice, he sobbed out a brief story of what had happened.

Her initial fears were right—it was really bad. Their chore man, Ben Whitehead, had bludgeoned his wife and son with something in his hand, and then Carver had shot Whitehead as he was coming after him.

Fighting to catch his breath, Lottie couldn't help but notice blood stains on both the front and back of Mr. Carver's white shirt. Standing just five foot four, her short, stocky neighbor guided her from the laundry room to his bedroom where he pointed down a narrow hallway leading to the bathroom and master bedroom. Without saying a word, he followed behind as she ventured forward and discovered first Whitehead near the bathroom, and then Mrs. Carver and her young son on the floor in the adjacent bedroom. Although a towel was wrapped around the boy's head, she observed that nothing had been done for Mrs. Carver, who rolled back and forth, with her arm occasionally swinging up into the air.

"What can we do?" Lottie reportedly asked Carver in that moment.

Slow to respond with a mind that was overloaded, Carver told her to call for a doctor, forgetting that he had already done so. The telephone operator informed Lottie that they were doing everything they could to get help to the Carver's home.

In that first bedroom she had come to, eleven-month-old Frances was crying loudly, scared by all the noise. Lottie picked her up and comforted the child as she looked around for Mr. Carver. She found him standing over the kitchen sink, splashing water on his face and neck, and then washing his hands and arms. Two telephone company linemen working nearby also heard the shots and entered the house just as Mr. Carver was washing. As he dried his hands on a towel, Carver gave a brief explanation of the tragedy to Ray Morgan and Paul Surgenior who helped him remove his blood-stained shirt as he spoke. The chore man and Carver's son were both dead, and the man's poor wife was in the bedroom alone, probably dying. And just as Lottie had, Morgan and Surgenior realized there was nothing they could do but wait for the authorities to arrive to help a family that nobody in Highlands County, Florida, really knew.

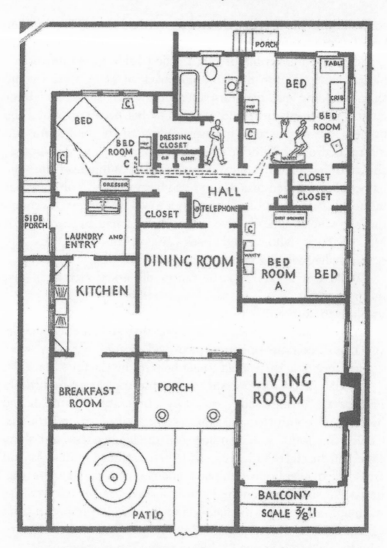

WILLIAM RAYMOND CARVER WAS BORN in 1891 in Philadelphia where his father was a successful steel manufacturer. Ray, as he liked to be called, graduated from the University of Pennsylvania in 1912 with a bachelor's degree in economics. He then took graduate courses at the University of

Pennsylvania, Columbia University, and Harvard. During the Great War, he was called up and served with distinction as an ammunition supply officer.

William Raymond Carver

When he returned home after the war, Ray worked with his father, Samuel Carver, who had become a successful real estate developer in south Florida. Although his passion was to be writer, Ray knew financial success was more attainable if he followed in his father's footsteps. In 1919, he returned to Pennsylvania to start his own real estate ventures. While there, he met his future wife. Following a one-year courtship, William Ray Carver married Ruth Stapff near Stroudsburg, Pennsylvania, in 1920. Ruth was a tender-hearted young woman from a proud family who were impressed with Ray's devotion to her. And like most mothers and daughters do, the two confided in each other and Ruth only had good things to say about her husband. Family and friends would later report their marriage was one of the happiest they had ever seen.

Ruth Carver *(Courtesy of family)*

As a real estate speculator using his father's money, Carver moved his family around a lot during the first ten years of his marriage, buying and selling land in Pennsylvania, California, Massachusetts, and New Jersey. In between these deals, Ray and Ruth would spend summers with her mother in the Pocono Mountains, or with his father in south Florida.

Samuel Carver made a lot of money during the 1920s Florida real-estate boom and was one of the few who survived the bust relatively unscathed. His success and foresight allowed him to purchase *Villa Serena*, a beautiful home once owned by three-time presidential candidate, William Jennings Bryan. He was also able to negotiate a good price for five thousand acres of land one hundred and seventy miles north, near Sebring and Lake Jackson in Highlands County. His plan was to build a subdivision of single-family homes there under the supervision of his son. To be near the large-scale venture, the younger Carver found a comfortable, Spanish-style home for rent three miles outside of Sebring and moved his family in during the first week of February, 1930. As their housing development project slowly got underway, Ray Carver enjoyed an easygoing lifestyle that allowed him to golf nearly every morning.

But as he stood there in the dining room with his neighbor's wife and two men he didn't know, the events of the last twenty minutes barely seemed comprehensible. When Sebring Police Chief Richard Stivender and Dr. John Mitchell arrived, their immediate focus was on all three victims. Whitehead and the Carver's little boy were clearly dead, and Ruth Carver was slipping away fast. As he knelt beside her, Dr. Mitchell watched helplessly as Ruth Carver let out one last painful moan before she too died.

Chief Stivender looked around at the carnage in the bedroom, gathered it all in, and then walked into the living room to talk to the husband. Highlands County Sheriff Oscar Wolff, and the former sheriff, James Hancock, were in the living room when Chief Stivender asked the dead woman's husband for an explanation.

According to Ray Carver's story, he arrived home at noon after playing a round of golf that morning. After they ate lunch, all four members of the Carver family lay down to take a nap. His wife, Ruth, and their two-year-old son, Lee Townsend, went to sleep in one bedroom, while Ray and his eleven-month-old daughter, Frances, rested in another room. The two bedrooms were separated by a bathroom and a closet, with a hallway connecting all four rooms. Ray instructed Ben Whitehead to wash the dishes and then mop the kitchen and bathroom floors, but to do so quietly. Shortly after drifting off to sleep, he was awakened by his wife's screams a little after 2:00 p.m.

"I got up and went to her room and saw my wife and my little boy on the floor," an emotionally charged Carver told the lawmen. "Whitehead turned and started for me. I had no weapon. He had something in his hand. I didn't know what it was but I knew he was after me. I knew he had done something to my wife and I had to get a gun. I ran back to my room and got a gun. I fired at the dirty skunk. I kept on firing until my gun stopped firing. I got more cartridges and put them in. Whitehead raised his head and shoulders from the floor and I fired again and again."

Whitehead was walking backward toward the bathroom when he was shot, Carver explained. And despite firing six bullets at him at point-blank range, Whitehead was only hit twice.

When they looked around for a motive to explain why Whitehead would murder Ruth Carver and her son, the lawmen found their answer in the small pile of jewelry that was gathered together on top of a vanity. In Whitehead's back pocket, they found a white beaded necklace and a small jewelry box. Chief Stivender and Sheriff Wolff surmised that Ruth had woken up from her nap to see Whitehead stealing her jewelry, which caused her to scream. Instead of running out of the house through an exterior door in that same bedroom, Whitehead responded by bludgeoning Ruth and Lee to death with a hatchet covered by a golf-club sock. The cutting edge was fairly clean but the blunt edge was soaked with blood.

During a coroner's hearing that was assembled a few hours later, at 5:00 p.m., Ray Carver told the same story he had told police. After Dr. Mitchell examined the bodies at a local morgue, he testified that the thirty-four-year-old mother of two had bled to death from five deep gashes to her cerebrum. The wounds were inflicted behind Ruth's right ear, and were administered by the hatchet covered with the golf-club stocking. Three of the five wounds were caused by the blunt edge, and two by the cutting edge.

Dr. Mitchell also told the coroner's jury that when he found her, Ruth Carver was lying on her back with her left arm at the side and the right arm extended. Her head was twisted to one side, and there was a slight wound on the cheek in front of her right ear. Ray's two year-old son, Lee, was struck by two blows behind the right ear—the same location as his mother's wounds. There were no bullet wounds to either Ruth or her son.

The coroner's jury concluded that Ruth and her son were murdered by Ben Whitehead, and that Whitehead was then shot to death by Mr. Carver. His killing was ruled justifiable homicide.

Although they came to their decision swiftly, and some members of local law enforcement considered it an open-and-shut case, there was one man who thought things were moving too fast. He wanted to take a second look for himself.

Grady Burton was a young, aggressive prosecuting attorney for the Nineteenth Judicial Circuit[1] which held Highlands County within its boundaries. Thirty-six hours after the incident, he met with Sheriff Wolff and Chief Stivender, who walked him through the crime scene.

With Carver's story as his initial guide, Burton found it strange that Whitehead was found on his back with two gunshot wounds—either of which would have been fatal. Burton decided this single peculiarity was enough for him dig into the incident more thoroughly.

"I wasn't satisfied that a person shot through the head and heart would fall on his back," Burton wrote in a 1932 magazine article. "I felt this point should be cleared up . . . and it started me upon an investigation that was to continue through several hours of intensive effort and study."

If Whitehead did in fact assault Ruth and Lee Carver in the bedroom where blood-splatter was found on the floor, walls,

---

[1] Highlands County was in the Nineteenth Judicial Circuit at that time. Today, Highlands County is part of the Tenth Circuit. Under the Florida judiciary system, felony cases, and civil cases that exceed a specific dollar amount, are heard in circuit court which is one level higher than the county courts.

ceiling, and furniture, then why was there more blood on Mr. Carver then there was on Ben Whitehead? The only blood stains found on the thirty-two-year-old laborer were from his own bullet wounds. With the exception of the jewelry in his back pocket, there was no evidence Whitehead was even in Ruth's bedroom.

By contrast, Lottie Alsymeyer and the two telephone company employees reported that Carver's shirt had blood stains on both the front and the back.

"The back of the shirt was crimson-stained in several places, especially between the shoulders," Burton wrote. "The stains bore out their statements. The end of the golf-stocking [which covered the hatchet] was also covered with stains."

What the state attorney was getting at in his article, without saying it directly, is that he believed those stains on the back of Carver's shirt likely came from raising the covered hatchet up to bring it down for each blow to the head of his wife and child.

After Surgenior helped Mr. Carver remove his shirt, that key piece of evidence was lost to investigators. Lottie's husband, Louis Alsmeyer, took the shirt home and put it in a pot of cold water to lift the fresh blood stains out of it.

"He did so without any intent to destroy evidence," Burton asserted. "He had found the shirt in Carver's home while helping to clear away traces of the horrible tragedy. Deciding it was a good shirt, he took it home and put it in the pot preparatory to having it washed."

When Sheriff Wolff later examined the golf knickers Carver was wearing that Wednesday afternoon, Burton learned he had found spots "that looked like blood spots that had been washed off." When Mrs. Alsmeyer and the telephone linemen told the prosecutor they saw Mr. Carver washing up over the kitchen sink, it only added to his suspicions.

News of the tragedy traveled fast, and two local newspaper reporters arrived at the house shortly after local law enforcement appeared. One of those reporters was snooping around when he discovered a $10,000 life insurance policy on Ruth Carver. He also found a golf-club stocking under the kitchen sink which matched the one that covered the hatchet. The policy had been taken out four months earlier and named her husband and children as beneficiaries. Like many life insurance policies, Ruth's paid double in case of accidental or violent death.

Chief Stivender told Burton that, while questioning everyone who was there that afternoon, he had heard Carver crying, "My God! I'm sorry I did it. Why did I do it?" This was later confirmed by one of the newspaper reporters who was in the house when it was said.

When Burton tried to question the widowed husband about the incident and get clarification on some of the issues raised by witnesses, Burton felt that Carver was evasive with his answers.

"He was reluctant to talk and appeared to dislike being questioned about the matter," Burton wrote in his magazine article. "He offered us little encouragement and seemed satisfied to let the matter rest as it stood."

Although he found circumstantial evidence which directed suspicion at Ray Carver, Burton also learned that on the morning of the day she was killed, Ruth Carver had been chatting outside with Lottie's father-in-law and had told him, "I'm afraid of that Negro." Whitehead, who was working in a flowerbed at the time, was staring directly at her while she spoke. Emanuel Alsmeyer also told Burton that Mrs. Carver appeared extremely nervous that morning.

Weighing this new evidence in his mind, the thirty-six-year-old prosecutor had William Raymond Carver arrested, and Burton called for a new coroner's hearing. Admittedly, he would later write, "the evidence I had at that time did not fully justify it."

In spite of this, Burton presented his circumstantial evidence, and the case was recommended to a grand jury which charged William Carver with all three murders.

"We are going clear to the bottom of this case, in order to uncover every angle," Burton boldly announced to the press while the grand jury toured the Carver's rented home.

As soon as Carver was indicted, news of the tragedy and his arrest exploded onto the front pages of newspapers nationwide. Reporters from New York, Pennsylvania, and all corners of Florida invaded quiet little Sebring to cover one of the most sensational murder cases the Sunshine State had ever seen. It was a high-profile crime that had all the ingredients of a sensation-driven story: racial tension, a defendant from a wealthy family with good social standing, an innocent wife and mother brutally murdered with her baby son by a hatchet, a dead black man who may or may not have been the perpetrator, and circumstantial evidence that failed to conclusively answer if Carver was guilty or not, which only deepened the mystery.

Everyone who followed the case had an opinion, and they weren't shy about expressing it either. "I estimate that I received approximately 10,000 letters," Burton wrote in 1932. "Some of them praised me for my efforts; others offered advice and suggestions; several hundred severely criticized me for having this man sent to jail and placed on trial. A few threatened me should I continue the case."

Because Circuit Court Judge William Barker was named in news reports as the presiding judge, he received a similar number of letters with the same mixture of sentiments.

When Ruth's mother and brother arrived in Sebring not long after Carver was indicted, there was no confusion over their opinion. Julius Stapff, and his mother, Marie Stapff-Boardman, stood firmly behind Ray. After visiting her son-in-law in jail, Ruth's mother scoffed at the "guilty or not" questions reporters lobbed at her.

"I spent two winters with my daughter and her husband and there was nothing but harmony in their married life," Marie told reporters. "He was a devoted husband and father and a wonderful son-in-law to me. If I thought there was one little inharmonious thing in their lives, I would be the first one to tell about it because I would want my daughter's death avenged."

Carver's brother-in-law also had strong words of support. "It is foolish to even think that he could have committed such a crime," Julius Stapff declared to reporters. He had known Ray for ten years, and described him as a "devoted and loyal husband."

When reporters were allowed into the jail to interview him, Carver held the same indignation over his arrest as his in-laws. "This is ridiculous. They ought to know better," he told them. "How can anyone think that I could have done it?"

For his son's defense, Samuel Carver hired Walter Bell, a state senator and former judge, and Mitchell Price, another defense lawyer who once served as a judge before going into private practice. Their first task was to file a writ of habeas corpus to push back against a no-bail order, and then free their client on a $15,000 bond. At Carver's preliminary hearing, Bell and Mitchell sought to get the charges dropped but were unsuccessful. They then requested a thirty-day extension to the start of trial, a move that Burton opposed. Unlike his own attorneys, Carver wanted a speedy trial without delay so he could get back to his life and care for his remaining daughter.

The State of Florida versus William Raymond Carver began on May 12, just forty days after the killings. The small courthouse in Sebring was packed every day of the trial with courtroom gawkers who came from all over the country. Those lucky enough to get a seat brought a sack lunch so they wouldn't lose their coveted place during the noon recess.

As part of his strategy to get a conviction, Burton tried Carver only for the murder of his wife. He knew jurors might acquit him of killing a black man, and for his son, there was no apparent motive. But for Ruth, the defendant had a $10,000 motive with double indemnity. Her family disagreed and their support of William had not wavered. Ruth's mother and brother were there every day, alongside his own parents and younger brother, Roy. It was a strong show of support noted by newspaper reporters who covered the trial.

"Carver, surrounded by relatives of himself and his wife, sat through the morning session with his eyes fixed on the floor, his lips nervously twitching, with little to say to those about him," the Associated Press reported.

After two days devoted to selecting a jury, Burton was blunt when he told those ten men his case was built around circumstantial evidence. He opened with Dr. Mitchell's account of the crime scene as he had found it that fateful afternoon. As the doctor directed the jury's attention to an architectural diagram of the house, the prosecutor saw that this was inadequate and made a motion to Judge Barker to reconvene the next day with the jury at the Carver home "so that they would have a competent understanding of a description of the scene as presented by witnesses."

To Burton's surprise, the defense concurred with his motion. Bell believed the jury would have a better picture of his client's claims of self-defense.

At the Carver house the next morning, Dr. Mitchell pointed out how he had found Whitehead dead with his head in front of the bathroom door, and his feet extended to an archway that opened to the hallway leading to Ruth's bedroom on their right and the defendant's on the left. In Ruth's bedroom, which was a master bedroom on the northeast corner of the house, Mitchell described how he had found Lee and Ruth on the floor between the front of the bed and a vanity desk against the wall.

Over the next several days, Burton called twelve witnesses, whose testimony helped him weave together the circumstantial evidence. The foundation of his argument was Carver's blood-stained shirt and the lack of blood splatter on Whitehead's shirt. He also built suspicion around Carver's washing himself over the kitchen sink, and a witness account of stains that looked like blood spots on Carver's golf knickers.

Bell countered the state's case with twenty depositions and twenty-seven witnesses. His first witness was Sebring Police Chief Richard Stivender, who described the scene, as well as the moment when he heard Carver sob, "I'm sorry I did it. So sorry I did it." Bell would get to the bottom of that statement later. The remainder of that first day of the defense's case was to call thirteen character witnesses and read to the jury eighteen depositions attesting to William Carver's good character. Nine of the character witnesses were from Miami, and all the depositions were taken from people in Pennsylvania who knew the couple.

"All of the character witnesses and the depositions stated that Carver's reputation was excellent and that he was known as a kind and considerate father and husband," reported the *Palm Beach Post*. "Several of the witnesses testified they had known Carver for as long as ten years. While others referred to him and his late wife as 'the happiest couple' they ever saw. All of them said they never heard him say an unkind word either to his wife or children, and that he was particularly fond of his small son Lee."

Over the objection of the state, Bell called Emanuel Alsmeyer to relate a conversation he had with Ruth Carver on the morning before the incident. She told him that the day before the tragedy, Whitehead had "made for me," or "went for me," as if he wanted to attack her. "I'm afraid of that Negro," she added. As the two were talking, Alsmeyer said Whitehead was staring at Mrs. Carver as he stood twenty feet away, leaning on a hoe near a flowerbed.

On Saturday, May 17, the second day of the defense's case, Carver's landlord, Tom Mitchell, testified that Carver seemed genuinely distraught over the loss of his wife and baby.

"'I can't see why I should have all this,'" Mitchell quoted Carver as having said. "'I wish I had got mine over there while I was in the army. I've been through hell once and now have nothing to live for.'"

Mitchel said he told Carver, "You have your daughter to live for."

Larry Whitener, another black yardman who worked for Tom Mitchell, testified that the day before the murders, Ben Whitehead was nursing a hangover. "[He] acted peculiar and had a sullen look about him," Whitener testified.

Mitchell's friend, Louis Evers, told the court he stopped by the house on the day of the murders to borrow some fishing poles, and he spoke briefly with Mrs. Carver who he said seemed nervous. "Ah, I am so glad you are here," she told him. She never explained why she was glad he was there, and since he didn't know her that well, he did not engage her in a conversation.

But the highlight of Saturday's testimony was when Ray Carver took the stand to tell his story. Although he started out appearing calm and composed, throughout his one hour and fifteen minutes of testimony he was overcome by grief, and the tenor of his voice rose as he fought to get his words out.

On the day of the murder he had played golf that morning. When he returned around noon, the family had lunch before lying down to take a nap. Before he went to his own bedroom, Carver said he told Whitehead to wash the dishes and then mop the bathroom and kitchen floors.

"I went into my bedroom to take a nap," Carver said, "and was suddenly awakened by screams. I ran into her bedroom and—oh, dear, there was my wife and boy!"

Carver broke down and sobbed and covered his eyes with his hand. It took him an entire minute to recover and resume his story. When he looked in the bedroom, he saw Whitehead with something in his hand, but he did not see him hacking his wife and son with the hatchet. He then ran back to his bedroom, grabbed his small revolver and fired at Whitehead who was coming at him down the hallway. He staggered backward but did not fall until Carver was out of bullets.

"When I shot, he screamed, and I shot him until he fell down," Carver told the jury. "Then, I saw he might get up again and I wanted to kill him—the dirty skunk—as any other white man would do."

At this point, Carver once again broke into tears. When he continued, he said he ran back into his bedroom to reload his pistol, and he shot Whitehead again as he lay on the floor. He then rushed into his Ruth's bedroom where he saw his wife and son with their heads bloodied by the sock-covered hatchet.

"At that point, Carver again broke down. His voice, which in the early part of his testimony had been low but distinct, now rose to a shrill falsetto as he tried to continue while struggling against his emotion. His face was distorted and beads of perspiration stood out noticeably on his forehead," an Associated Press report revealed.

Seeing that his wife was still alive but unconscious, Carver said he got a towel and wrapped it around his little boy's head. Then, he telephoned for police, a physician, and his neighbor, Mrs. Louis Alsmeyer, who did everything she could to console him after the police arrived. He admitted he couldn't remember much about what had occurred in the house when everyone was there. His memory was foggy.

"Mr. Carver, did you kill your wife and child?" Bell asked him.

"No, sir," he replied loudly. It was "that dirty skunk of a Negro."

He then repeated to the jury that when he went to his wife's bedroom, Whitehead had something in his hand and started after him.

"I don't know what it was," he said, "but I know he was after me and he had done something to my wife and I had to get my gun."

When he met Whitehead in the hall, he started shooting at him, and Whitehead threw up his hands and "screamed like a wildcat."

On redirect, Bell brought into evidence the life insurance policy and questioned Carver about it, who said his wife had signed up for it on her own accord. Taken out on December 13, 1929, the policy, with her signature, named her husband and both of her children as the beneficiaries. Bell also introduced into evidence checks Ruth had written from her personal bank account to pay the premiums herself.

Bell continued by asking Carver what he meant when witnesses testified that he said, "I'm sorry I did it—so sorry I did it."

Carver answered that he was sorry he took a nap while leaving Whitehead in the house unattended.

Later that same day, Ruth's mother explained to the jury her daughter had a distinctive, high-pitched soprano voice. Earlier in the trial, state witnesses said the screams they heard could not be identified as male or female. If observers thought this was a barely relevant point, to Bell, it wasn't. It was meant to pick apart the state's theory that Carver shot Whitehead first, and then bludgeoned his wife and son to death, and it was her screams that witnesses had heard. Instead, he wanted to show it was possible the screams had come from Whitehead.

Monday saw more witnesses and rebuttal witnesses testify before closing arguments were presented on Tuesday, May 20. As Bell reviewed Carver's character and the entire case over several hours, his key point noted by observers was that Carver was wealthy enough from his own real estate endeavors, and "would not have to do a thing like this for a paltry $10,000 life insurance policy."

Bell also proposed a simple counterpoint to the prosecution's main argument. If this were in fact an elaborate scheme to collect $10,000, what did William have to gain by murdering his son? Why not wait until Ruth Carver was alone to "stage" the crime scene and shift blame to Whitehead? As for the blood on his shirt, it came when he inspected his wife and then aided his son by wrapping a towel around his head.

State prosecutor Burton closed with the assertion that Carver had planned the murder because his success had always been dependent on his father and wasn't his own. On April 2, he first shot Whitehead in the bathroom, which woke his wife who grabbed her son and ran around to the front of the bed where Carver beat them to death with the hatchet. Then, he fired several more shots to stage the crime.

The ten-man jury deliberated all night long until the morning of May 21, when they returned a guilty verdict with a recommendation of leniency. Carver grew pale when he heard the jury's decision, but he showed little emotion. His family, as well as Ruth's mother and brother, gathered round to comfort him as he sat back in his chair, stunned by the news.

Outside, Ruth's mother continued to voice her support. "I know William is innocent. Nothing that could ever happen will convince me otherwise. My years of intimate knowledge of the married life of William Carver and my daughter give me a confidence which nothing can alter."

Ruth's brother, Julius, was appalled by the verdict, and could barely hold back his anger.

"I have listened to every speck of evidence produced in this trial," he began as he stood outside the courthouse. "I have personally investigated the case. I loved my sister as much as any man in this world could love a sister and I would be the first one to feel bitter toward her slayer. But I know beyond any shadow of doubt that Bill Carver is as innocent of that crime as I am, and I know that the evidence produced upon the witness stand was not sufficient to justify such a verdict. The plain fact remains that an innocent man has been condemned."

Judge Barker delayed sentencing until after he had heard defense arguments for a new trial that were to be presented on June 9. Carver, in the meantime, remained in the county jail awaiting the judge's decision.

Not wanting to see his career-building case get away from him, prosecutor Grady Burton told reporters he would try Carver on the two still-open murder charges. But as June rolled into July, both sides waited as the judge reviewed the new trial motion. Most judgments on new-trial motions come quickly, often the same day they are presented, but Judge Barker seemed to be considering the motion.

Finally, on July 21, Judge Barker denied the defense's motion for a new trial. One month later, on August 18, nearly three months after the trial ended, Carver was brought to court to hear his sentence. Before doing so, he was asked if he had anything to say to the court.

"Yes," he replied. "This sentence should not be pronounced. I swear before God and man that I am not guilty of this hideous crime."

Taking up the jury's recommendation, Barker sentenced Carver to a life sentence in prison.

Denied bail, Carver was allowed to stay in the Highlands County Jail as his attorneys appealed his case. In April 1931, the appeals court upheld the circuit court ruling. Undeterred, Carver's defense attorneys petitioned the state supreme court for a rehearing of the case and, to everyone's surprise, their request was granted. This ultimately resulted in a three-to-two decision for a new trial.

With his second trial scheduled for March 1932, Carver's attorneys obtained a change of venue to DeSoto County. In a surprise move, defense attorney Bell subpoenaed Judge Barker as a defense witness, which forced the state to name Judge James Koonce to preside over the case. He set Carver's bond at $15,000 and after serving 563 days in jail, Carver was released.

Jury selection began on March 2. This time around, the press took no real interest in the case, and the top headlines during the ten days of the second Carver case were for the missing baby, Charles Lindberg Jr.

In his magazine article published later that year, prosecutor Grady Burton said his case was handicapped by the absence of two key witnesses. Sebring newspaper reporter Jack Cleaver had been killed in a car accident several months before, and Dr. John Mitchell lay dying in a Texas hospital.

After Burton presented a shorter version of his case, Walter Bell put on an aggressive defense which began with two days of testimony from witnesses who tore holes in the state's case.

One of the central points in the second trial was the fact that witnesses had heard screaming. Defense expert Dr. L.W. Martin testified that the blows to Ruth Carver's head were so severe they would have immediately rendered her unconscious. The scream Carver heard which awakened him likely occurred when Ruth woke to find Whitehead in her room stealing her jewelry. Ruth Carver's fears of Whitehead were also more thoroughly established in the second trial. It also came out that Carver was going to fire Whitehead later that day, and that the laborer may have known this.

On the third day, Carver took the stand to tell his story again.

"Did you kill your wife and baby?" Bell asked him.

"No, I did not," Carver replied in a loud voice.

"Who killed them?"

"Ben Whitehead," Carver answered.

"And did you kill Ben Whitehead?" Bell asked.

"Yes, sir."

Carver also testified that when he heard his wife scream, he ran into the room and saw his wife and child on the floor, and Whitehead "had his arm raised and was holding some dark instrument."

This time, the DeSoto County jury sided with Carver, and he was acquitted of his wife's murder. State Attorney Grady Burton dropped the two remaining charges against Carver.

Epilogue
According to a 2014 interview with William Carver's granddaughter, Carver's daughter, Frances, is still alive and eighty-five years old at the time of this writing. Frances passed

on to her daughter the story of her life after her father was acquitted.

"He told my mother that he was going to fire Ben Whitehead before the incident happened and that he felt Ben was angry and this was how he was going to pay them back," she recounted. "He was heartbroken and always said Ben Whitehead did it because he was disgruntled. My mom believed she was to be killed next."

For reasons that are unclear, William Carver was ostracized from his own family, as well as Ruth's, after his acquittal. His ordeal, and his estrangement from both families, embittered him.

"She [his wife's mother, Ruth Stapff-Boardman] blamed him for what happened—because it happened, not because he did it," the granddaughter explained.

With his name attached to a murder conviction, despite being later found innocent, and with employment opportunities made scarce by the depression, William Carver left his daughter in Ruth's care as he wandered the United States looking for work. He did odd jobs and jobs that paid cash, and learned to use an alias because no one would hire William Raymond Carver from Sebring, Florida.

When Frances was five or six years old, her father came back for her and brought her out to the Los Angeles area where he did odd jobs for the movie industry, sometimes working as an extra in films. He also did a little script-writing and editing but never received credit for his work. Frances never saw her grandmother again. Since neither family would have anything to do with William, their exclusion extended to his daughter, who became an innocent pawn in a grownups' game of selfish bitterness.

As hard as life was for William Carver, he made it even harder on Frances, who was forbidden to go to school until she was ten years old. Her existence had to be kept a secret in order to keep William's secret—that he was once convicted of a horrible murder.

"Mother had to stay at home," the granddaughter explained. "She was not allowed to go outside. She was told to stay in the house and nobody could know she was there."

It was a lonely, sad time for Frances, who learned how to read and write from her father. At the age when other children have friends and play outside, Frances had to stay indoors and do all the housework. When she was ten, Frances was allowed to go to school but was under strict orders to come home as soon as it had ended.

When she was twelve or thirteen, she came home from school one day to find a note that said: "I can't take care of you anymore. Go live with the neighbors." It was a harsh way of telling his daughter he had cancer. He would be in and out of a Veteran's Administration Hospital for the rest of his life.

When Frances was seventeen, William wrote to her, requesting a visit. By then, she was living in Santa Monica, California, with a foster family that showered her with love and care. Despite her conflicted feelings, she was encouraged to visit her father by the man who would soon become her husband. Not long after that visit, William Carver died in Los Angeles on October 8, 1950. He was fifty-nine years old.

"He was very depressed his entire life for losing his wife and child," the granddaughter learned from her mother. "He didn't know what to do with himself. He was just going through the motions of life."

At the age of seventeen, while living with her foster family in Santa Monica, Frances Carver worked in a Macy's department store as a clerk and occasional model (see photo on next page). She married in 1949, and the couple had two boys and two girls, one of whom was interviewed for this story.

Grady Burton: Four years after he lost the second trial, Grady Burton ran for the Democratic nomination for governor but lost, taking seventh place with just 7.6 percent of the vote.

He remained a prosecutor and handled many important cases for the state of Florida. He died in 1981 at the age of 87.

Frances Carver, 17, modeling a fur coat for Macy's Department Store.
(Courtesy of family)

Chapter Four: Mr. Secret Agent Man, 1930

ON THE EVENING of Wednesday, June 11, 1930, Joseph Mozynski was in a place he shouldn't have been, doing something he wasn't supposed to do. The thirty-nine-year-old owner of a small grocery store in Queens, New York, told his wife and mother of his two children that he was off to run a few errands. Instead, he picked up his nineteen-year-old mistress, Catherine May, and drove his four-door sedan to a secluded spot near Whitestone in the College Park area of Queens. The small, wooded area was just one of many locations throughout the borough that lovers adjourned to for nighttime trysts in parked cars. The couple's two-year-old affair had produced many amorous moments like this one, and they knew just what to do: they moved to the back seat where they could settle in and get comfortable for making love.

A few minutes into their heavy petting, a small, slender man appeared out of the shadows and startled the couple when he poked his head into the car through the open driver's side window. With gun in hand and a thick German accent, he ordered Joe to get back into the driver's seat while he let himself in and sat next to Catherine.

"Start the car," the intruder ordered.

Joe complied, and when the engine sputtered to life, the gunman pointed his pistol behind Joe's right ear and pulled the trigger. The force of the bullet spun Joe around until he was facing the back seat. When his mouth dropped open in shock and pain, a second bullet crashed through his teeth and exited out his cheek. Two bullets to the head should have been enough to kill him, but they didn't. And as Joe sank down behind the seat, Catherine could hear her lover rasping and moaning.

The stranger then turned his attention to the pretty nineteen-year-old girl beside him and raped her while her dying lover could do nothing but listen. After he had satisfied himself, the attacker exited the vehicle and opened the driver's door. When he did, Joe's bleeding, hard-breathing body fell partway out of the car. The gunman stood over him, reached into his victim's inside coat pocket, and pulled out some papers—as if he had expected them to be there all along. He studied their contents for a few moments before taking a match to each of them, scattering the ashes to the ground.

Joseph Mozynski

As he burned the papers one by one, he caught sight of Catherine trying to sneak out of the car. "I'll have to murder you if you don't behave," he warned her.

The gunman pressured Catherine for her home address and, with a flashlight retrieved from his pocket, he calmly walked the terrified girl to the village of Bayside where they boarded a bus bound for Flushing, Queens. Once they were seated, the strange man handed her a folded sheet of paper.

"Don't read this until tomorrow," he ordered.

After the bus reached the Flushing terminal, the stranger dutifully escorted Catherine to a trolley that would pass through her neighborhood in College Point. As the trolley began moving, her rapist gallantly bid her goodnight, hopped off, and disappeared into the darkness.

Still in shock, the young woman sat silently in her seat, too afraid to move until the trolley was several blocks away. When she felt it was safe, she opened the folded piece of paper in front of her. The message was stamped in red ink.

JOSEPH MOZYNSKI
3 X   3-X-097

Too traumatized to know what to do, the terrified girl went home and went to bed, but she was unable to sleep. A few miles away, her lover lay on the ground beside his car, dying slowly, but still alive.

Police found Joseph Mozynski's body the next morning and determined he had died sometime in the last hour. The detectives at the scene were Inspector John Gallagher, and Lt. James Smith, the same duo who years before had sent Ruth Snyder and her lover, Judd Gray, to the electric chair following one of the most sensational murder trials in New York history.

In the front seat, they found a woman's velvet coat stained with blood. Because the area they were in was known as a "lover's lane," Gallagher and Smith wanted to find the woman who owned the coat. They got their answer when they looked through the dead man's wallet and found a photograph of Catherine which they were able to use to track her down to her home in College Point later that evening. After establishing that she was with Mozynski when he was killed, Catherine was brought to the precinct for questioning. There, she told skeptical detectives the entire story of what had taken place the night before.

"I didn't know what to do," Catherine reportedly told them, "so I went home and went to bed."

Of course, they didn't believe her, even when she showed them the bizarre note.

"Why didn't you call the police?" Inspector Gallagher asked her.

"Because I didn't want my parents to know I was mixed up with a married man."

In spite of all their best efforts, detectives were unable to break Catherine from her story, but only at first. Arrested as a material witness, they held the young Civil Service Bureau employee on a $50,000 bond. What followed were three days of sleep-deprived, nonstop interrogation by police.

"The detectives saw to it that she had little sleep until they had finished questioning her," reported the *Brooklyn Standard-Union*. "All night and day Thursday, Friday, Saturday and Saturday night [June 12, 13, and 14] until after midnight, they questioned her until it seemed that she must break down."

The nonviolent form of third-degree tactics that were acceptable during that era for use on a woman slowly began to work. By Friday and Saturday, Catherine was weakening, just wanting the interrogation to end. The detectives' theory was that Mozynski was murdered by a jealous sweetheart of Catherine's. Without knowing this, she gave them the name of the man whose adoration of her had gone unrequited, Joseph Moissette. By Saturday, Catherine was blaming her lover's death on a made-up Italian gangster named Alberto Lombardo. She had told them the truth but they didn't want to believe it. If she could tailor her story to what they wanted, maybe she could go home.

Police found Moissette in Chicago aboard a California-bound train and brought him back to New York. Lombardo, they quickly realized, was a fictional person. Exhausted, and with barely any sleep since the night before her fatal rendezvous, Catherine next tried to confess she had killed her lover by herself. By then, fortunately, police didn't believe that either.

In another part of the city, events were unfolding that would not only exonerate Catherine but create a drama that would make New York City history.

On the Friday afternoon of June 13, the day after Mozynski's body was discovered, *New York Evening-Journal* city editor Amster Spiro sat down at his desk to sift through the day's mail. The *Evening-Journal* was owned by William Randolph Hearst and was one of the original muckraker newspapers of New York. By 1930, the *Journal* boasted the largest newspaper circulation in the United States. If a murdering maniac wanted to taunt police, shock readers, and bask in the publicity of his crimes, the *New York Evening-Journal* was the go-to newspaper of the day.

Mixed in with the usual press releases, reader complaints, letters to the editor, and crackpot manifestoes was a bizarre message on pink stationery that read:

> City Editor:
> Kindly print this in your paper for Mozynski's friends.
> CC-N Y ADCM-Y16a-DQR PA --241 PM6 Queens.
> By doing this you may save their lives. And the women may know where the missing papers are and who has them since they were given to Mozynski.
> We do not want any more shooting unless we have to."
> Signed,
> 3X, The Man Behind the Gun.

Spiro crumpled up the nut job's letter and was about to throw it in the trash when his brain made a connection.

Mozynski? Wasn't that the name of the guy they found out in College Point?

Spiro read the note again and then examined the envelope it came in. To his horror, he saw the postmark showed the letter was mailed several hours before the body was discovered. Soon, a dozen detectives were in his office to have a look at this new piece of evidence. No fingerprints were found on the letter and, at the time, police were unsure of what to make of the killer's odd message.

At first, the Mozynski story was relegated to the inside pages of the city's many newspapers. On the day the *Evening-Journal* received the letter from 3X, the newspaper made no mention of the note, and their front-page story on the case emphasized that Mozynski and his companion were caught *in flagrante delicto*. The *Evening-Journal* also spoke to one of Mozynski's relatives who knew about the affair and reported that Catherine was just one of his two extra-marital companions. The paper also sneeringly dubbed the dead man as "the Don Juan grocery man of College Point." The *New York Times*, less concerned with moral issues, devoted just one paragraph to the story when it noted the lack of progress in Miss May's questioning and made a brief mention of Moissette's arrest.

On Saturday, June 14, the *Journal* received another letter from 3X, written on stationery that came from the Civil Service Bureau office in College Point, the same place Catherine May worked.

> Ref: Mozynski Queens
> Gentleman:
> For your information, the young lady, Miss C. May, involved in the case is innocent and a victim of unfortunate circumstances. We always get them through their women friends. Mozynski was nothing but a rascal (obscenities omitted)–a dirty rat. Not two women as stated in the papers, but six, and two young girls, one 14 and one 15, were with him in that same place. I am the agent of a secret international order and when I met Mozynski that night it was to get from him certain documents but unfortunately, they were not in his possession.
> If his relative knew so much of his luck with women, maybe he would tell us what became of the following items:
> NYX-26-73; NJ 4-3-44; Philadelphia XV 346.
> These papers must be returned to us at once or 14 more of Mozynski's friends will join him. Mozynski's relatives and friends have up to Monday, 12 pm to bring these documents to us or to have someone get in touch with us, and tell us where to find

them. If no answer is received by that time, we will start merry
hell for all of them.
Signed,
A V 3X,
The Man Behind the Gun

*Kill fourteen more people? And what in the hell did the letters and
numbers mean?* Inspector Gallagher and his detectives didn't
believe the ramblings about a "secret international order," but a
lunatic on the loose was even more dangerous, and officers
were sent to guard all of Mozynski's relatives as a precaution.
Those same relatives told police that Joe had never been
affiliated with or betrayed any secret organization. The *Journal*
wasn't the only one to get a letter from 3X that day; Inspector
Gallagher received one as well. His was more brief and to the
point—Catherine May was innocent, and more people would
die in Queens if they didn't return his code-labeled documents.

Not wanting to play into the maniac's hands, the *Journal* kept
the letters a secret, a move that would later prove to have
frustrated 3X. Over the weekend, the daily newspapers were still
giving the story minimal copy space. On Monday morning,
June 16, the *Brooklyn Standard-Union* had only a seven-paragraph
story on page 16 which reported on Catherine's three-day face-
off with detectives and her false confession.

True to his word, 3X struck again later that Monday night
under familiar circumstances.

The following morning, a motorist on his way to work
spotted the irregularity of a new car parked among old wrecks
in an auto salvage yard near Floral Park in Queens. When the
passerby investigated, he found a dead man slumped behind the
wheel of a two-door coupe. Arriving officers inspected the
man's billfold and learned his name was Noel Sowley, a twenty-
six-year-old radio mechanic from Brooklyn. He'd been shot
twice in the head. They found something else: a calling card of
sorts left by 3X in the form of a newspaper clipping about the
Mozynski murder. Stamped directly on the article in red ink was

the name **MOZYNSKI**. In the margins, the killer wrote, *"Here's How,"* in pencil

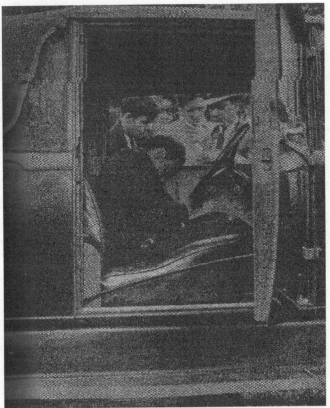

Noel Sowley slumped behind the steering wheel of his coupe.

At exactly the same time that Inspector Gallagher and his detectives were processing the crime scene and newspaper photographers were snapping pictures, city editor Amster Spiro was at his desk reading another dispatch from 3X.

> Dear Sir:
> You have not published the code message sent to you. Too bad. For your information, there is more work for the police. Tonight at 10:00 p.m. Sowley was bumped off near Floral Park, and not far away from a police signal station. You will find him

near an auto junk pile. We have selected this night to do it as Mozynski was buried today. This is our second warning to them. Thirteen more men and one woman will go the same way if they do not return two of the missing papers. N.Y. document was found on Sowley last night and also some of our money. As in the case of Mozynski's girlfriend, the girl was put on a bus and sent home.

We always get them through their women friends.

3X

When Inspector Gallagher returned to his office, he found a letter addressed to him from 3X. It was similar to the *Journal's* letter but it also contained an evidentiary present.

Inspector J.J. Gallagher
Lieutenant J. Smith
For your information, one more of J. Mozynski's friends was sent to meet him. V-5 Sowley was shot to death near Floral Park, and not very far away from police signal station. Some of our money was found on his person and the N.Y. document. This is the shell that killed Noel Sowley. I apologize for not sending the other shell but I lost it in my excitement. The girl was, as in the case of Miss May, put aboard a bus and sent home—but no clues were left for you this time. Thirteen more men and one woman will go if they do not make peace with us and stop bleeding us to death.

The shell was a .32 caliber, the same type used to kill both men. Police found "the girl." Her name was Elizabeth Ring. She was an eighteen-year-old divorcee who had recently rekindled a romance with Noel, a boyfriend she had dated before her brief and failed marriage to someone else.

According to the story she told police, a stranger appeared at the window of Sowley's car and, with a gun pointed at him, demanded to see his driver's license. Sowley complied and asked the man if there was a problem. The stranger then faced the rear of the car and flicked his flashlight on and off as if he were communicating by Morse code. When Sowley asked him what he was doing, the man with the German accent replied that he was signaling his friends on the hill that he did not require assistance.

"Then he handed some cards to Noel, asking, 'You know Joe Mozynski?' Noel said he did not know Mozynski. As Noel was saying that, the man shot him in the mouth," Elizabeth told police. "Noel gasped—but managed to mumble, 'I'm not the man you're looking for.' The gunman stepped away from the car, looked at the license plate, came back and said, 'You're Sowley all right,' and then shot him in the head again. He searched Noel's clothing, found a sheet of paper and exclaimed, 'I have it!'"

As he had done with Catherine, the stranger was about to rape the young girl but changed his mind after she pleaded with him while she displayed a religious medal she wore around her neck.

"He ordered me out of the automobile, then walked me more than a mile to a bus station, and put me aboard a bus for Jamaica," Elizabeth continued. "He handed me a piece of paper and warned me under threat of death, 'Don't open your mouth.' On the bus I looked at the piece of paper and shuddered. Rubber-stamped in red ink was the name of my friend **SOWLEY**. And under the name was penciled, 3X."

Miss Ring didn't call police for the same reason Catherine didn't: the shock and fear that comes after seeing your companion murdered were powerful motivators to keep quiet. It wasn't until police found her that she told them what happened.

Now that 3X had murdered two men, the story that had been simmering below the surface exploded onto the front pages of New York City newspapers. Newswire reports carried the bizarre tale to dailies across the United States. Agent 3X was now getting the attention he desired.

"What had started out as an insignificant homicide had now become a sensational drama," wrote one observer years later. "The case had all the elements of the most lurid type of mystery fiction: taunting notes to police, an international secret organization, all surrounded by an aura of sex."

Large, block headlines from the tabloids screamed fear into New York residents. A photograph of Noel Sowley slumped behind the wheel of his death-car suggested to other couples "this could be you." The *Evening-Journal* published all the letters and revealed the entire story of 3X and his two murders. Reporters worked late into the night, while Amster Spiro never went home at all. The next morning, he received another letter from 3X that would create mass hysteria and launch one of the largest manhunts in New York City history.

> Sir: I advise you to publish this code message: A V 3-X. Tonight one more will go. You may let them know 3X is the man behind the gun. He asks for no quarter but will give none. On June 18 [that day] at 9 p.m., I will be at College Point to get WR V-8.

Although it had taken police a while to regard 3X with the significance his letters demanded, Police Commissioner Edward Mulrooney threw everything he could into the case and ordered a small army of police officers to invade College Point that night to prevent the execution of agent WR V-8, whoever he was.

"The police seemed to join in the general hysteria and Queens took on the appearance of a beleaguered city," Jack Mauder would later write for *American Mercury* magazine. "An extra force of 425 detectives and 2,000 policemen were assigned to the less-frequented areas of the borough. Two emergency squads and a fleet of automobiles equipped with machine guns were pressed into service against the lone killer."

According to a 1955 story written by veteran crime writer Carl Sifakis, "100 officers were dolled up in women's clothes, wigged, rouged, and lipstick. Together with 100 detectives in male attire, they were sent in individual parked cars to isolated spots all over the neighborhood. From 6:00 p.m., the 'couples' sat facing each other, as if embracing. Actually, they each watched the window opposite them with loaded pistols. Any stranger who approached the car menacingly would likely get his head blown off."

In neighboring Nassau County, 600 officers and detectives kept close watch on all the petting places bordering Queens.

To make matters worse, the *Evening-Journal* ratcheted up the widespread panic and morbid excitement with a face-slapping headline blazoned across their afternoon issue:

TWO DEAD! FOURTEEN MORE TO DIE
AND ONE OF THEM A WOMAN, KILLER SAYS

"The *Journal's* harrowing story caused almost every College Point window to be shuttered that night, and hysteria swept the area," Sifakis continued. "There was a run on the gun-permit office and petters deserted their usual lovers' lane haunts."

The police invasion of College Point and Queens was hardly kept a secret, with headlines like this one from the *Brooklyn Daily-Star*:

2,000 POLICE IN HUNT FOR MANIAC 'PETTER-
SLAYER' WHO THREATENS TO MURDER THIRD
VICTIM TONIGHT

Now that police finally believed her story, Catherine's recollection of 3X was combined with Elizabeth's and printed on a police circular that went out to all officers, who were ordered to keep a copy with them at all times until the case was solved. Catherine's description was followed by Elizabeth's.

(A) Forty-years-old, five-feet six-inches, 125 pounds, pale complexion, wrinkled face, dark clothes, dark gray soft hat, speaks with foreign accent.

(B) Thirty-years-old, pale complexion, thin face, sunken cheeks, lanky build, little hump on bridge of nose, small eyes, thick lips, peculiar teeth, wore black suit, black bow tie, white shirt, soft white collar and black fedora hat with telescopic brim. Speaks with accent indicating German extraction. Wore a small, round bronze button on left lapel of coat marked "Rifle Association."

Artist rendering of secret agent 3X, "The Man Behind the Gun."

As the evening hours approached, Elizabeth and Catherine were taken to the Creedmoor State Hospital for the Insane [war veterans] where all 1,931 residents were brought into the large dining room and slowly paraded past the two women. None of them resembled 3X. The women were then shuttled back to court in secret, where their bonds were reduced and they were released but placed under heavy protection by police. Guards were posted at the girls' homes. A police matron was assigned to Elizabeth, and the cops even prevented newsmen from taking pictures of their star witnesses, which ruffled a few feathers.

"At the Jamaica headquarters the police took extra precautions to prevent photographers from getting a picture of her [Elizabeth]. A squad of twenty-five men under the command of Captain John Boyle cleared the sidewalks in front of the building of all newspapermen, jostling them in a fashion they regarded as unnecessary in most cases," reported the *Brooklyn Daily-Star*. "One reporter protested against the roughness of the officers, and he was taken into the station house, presumably under arrest. Inspector Gallagher intervened, however, and he was released."

As the army of police officers fanned out and took up positions, patrolled beats, hid behind trees, or sat in cars dressed in drag, all waiting for 3X to make good on his promise to assassinate another traitor to his organization, thousands of residents from all parts of New York drove to College Point that Monday night in the hopes of seeing some action.

"Attracted by the murderer's threat, several thousand curious persons motored to College Point and spent hours along Thirteenth Street and intersecting avenues waiting for something to happen," The *Daily-Star* continued. "During a period of two and one-half hours, more than 2,200 automobiles passed over the causeway into College Point. The main streets gave the community a carnival appearance with crowds moving slowly along the sidewalk for hours in the hope of 'being in on' the killing."

Everyone was watching, listening for a gunshot, a scream, maybe a speeding car. Six p.m. came and went, and then seven and eight ticked by. As the promised hour of the nine o'clock execution of agent V8 got closer and closer, the excitement was building. Officers with shoot-to-kill orders were on edge. The crowd of morbid spectators kept their voices low and strained to hear the inevitable gunshots and screams. In a few moments, somebody was going to die . . . Nine . . . Nine-thirty . . . Ten.

But nothing happened.

Although the promised third murder did not occur, newspapers the next morning revealed that the largest dragnet in New York City history did catch some fish. All of them were eventually thrown back.

"Some brave 'petters' braved the wrath of the so-called 'moral avenger' and held their usual trysts. Most of them gave Queens, especially College Point, a wide berth. Police ordered all occupants of parked cars to 'keep moving,'" the *Daily-Star* reported the next day. "Pedestrians were closely scrutinized, and many were questioned until they had satisfied officers to their business in the area. Some had to call on neighbors and friends to vouch for them."

When officers surprised a lone man sitting in his automobile in the Richmond Hill area, he jumped in his seat and the first words out of his mouth were, "I didn't kill anybody!" He was taken in for questioning just to make sure. Another man found crawling in a clump of weeds and tall grass near College Point was also taken in. Both were put into a line-up for Catherine and Elizabeth, who didn't recognize either. Three teenaged boys thought it would be fun to play on everyone's nerves by setting off some fireworks, but they weren't even able to light a match before police did a stop-and-search. They were told to go home.

As he would soon explain in a *Journal* bound letter mailed a few hours before the scheduled execution, it wasn't necessary for 3X to take out his intended target after all. There was a twist to his drama that all of New York would read about the following afternoon in the *Evening-Journal*.

> WR V8 of CP has returned the Philadelphia XV346 to me tonight after reading your paper—also 37,000 dollars of blackmail money—thanks to God—if I may use his name.

In the same letter, 3X explained that the return of the money and secret document "Philadelphia XV346" were enough to spare the lives of WR V8, the woman, and five other men. But in 3X's world, that still left seven operatives who needed to be killed. Fortunately, he also gave them a way out. Maybe.

> The following document still is missing N. J. 4-3-44 and 39,000 dollars for this document. The following people still are marked for death, X14, X21, Y2, O6, X7, S1, V4.
>
> The only way they may continue to live is to follow the directions in this code message: N.J. — CC.KZMAWAEEAA.V.—3X—R.G.—4 MYT—RP 49-6.

If the seven targets of 3X's wrath believed they would be allowed to live by simply returning whatever money and documents he was demanding, he flat-out contradicted himself when he wrote, in the same letter, that he asked his superiors for mercy in certain cases "but the word came back, 'No, Fire.'"

Live, not live, mercy, no mercy—all in the same letter. If 3X lacked the self-awareness of his own apparent contradictions, it wasn't lost on experts who were keeping up with his every move as told through the newspapers. One leading psychiatrist diagnosed 3X as a paraphrenic—an early 20th Century mental illness classification similar to what is known today as paranoid schizophrenia. The psychiatrist went on to explain this condition to newspaper readers.

> Persons suffering from the former are obsessed with delusions and hallucinations and the delusions may be either groundless or persecutory. The patients commonly complain that their thoughts are read or that their brains are controlled. The hallucinations may affect all senses, and, like the delusions, are bizarre and mysterious.
>
> If the killer belongs to the latter class he is suffering from a disorder which is a progressive condition and in which incidents in his life are misinterpreted and distorted so as to fit into a basic delusional system.

If this is true he is probably an egocentric who displays dangerous propensities because he has delusions of persecutions and that some persons are plotting against him.

Even if the police didn't believe 3X was a secret agent on a mission, 3X believed he was, and in his world all of it was very real.

Approximately three hours after detectives received his letter that agent WR V8 was spared, they received yet another letter from him in which he couldn't resist antagonizing the police with a claim that he had been watching them on the night they invaded College Point. The letter was addressed to a patrolman by name who had spent the night of June 18 in a police signal station.

"I saw you cleaning your gun last night," he wrote the officer. "I hope you didn't expect to shoot me. You will never find me."

As police were studying the letters for possible clues, on Thursday, June 19, 3X took a train ride to Philadelphia where he mailed a letter to Joe Mozynski's brother, John. The special-delivery letter told John he was "next on the list" and ordered him to leave the valuable papers in the lavatory of the Broad Street train station in Philadelphia, or "death will follow." John wasn't a secret agent; he was a plumber who lived in the Philadelphia suburb of Port Richmond with his wife and four children. His friends created a human barrier around his home that night to protect him against 3X.

Philadelphia detectives moved fast by trying to back-track the special-delivery letter to the sender. By sheer coincidence, 3X wasn't the only mentally unbalanced person using the Philadelphia special-delivery mail system that day. John Clarke, a thirty-four-year-old escaped inmate of Kings Point Mental Hospital in Long Island, was arrested after police traced some of his bizarre letters to his rooming house address in Philadelphia.

"Clarke's ravings, when he was overcome by detectives in a desperate battle, were on subjects which recalled some of the statements of the Queens maniac murderer's newspaper letters," the *Daily-Star* reported on June 20. However, Clarke's own doctor helped to clear him as a suspect when he was interviewed by a different *Daily-Star* reporter for the same issue.

> Clarke has always been a confirmed letter writer, but he never gave any indication while he was here that he would ever resort to violence. He is afflicted with a "persecution complex" and is otherwise harmless. He spent most of his time here writing letters to various officials in which he harangued the superintendents of the numerous institutions in which he has been confined.
>
> He is simple-minded and has the mentality of an eight-year-old child. It would have been impossible for him to write the letters received by the police and newspapers.

On June 19, the same day all eyes were on Philadelphia, Morris Horwitz, a fifty-year-old insurance salesman from Brooklyn, was about to put his car in the garage when a stranger appeared out of nowhere and pointed a gun in his face.

"Get going," he commanded.

Although he was sitting behind the wheel, Horwitz tried to lie his way out of the predicament. "I don't know how to drive a car."

The gunman reached in, pistol-whipped Horwitz, and then shot him once in the shoulder. He fired a second time but missed. Mrs. Horwitz, who was sitting on the front porch, stood up, screamed, and then promptly fainted. The would-be carjacker ran off down Carroll Street to Brooklyn Avenue and disappeared up an alley.

"Within a few minutes, 300 policemen had formed a cordon around the scene and a house-to-house search for the attacker followed," an Associated Press report stated.

From his hospital bed the next day, Horwitz told police the shooter was "wild-eyed as if he were crazy." He also described him as a short, slender man with blonde hair—a description that somewhat resembled 3X.

Although the attacker was never found, police did recover two .45 shell casings. Mozynski and Sowley were killed by a .32 caliber pistol. In spite of the difference in calibers, police and newspapers treated 3X as the number one suspect over the next few days.

The Horwitz incident was just one of many misdirected leads police received. When a man in the Bronx got a threatening letter from 3X, police quickly matched the handwriting to his own wife. "The dirty bum was two-timing me again and I figured if I gave him a good scare, he'd stay home at nights," wrote Carl Sifakis in his 1955 crime-magazine article.

After a man was murdered in New England, four different letters were mailed to police and newspapers claiming he was killed by 3X because he betrayed the group. All of them were fakes.

Paranoid residents of Queens called police every time they saw a suspicious-looking man lurking in the shadows. For their part, police were rounding up anyone who matched 3X's description and parading them through the Jamaica precinct for Catherine May and Elizabeth Ring to scrutinize. Complete copies of the 3X letters were sent to government code-breakers in Washington DC and Chicago. New Yorkers who delighted in doing crossword puzzles were looking over the codes and sending suggestions to area newspapers. The CCNY reference could mean College of the City of New York, they proposed. The NJ 4-3-44 document could mean it concerned New Jersey. The V8 in WR V8 could be a type of automobile engine.

While police were hunting what some newspapers were calling the "petter slayer," or "morality murderer," agent 3X was focused on his own mission and by nine o'clock at night on June 19, a few hours after Horwitz was shot in his driveway, 3X was getting back what he needed from those who had betrayed his secret organization. In a letter received by the *New York Evening-Journal* on June 21, 3X proclaimed his mission was over in a bizarre letter in which he first boasted of his exploits, and then described himself with false modesty.

Dear Sir:

The last document, NJ 4-3-44 returned to us the 19 at 9 p.m. My mission is ended. There is no further cause for worry. I do not know Doctor Williams and the others. The first sign means A, the supreme tribunal of the order. The second V, its special agent. The two combined form the Red Diamond of Russia, a secret organization all over the world. Anyone breaking its rules is marked for death. These men were dismissed for treason. They were all our friends but came in contact with a gang of blackmailers and a drug ring and turned against us. One of them stole the documents mentioned before and they tried to use them for blackmailing our men here. Most of us are soldiers and every nation in the world is represented in our ranks.

Word came to us at the supreme council in Russia of the peril in the U.S. Twelve of us picked one card. Mine was the king of diamonds. I was the one selected to punish, and inflict death if necessary. I have patiently waited. I have warned them all of danger. Instead of heeding the warning they answered me by blackmail. They were requested many times for the return of the papers but refused to surrender them. It was when Mozynski died that they found out who I am. Now it is all over. The documents in question—one is a military document, another is political and the third one just surrendered is commercial.

Who am I? Not much. An ex-German Army officer of the Wilhelm St. Office, Berlin, during the war. Now in the service of the Red Diamond of Russia. Yes the code was addressed to Sowley. Now it is all over. You show me to be brave. Any man who took orders from this 77 is fearless. Your policemen are brave men only they need training. I was watching them at C.P. [College Point] on the 18th at 9 sharp.

A German officer never breaks his word—yes, right there. Have you heard a plane? It was a monoplane, small, very fast. The plane circled twice over Flushing, C.P. Bayside, then went away. If you did then you will know I was there . . . I have no fish eyes. The police have fish eyes . . . They have always been wrong from beginning to end. That is why they have lost from beginning to end. For two reasons. One I have stated to you. The other, they are too slow.

I am deeply sorry for having stained your country with blood but let this be a warning to all concerned—treason of one means death. The next time no mercy will be shown. Death only will be the penalty, but I hope I will not be the one to inflict it next time. We are not maniacs or bandits or robbers—robbery never was the motive and we do not belong to any dope ring. This is final. You know what we want you to know. Quiet your people and tell them that 3X is no more.

H.P. 12W.A.

PS: Do not let anyone fool you, if any more letters come they are fakes. I am leaving today on my way back to Russia. Please note I do not write USSR. We do not recognize them. There is no one else to begin trouble. It is settled.

H.P. 12W.A.

From his letter, it was obvious to all that 3X took special delight in having outwitted police while successfully completing his mission in a drama where he portrayed himself as the dashing and gallant hero. He may have seen himself that way, but the public did not, and other New York newspapers characterized him as "a lover's lane killer," or the "petter-murder maniac." There was nothing heroic about ambushing two men, or gallant about raping Catherine May.

Despite the claim that his mission was over, detectives did not believe it and Commissioner Mulrooney publicly declared the widespread manhunt for the killer of Mozynski and Sowley would continue for thirty more days. Out of the invasion force of twenty-five hundred police officers and detectives sent in to College Point, two hundred were kept on to patrol the "petting lanes" of Queens.

Over the next few months, dozens of letters claiming to be from 3X were mailed to police, newspapers, or various individuals. Each one had to be taken seriously until it was proven to be fake. From these, a pattern emerged in which it became obvious that, in some cases, the sender held a grudge against the receiver whom they wanted to get revenge on by causing stress and fear.

A few days after 3X bid farewell, a potential break in the case came when Elizabeth Ring spotted a man in a "Rogue's Gallery" mug shot book whom she said was similar in appearance to 3X. His name was Nicholas LaRoche and he was a thirty-eight-year-old church sexton from Mount Vernon, a small community north of the Bronx. LaRoche had once forged a prescription to obtain narcotics and his handwriting on the prescription was a close match to the killer's, who addressed his envelopes in longhand.

LaRoche was picked up by police and brought in, where he was examined for a full thirty minutes by both witnesses. He was even made to dress in clothes similar to what the killer wore on the nights Mozynski and Sowley were murdered. Eventually, the girls decided LaRoche was not 3X.

Over the next few weeks, police followed up on leads, tips, sightings, and even false confessors—all of which were blind alleys. After a $5,000 reward was announced, a Bronx fingerprint examiner and a civil engineer from New Jersey were arrested in separate cases when the schemes they concocted to get the reward money backfired on them.

On July 8, Commissioner Mulrooney pulled the 200-man detail from Queens with the statement that he believed 3X had in fact left the area, just as he had claimed in his final letter. Despite this move, the commissioner assured the public that the search for 3X would continue. It was an investigation that was costing the city of New York $10,000 a day, and would eventually top out at $1 million before police quietly gave up.

After all the remaining clues and suspects had been cleared, the investigation stalled. "The hue and cry in the newspaper subsided; lovers returned to their trysting places and the mysterious figure of 3X sank into limbo," Jack Mauder wrote.

The 3X story would pop into the newspapers again after convincing letters were received in October of 1930, and again in October of 1931. In each of them, the writer warned of murders to come that were never fulfilled, and no follow-up letters arrived to explain why they hadn't. It remained unclear who had sent them.

New Yorkers forgot about the "petter slayer" for six years, until the afternoon of October 3, 1937, when two young sweethearts were found shot and stabbed in a parked car in a secluded area in Hollis, Queens. Twenty-year-old Lewis Weiss and his nineteen-year-old girlfriend, Frances Hajek, had both been shot in the right temple. The killer then took the girl's lipstick and drew a crimson circle on the forehead of each victim. After a thorough investigation and an appeal to the public for help, police could find no motive for the murders and no connection to 3X.

"These strange symbols, coupled with the surrounding circumstances, were strongly reminiscent of the 3X murders," Mauder wrote. Eventually, this theory was dropped and the "lipstick murders," as they became known, went unsolved.

In the absence of actually solving the 3X murders, detectives and reporters who had worked on the case put forth their theories, which ranged from 3X was a sex maniac, to the belief that he was a clever killer whose motivation to slay one of the two men was obfuscated by a second murder. They also believed his bizarre letters claiming a secret international organization was behind his actions was all part of his elaborate ruse—whether it was for sex or murder, or both.

Nobody really believed the secret agent theory—unless one considered it strange that one month before his death, Mozynski had mysteriously deposited more than $8,000[1] in his bank account. After he killed "V5" Noel Sowley, 3X reported in his letter to the newspaper, "N.Y. document was found on Sowley last night and *also some of our money.*" He may have been telling the truth about recovering "some of our money." He didn't get all of it, though, because police found a wadded-up

---

[1] $114,000 in 2014.

roll of cash stuffed inside a blood-stained magazine near Sowley's car.

Secret agent or not, 3X may actually have been trying get his money back.

Chapter Five: Spree Killer Chester Comer, 1934-1935

THE BULLET IN CHESTER COMER'S head made it difficult for him to speak. As he lay on the floor of a mechanic's garage in Blanchard, Oklahoma, his head bandaged with a bloody towel, state crime bureau agents and lawmen from four counties gathered around to try and make sense of his mumbling, incoherent words.

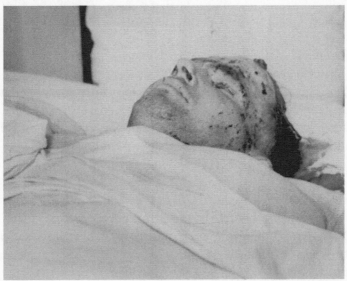

Oklahoma Spree Killer Chester Comer in a hospital bed with a gunshot wound to the head. *(Courtesy: Oklahoma Historical Society)*

"Chester, is Ray Evans's body in the Canadian River?" agent Clint Miers asked the hitchhiking murderer. He was desperate to learn the location of five dead people before the killer himself died on the floor.

Chester shook his head "no."

Miers pressed the twenty-three-year-old gunman further but yielded to Oklahoma County Sheriff Stanley Rogers who had better luck when he heard Chester mumble the words: "North of Ada... bunch of bodies. Three bodies... oh, piles of bodies."

That would be enough information to send hundreds of volunteers searching the back roads, creeks, and fields near Ada, Oklahoma, looking for Chester's victims. But now it was time to get him to the hospital. Blanchard didn't have the medical facilities for a man with a gunshot to the head and four other bullets in him. As much as they hated him for what he'd done, they needed to keep Chester alive. He was bleeding out all over the place. Oklahoma City, with the best doctors and hospital in the state, was thirty-miles away, but the small hospital in Chickasha was closer to Blanchard.

They chose Oklahoma City.

State investigators loaded Chester in a dead man's car he'd been caught driving and, with a police escort, drove north to Oklahoma City. The devil was dying in the back seat, and they needed to keep him alive long enough to find his victims.

CHESTER L. COMER WAS BORN IN 1909 near Center, Pennsylvania, thirty-miles northwest of Pittsburgh. He was the fourth of seven children born to John and Carrie Comer. By 1920, the family had moved to northern Arkansas where they settled near Buffalo in Marion County, close to the Missouri border.

In December 1925, Chester's younger brother, Arnold, murdered a man, woman, and baby, and wounded three others in what the newspapers described at the time as "A tragedy that shook the Ozark section of northern Arkansas like nothing has in years." An Associated Press story summarized the deadly crime spree.

> The boy, little Arnold Comer, who says he is "about 13 or 14," has admitted to officers he is the author of a succession of lawless acts, culminating Sunday in the slaying of three persons. Arnold's story, told to Sheriff Willingham here [Buffalo, Marion County], was a thriller to match any outlaw's tale. This is the gist of it:
>
> The boy, discontented with home conditions, fled from the Comer home Wednesday night [December 9, 1925], taking a pistol with which he was a practiced shot. Thursday afternoon he entered a rural home and took $17.50 and a shotgun while the occupants of the house were absent. That night, he plundered a little store, increasing his armament.
>
> Friday night, seeking food, he went to another mountain home to assuage his hunger but became afraid when a man opened the door. He fired his shotgun, wounding the man, and his wife and child, and retreated into the darkness.
>
> Hungrier still, Sunday the boy approached the house where Mrs. Tom Boyd lived with her infant granddaughter, shot and beat the aged woman to death—he didn't seem to know why— and then killed the baby because it cried. A quarter of a mile away, as he ran from this tragic scene, he met Charles Moore, dealer in pelts, and shot him to death.

During his pre-trial hearing in late January, 1926, Arnie's insanity defense was shattered when a doctor found him "not unduly subnormal." At the end of his two-day trial, he was sentenced to twenty-one years for the second-degree murder of Charles Moore. The indictments for the murders of Sarah Boyd and her granddaughter were kept in reserve until his release in 1947. The first four years of his sentence were served in a reform school in Pine Bluff.

Shortly after his trial, Arnie said he could give no explanation as to why he went on his killing spree. Later, he blamed "the mistreatment on his brothers, Austin and Chester," as the reason he ran away from home.

Despite the fact that he was declared sane at his first trial, by 1933, Arnold resided in a state mental hospital where he murdered his fourth victim on January 12 of that year. Millard Stanley, his roommate, was beaten to death with a six-pound, cast-iron window weight while he slept. Arnold had been a model inmate until that day. Although the coroner found him not responsible due to his insanity, Arnold had to be forcibly restrained from attacking the doctor.

Arnold's ordeal and the tragedies he inflicted had reportedly aged his father's face, which "appeared to take on added years." The shame of their son's crimes drove the family to leave northeastern Arkansas and move to the small town of Asher, Oklahoma, where Mr. Comer was employed as a night watchman in the booming oil fields of Pottawatomie County, sixty-miles southeast of Oklahoma City.

By 1930, Chester had moved out of his parent's home, and varied reports have him working as a farm hand and itinerant laborer that year. It didn't take long for Chester to grow tired of hard work, and on March 12, 1931, he was sentenced to serve three years in a Huntsville, Texas, prison under the alias "George Jones" for attempted robbery and assault. His fingerprints, photo, and given birthplace of near Center, Pennsylvania, would later identify George Jones as Chester Comer. False names would become a common ruse that Chester would use over the next four years to cover his true identity as he worked various schemes.

After serving his time, Chester was paroled and, with nowhere else to go, he moved in with his parents and siblings who by then were living in Oklahoma City. Fresh out of prison and filled with lust, Chester met seventeen-year-old Elizabeth Childers and, after a brief courtship, the two were married on Valentine's Day, 1934.

Four to six weeks later, the new Mrs. Comer announced to her husband she was pregnant, and would give birth in November. She shared the good news with her grandmother,

Grace Childers. Mr. Comer was less excited. This was a big problem for Chester. He liked having sex with his new wife, but loathed the idea of supporting her and a child by making an honest living.

When Elizabeth's father died in May, the couple moved in with her grandparents, James and Grace Childers, in Oklahoma City. Three months later, the couple moved out. Chester told his wife's grandparents that he had a job waiting for him in Amarillo, Texas.

Chester Comer with first wife, Elizabeth Childers, in 1934. *(Courtesy: Oklahoma Historical Society)*

On October 6, 1934, a pregnant woman's body was found next to a lonely highway in Wyandotte County near Kansas City, Kansas. She had been shot five times in the head with a .38 caliber pistol, mostly in the face, as if her killer were trying to obliterate her identity. She was last seen alive sitting in the passenger seat of a car with California or Oklahoma license plates that was parked near the location where the body was discovered a short time later.

The mystery woman was viewed by more than 15,000 people who passed through a Kansas City morgue where her body was kept for eight months. In May, 1935, she was buried in a potter's grave in a Kansas City cemetery. Her clothing and the five .38 caliber slugs were kept as evidence, and her photograph was published in a national magazine for police officers.

Chester found his way back to the Childers's home around the same time his wife was due to give birth.

"We asked him where Elizabeth was and he said, 'we have a fine big girl now and she didn't feel like coming with me,'" Grandma Childers would later tell a newspaper reporter. They never heard from their granddaughter again after they saw her leave with Chester in August.

Not long after the unidentified body of the pregnant woman was discovered west of Kansas City, a "Jack Armstrong" found work as a laborer on the Oliver Fain farm ten miles south of Blanchard. Jack was a clean-cut, hardworking, young man with good manners. While he worked for the Fains, Jack turned on his charm for a too-young neighbor girl with a last name that sounded a little familiar to him.

"I liked him because everybody thought he was such a good, kind boy," Odessa Childress would later tell a female newspaper reporter. She was just thirteen-years-old when she met Jack. "I thought he was only nineteen—that's what he told me."

"He helped us through watermelon season," seventeen-year-old Otis Fain later recounted. "He was a good worker and easy to manage. I didn't see any signs of a temper. He was always a little nervous and we remarked among ourselves that he was only half-bright, but it didn't occur to us he was crazy."

Although Chester Comer, aka Jack Armstrong, took a strong liking to the Fain family, who seemed different from his own, he only worked with them two months before he left to toil in the oil fields in south-central Oklahoma. There, he found a good job paying 85 cents an hour[1] laying an oil pipeline between Ada and Fittstown. He soon became friendly with Charles Stevens, an older coworker, who invited him back to his home

---

[1] The equivalent of $14 an hour in 2014.

in Maysville, Oklahoma, for supper. At the dinner table, Chester met the Stevens's seventeen-year-old daughter, Lucille.

Odessa Childress, fourteen-years-old in photo above. *(Courtesy: Oklahoma Historical Society)*

Like his first wife, who hadn't been seen or heard from the last few months, Lucille Stevens was young and naïve enough to believe the smooth-talking ex-convict. He even gave her some clothes that belonged to his sister who had died recently. Four weeks later, Chester approached Charles about marrying his daughter.

"I guess I don't mind, as long as you are good to her," Charles told him. The two were married in the spring of 1935. Just a few weeks later, Chester got himself into trouble and had to quit his good job and go on the run.

"Right after they were married," Charles Stevens later told an Oklahoma City newspaper reporter, "Lucille came to me and said Chester was in trouble—that he'd forged some checks. They lit out for the east," He learned from his daughter that the pair stayed two weeks in Tennessee at the home of his father, then two weeks in Little Rock, Arkansas, and then spent some time in Kentucky.

The young newlyweds eventually returned to Maysville, Oklahoma, where they moved in with Lucille's parents in July 1935. When Charles asked him what they had used for money while running from the law, Chester told him they didn't have any and had "bummed" food and hitchhiked all the way.

His daughter's marriage was off to a bad start. Charles grew concerned about his new son-in-law.

Marriage didn't stop Chester from his attempts to seduce thirteen-year-old Odessa, whom he still visited on occasion during that summer under his alias, Jack Armstrong. The Fain farm near Blanchard was just twenty-five miles away from the Stevens home near Maysville.

"When he would come to see me, he would always seem to have plenty of money. We would go to picture shows in Lindsay [halfway between Blanchard and Maysville] and he was always buying me little things," Odessa later said. "He told me he didn't have any other girls and that he always came to see me as often as he could get off from the oil fields. I didn't have any other fellows. I didn't want to have any others except Jack."

It was all a lie, of course. "Jack" didn't have a job in the oil fields anymore. He was mooching off his new in-laws. In August, Chester's brother Austin, with whom he used to torment his younger brother Arnold, came to Maysville to pick up his brother and Lucille. After speaking with his brother in private, Chester told his in-laws he had a good job waiting for him back in Oklahoma City. Shortly after the couple left Maysville, the marriage ran into a familiar problem: Lucille became pregnant. For a man that didn't like responsibility or hard work, Chester knew just the solution to this problem.

One month later, on September 14, Charles Stevens and his wife received a letter from their daughter that was mailed from McLean, Texas. It was a bit of a surprise to them since they believed the couple was in Oklahoma City. Lucille wrote her parents that she was pregnant and excited to be a mother.

The Stevens family never saw or heard from their daughter again.

With no job, no place to live, and no wife to take care of, Chester moved back in with his family in Oklahoma City in October 1935. He informed them that he and Lucille "had separated." For the next six weeks, the ne'er-do-well moped around the house and looked for work but it wasn't going well. The federal Emergency Relief Appropriation Act had recently extended the age limit of the Civilian Conservation Corp from 25 to 28. Even though the twenty-six-year-old was guaranteed to get a job under the new expansion, the work only paid $30 a month, with $25 of that allocated for his parents.

The ominous half of his Dr.-Jekyll-and-Mr.-Hyde personality influenced his thoughts. He was twenty-six years old and his discontent with the harsh realities of life fed his warped soul, turning it colder and darker. *Thirty-dollars a month!?* He used to make that much in just three days working in the oil fields. He had stolen and he had murdered. It was now time to combine the two—and push back against an unfair world.

On Monday, November 18, Chester Comer told his family he was going on a "hitchhiking tour looking for work." He packed a small bag, wrapped his .38-caliber revolver in his clothes, tucked his small .32-automatic pistol in his pocket, and headed southeast.

By the following morning, Chester had traveled forty-five miles to the outskirts of Shawnee, Oklahoma, where he hitched a ride with prominent Shawnee citizen, attorney, and trustee of the local Oklahoma Baptist University, Ray Evans. Evans was known by his friends to "never refuse a ride to anyone." He was on his way to Ada to interview a client when he picked up Chester Comer.

North of Ada, Evans stopped at a filling station to ask directions to the home of the client he was scheduled to meet with. In the car with him was a man who "looked like a hitchhiker," the station attendant would later tell police.

Ray Evans

Somewhere between the few miles that separated the filling station and Ada, Chester Comer hijacked the forty-year-old attorney. Exactly where and when is unknown but a short time after he was seen at the filling station, witnesses reported seeing the tan-colored Evans sedan speeding through Ada with only the driver visible—and he didn't look anything like Ray Evans.

Around 8:30 in the morning, Wednesday, November 20, Chester arrived at the Fain farm, ten miles south of Blanchard.

When he pulled up in Evans's tan Ford sedan, he told Otis and his mother, Minnie Fain, that he had driven in from Oklahoma City. However, neighbors would later report seeing him drive in from the south on the road from Lindsay, where Chester used to take thirteen-year-old Odessa to the movies.

All that day, Chester sat around the house while Otis and his thirty-six-year-old mother went about the ordinary duties of their farm work. The Fain family could see no difference in his appearance and actions from what they had observed when he worked for them nearly a year before, or on his frequent visits afterwards.

Chester spent the night in the bed he had occupied when had worked for his room and board one year before. Thursday morning, he loitered around the house until lunch time, when he carried Otis's meal out to him in the field. By two in the afternoon, Chester had grown bored and proposed a car ride to Opal Fain, Otis's sixteen-year-old sister, and his too-young sweetheart, Odessa, who had recently turned 14. The trio drove to Lindsay, where they watched a movie, and then returned to the Fain farm at 5:30 p.m. When they arrived, Otis walked up to the car and looked inside where he noticed a small duffle bag in the front seat. Inside the opened bag was a coil of rope and a revolver. The two items were a peculiar find, which prompted Otis to ask Jack where he'd gotten the new car. Chester answered that he had bought it in Oklahoma City for $475.

After dinner, Chester offered everyone another car ride. His passengers this time were Otis and his eight-year-old brother Garland, their mother Minnie, and Odessa. After an hour of driving along the country roads of Grady County, Chester dropped Minnie and Garland off at the home of a neighboring farm family that Minnie wanted to visit. With only Otis and Odessa in the car, Chester soon transformed to his Mr. Hyde personality.

Four miles down the road, Chester turned to Otis with a scowl and ordered him out of the car. "We [Chester and Odessa] are going on alone," Jack told him. When Otis protested, Chester pushed him out of the car and drove off with Odessa.

"It was the first time in his life he ever spoke harshly to me," Otis later told a newspaper reporter. He continued to walk in the same direction the car had traveled. Twenty minutes later, he saw it coming back. In those twenty minutes he was alone with Odessa, Chester threatened to rape the young girl. Unsuccessful in his attempt after she talked him out of it, Chester drove back the spot where he had left Otis and picked him up.

"His face was flushed angrily and the girl was obviously frightened," Otis continued. On the way to the farmhouse where Minnie and Garland were visiting, he never said a word to the girl for fear it would trigger Chester's anger. When they arrived, Odessa jumped out of the Ford and ran into the house, where she grabbed hold of Minnie and refused to let go. She said Jack had tried to tie her up with a rope.

"The child told Mother that Armstrong had threatened to kill her unless she did what he wanted her to do. She talked him out of his mood," Otis recounted. "We were all pretty nervous by then because we could see that he had changed in some manner from the man we had known. The whole group piled into the car and started to my home."

Two miles further down the road, Chester slammed on the brakes, sending everyone boomeranging forward, then backward. He turned to Odessa and said, "Unless you do what I want you to, I am going to kill all of you!" Otis tried to talk him out of it but Chester told him to shut up, "or you'll go down too."

Otis said he and Jack started to argue for a few minutes until Armstrong took off again, but one mile later, Jack again stopped the car.

"This time, he leaned over the back seat and opened a zipper bag and pulled out an automatic pistol. He held open the bag so that I could see a revolver inside it. Then he said, 'I've got a .45 too—in case you're thinking of getting funny.'"

He didn't have a .45, but Otis didn't know that.

Chester again ordered everyone out of the car except Odessa, but the girl clung to Minnie and refused to move. "She told him to drive to our house and she would go with him if only he wouldn't kill us," Otis said. "That calmed him down a minute and he drove on."

About a quarter of a mile from the Fain and Childress homes, and directly in front of the Bradford residence, Chester stopped the car and again ordered everyone out except Odessa. It was then that he noticed Roy Bradford sitting on his porch, watching them.

"If he comes out here and starts anything, you're all going down," Chester told them.

By now, Minnie was too upset to be quiet anymore. She began to reason with Chester and begged him to drive them home and be on his way.

"If you give me $3, I'll take you home," he told her.

Minnie gave him the $3 from her purse and he took them home. Relieved to still be alive, they scrambled out of the Ford as fast as they could.

"Don't you go into that house until I'm gone, and don't you go away from the house tonight," Chester ordered them as he pointed the .32-caliber automatic at them through the driver's side window.

There was no telephone in the Fain, Childress, or Bradford homes, and Otis presumed Chester's orders were meant to prevent them from warning the authorities. About a quarter of a mile away, the group watched as Chester stopped the car, got a flashlight out of the trunk, then got back in the car and drove away.

"After he left, we all huddled into the house," Otis recounted. "Odessa said Armstrong told her when they were alone that he was mad at her and had come back for revenge."

About an hour later, a flashlight beam was creepily directed into both the Fain home, then later the Childress house. It was Chester, still determined to get his sexual gratification from young Odessa. He thought better of going inside and finally drove away.

If he couldn't have Odessa, he knew just where he could go to try and force himself on another young girl.

Chester arrived at the Maysville home of his second wife around eleven o'clock, Friday morning, November 22. It seems unlikely that Charles Stevens was home at the time since he had spent the last two months looking for his daughter and Chester. He had talked to lawmen in several counties and searched for her in nearby Pauls Valley and then in Oklahoma City. The last news they had from her was a letter she had mailed them from McLean, Texas, on September 14. If Charles had been home when Chester showed up, somebody could have gotten hurt or killed.

But Chester didn't care about the risks he was taking by now, and he was going to get what he couldn't get from Odessa. Lucille's thirteen-year-old sister, Elizabeth Stevens, would have to take her place.

As the Dr. Jekyll half of his personality played the congenial guest to Elizabeth and her mother, it's unclear if he knew about the search parties looking for the owner of the nice car he was driving. Forty-five miles to the east, fifty men had gathered Wednesday morning to search for clues that would lead to Ray Evans—dead or alive. On Thursday, two hundred people had volunteered to search for the popular attorney along the back roads and fields of three Oklahoma counties, and as far south as Denison, Texas. The news of his disappearance was covered by radio stations and newspapers, which carried descriptions of both the missing man and his tan Ford sedan. When Chester arrived at the Stevens's home Friday morning, another large search party was being assembled.

Chester told Mrs. Stevens and her daughter a story about how Lucille had left him to go to Oklahoma City, and that he was on his way to look for her. He played dumb and asked if they had heard from her.

No? They hadn't? Hmmm, that's odd.

Before he left for Oklahoma City, Chester told them he wanted to go to the local grocery store to buy some oranges and asked if Elizabeth cared to ride along with him. She agreed but not long after they left, Chester switched to Mr. Hyde and told Elizabeth they were actually going to Oklahoma City. Scared, the young girl tried to jump out of the moving car. Chester grabbed her and the two struggled violently, which sent the Evans car veering off into a ditch. Elizabeth was able to break free and ran back home.

Center, young Elizabeth Stevens, the thirteen-year-old-sister of Chester's second wife, was to be his next victim. She caused Chester to crash his car and escaped. She is seen here flanked by her older brothers, Francis and J.C. *(Courtesy: Oklahoma Historical Society)*

Chester didn't have time to chase after her. A dead man's car was in the ditch and the second girl he wanted to rape had gotten away. He needed to get away, too. To his good fortune, he was able to hitch a ride with a farmer to nearby Lexington where he caught a bus to Oklahoma City. Witnesses would later tell police they saw a man answering Chester's description— five-feet six-inches tall, weighing 135 to 145 pounds, dark brown wavy hair, brown eyes, and a prominent nose—getting off the bus at the Capitol Hill area of Oklahoma City.

When news that the Ray Evans car was discovered six miles north of Maysville in a ditch, the center of the search shifted from Ada to forty-five miles east. The Stevens family was able to tell investigators that it had been driven by Chester Comer. They also told state investigators that Chester had also tried to kidnap their Elizabeth and had probably murdered the oldest daughter, Lucille. Inside the car was an ominous clue: a bloody sock that belonged to Evans.

Chester's anonymity for his four-day crime spree had just been blown.

By the morning of Saturday, November 23, as investigators were putting together the pieces of the puzzle, Chester was seen by a filling station attendant in Piedmont, twenty-seven miles northwest of Oklahoma City. A short time later, he was given a ride by farmer Frank Lushen, who gave Chester a three-mile lift and dropped him off near the rural home of sixty-five-year-old Sarah Simpson. Lushen, who drove an old, slow, farm truck, was deemed an unsuitable target by Chester.

Not long after Lushen had dropped Chester off, a witness later told police a hitchhiker was seen getting into a dark-colored 1935 Chevy sedan driven by Mrs. Simpson's thirty-eight-year-old son, Lester Simpson, and her fourteen-year-old grandson, Warren. The two had visited her that morning and left at noon to return to their home two miles away. Like Evans, Lester Simpson was known to give lifts to hitchhikers.

They were never seen alive again.

By Saturday evening, one thousand volunteers were searching for Ray Evans and Chester Comer in what statewide newspapers were calling the greatest manhunt in Oklahoma history. Although they hadn't yet connected him to the disappearance of the Simpsons, he was their prime suspect for the murder of Ray Evans and disappearance of Lucille Stevens. Friends of the prominent Shawnee attorney had donated $500 for information leading to the whereabouts of Evans, and five thousand cards with his description were mailed to law enforcement agencies in seven nearby states.

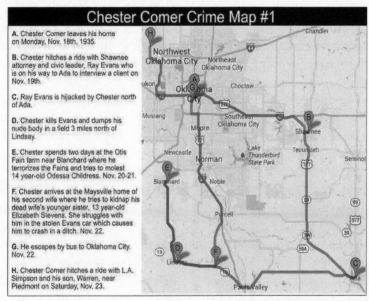

Chester Comer Crime Map #1

A. Chester Comer leaves his home on Monday, Nov. 18th, 1935.

B. Chester hitches a ride with Shawnee attorney and civic leader, Ray Evans who is on his way to Ada to interview a client on Nov. 19th.

C. Ray Evans is hijacked by Chester north of Ada.

D. Chester kills Evans and dumps his nude body in a field 3 miles north of Lindsay.

E. Chester spends two days at the Otis Fain farm near Blanchard where he terrorizes the Fains and tries to molest 14 year-old Odessa Childress. Nov. 20-21.

F. Chester arrives at the Maysville home of his second wife where he tries to kidnap his dead wife's younger sister, 13 year-old Elizabeth Stevens. She struggles with him in the stolen Evans car which causes him to crash in a ditch. Nov. 22.

G. He escapes by bus to Oklahoma City. Nov. 22.

H. Chester Comer hitches a ride with L.A. Simpson and his son, Warren, near Piedmont on Saturday, Nov. 23.

On Sunday morning, investigators from the state crime bureau banged on the door of the Comer family home near Southeast 44th Street and High Avenue in Oklahoma City, and questioned the six relatives who lived inside. They hadn't seen Chester since he went on a hitchhiking tour looking for work the week prior, the family told investigators. Unsatisfied with the little information they could provide, the agents took Chester's sister, Edna, 24, and twin brothers, Larmer and Armor, 19, into custody on the trumped-up charge of "vagrancy." Even after they were booked in jail, they were still unable to tell police any more than they already had.

Other state and county investigators also spent that Sunday gathering the clues, witness statements, and reports that connected Chester to the disappearance of five people in total, including his first wife Elizabeth Childers, with the body of a mystery woman discovered outside Kansas City on October 6, 1934, as well as the disappearance of Lester and Warren Simpson. Just like twelve years before, when Arnold Comer went on his rampage in northern Arkansas, Oklahoma authorities had a maniac killer on the loose that they needed to stop before he killed anyone else—if they only knew where he was.

For his part, Chester broke his usual pattern that Sunday, November 24, of doubling back to south-central Oklahoma and made a 105-mile drive east to Sapulpa. Sapulpa was another booming oil town that lay just fourteen miles west of Tulsa where news of Chester's crimes had already reached. Detectives would not learn for several weeks why he traveled to the Sapulpa area.

By Monday, November 25, all the information and clues investigators had pieced together over the weekend were front-page news throughout Oklahoma's daily newspapers. The story had also gone national from the *Binghamton Press* in New York, to the *Oakland Tribune*, all throughout Chester's home state of Pennsylvania, and to many daily newspapers in between, with a concentration in the southwest.

That Monday would also be the last day of Chester Comer's crime spree. As always, he eventually doubled back to his hunting grounds near the Fain farm outside of Blanchard, arriving there late Sunday afternoon. Jack Stanley, a twenty-year-old oil field worker, spotted a suspicious-looking car parked by the side of road five miles southwest of Blanchard.

"When I passed him in his car, he sort of ducked his head and crouched down, but of course I didn't know it was Comer, although the case did flash through my mind," Stanley later told a reporter from the *Daily Oklahoman.*

"Then Monday morning I went out on business and saw the same man two or three miles south of Blanchard. I recognized the car right away as the one I had seen Sunday. And this time I got a look at the license plate number which I had seen in the newspaper and knew it was the car missing from Piedmont.

"He was headed south when I passed him so I headed on north into Blanchard. There was no question of what to do. I saw J.L. Saunders and we headed to Oscar Morgan's house."

Saunders was the nineteen-year-old nephew of Ray Evans. He had spent the last few days searching for his uncle. Earlier that morning, Saunders had been talking to Oscar Morgan, the town marshal of Blanchard, about his uncle's disappearance and the hunt for Chester Comer.

Although he was the only officer for the small town of one thousand residents, Morgan was no slouch. He was an old-fashioned, western-style lawman known to locals as "Blood Hound Morgan." In 1924, Morgan shot and killed bank robber Claude Lee during a gunfight with Lee and his accomplice. Morgan was shot in the leg during that shootout. He played a large role in other arrests and gunfights, and he had once spent twelve months tracking down a notorious local criminal to Colorado, where he arrested him and put him in the Oklahoma State Penitentiary in McAlester. That same criminal was later paroled and broke the law again, forcing Morgan to hunt him down a second time. After he jumped bail following the second arrest, Morgan hunted him down a third time and arrested him six months later in Florida.

But when Stanley and Saunders burst through the door of his house around eleven o'clock that morning, Morgan was soaking a sore foot in a bucket of hot water. When Stevens told him about spotting the Simpson car a few miles outside of town, Morgan put on his clothes, strapped on his gun belt, and got in Stanley's car with Saunders tagging along. Two and one-half miles south of Blanchard, the trio spotted the suspect's Chevy through the rain and chased him for two miles.

"Finally, he must have noticed we were gaining so he pulled up to the side of the road near a little ravine. We stopped about ten feet from the other automobile," Morgan said. "I told Stanley and Saunders just to sit still while I go see who the driver was."

The two young men had a front row seat to what happened next and would later describe the series of events to a *Daily Oklahoman* reporter.

"Oscar stepped up to the driver's side of the car and took hold of the door handle," Stanley said. "Just then, I saw this guy move, saw a gun and he fired."

Morgan was hit in the arm once when Chester fired two shots from a .32 automatic. The Marshal frowned, stepped back, pulled out his .38 and fired three shots from the hip while dodging seven more bullets from Chester. Morgan, seeing that his first three shots hadn't stopped Chester, walked around to the front of the Chevy, and fired two more times through the windshield, with one of the bullets hitting Chester above the right eye. It would later be reported that all five of Morgan's bullets hit their target.

"Oh it was just a blaze of fire," Stanley recounted with some excitement. "All at once, the shooting stopped and I saw that fellow slump in the front seat. Morgan was standing there ready and just as calm as an old lady in church."

Stanley and Saunders got out of their car and tried to get in the Simpson's Chevy but it was locked. They used Morgan's gun as a hammer and broke through the back-door window. Stanley took the automatic out of Chester's hand, pulled him out, and loaded him into the back seat.

"Comer's brains were oozing out and he was unconscious," Stanley said. "The motor was running and the radio was going full blast. It was gruesome; blood every place and the radio blaring out 'Sweet Adeline' the whole time."

Stanley drove the Simpson's Chevy back to Blanchard while Saunders drove the deputy back in his car. On the way back to town, Stanley got the scare of his life.

"I kept watching that guy in the mirror when he sat up suddenly with a desperate look," Stanley said. "I did not know until after we got back that he had another gun. He mumbled something, I never could understand it, but he sure seemed to come to in a hurry."

In Blanchard, Chester was laid out on the floor of an auto mechanic's garage, where he was kept for a short time while being questioned by lawmen.

"North of Ada—bunch of bodies," Comer told them.

But Comer, even with a bullet in his head that had fractured into five pieces, was still trying to confuse and misdirect his pursuers. When Jack Stanley helped pull his body from the Simpson's Chevy into the garage, he asked Comer, "Where is Ray Evans?"

"Fittstown . . . east of Fittstown . . . (incoherent mumbling) . . . in a creek, pipeline, ditch."

Fittstown? How could Evans's body be there, when Fittstown is south of Ada? North of Ada? East of Fittstown? None if it made any sense.

On the garage floor, investigators searched Chester's pockets and belongings and found a note that read: "If I am not killed in this car, it will be a surprise to me. I have nothing to regret. I had rather be dead than to be a public slave."

In Chester's mind, working for the Civilian Conservation Corps for $30 a month was the equivalent of being a public slave.

As Comer was being driven to Oklahoma City General Hospital, he was still being questioned by lawmen, who feared he wasn't going to make it. For a third time, they asked him where Evans was.

"I buried him."

"How about Simpson?"

"Simpson? That guy is just a dirty . . ." Comer replied.

For the most unpopular man in Oklahoma, Chester Comer had dozens of people surrounding his hospital bed. They crowded his hospital room, choked the doorway to his room, and stretched far down the length of the hallway. State crime bureau agents, deputies, policemen, family members of his victims, his own family members, and even Odessa Childress all wanted to see him, ask questions, and find out where the bodies were.

"Where is Ray Evans?" a physician asked him.

"I buried him."

"Did you kill Ray Evans?" agent Clint Miers asked him.

"Yes."

Then, his broken-hearted mother, Carrie Comer, urgently pushed her way into the room to see her son.

"Talk to me, son," she implored. "Tell me what happened. Tell me all about it. I'm your mother, do talk."

Chester took one look at his mother, rolled his eyes, and stared off in another direction. It's hard to be a desperado when your mother is there nagging you.

As she was led out of the room, Mrs. Comer said to a newspaper reporter, "Oh, I know he will die. There's nothing that can save him. I don't know why he did it."

Charles Stevens was later permitted to visit and asked his one-time son-in-law: "Where is Lucille?"

Comer raised himself up, looked at Stevens, compressed his lips as if he were about to speak, and then fell back in bed. He wasn't going to tell anyone what he'd done with his first two wives. They could figure it out for themselves.

By Tuesday morning, November 26, doctors said his chances of survival were very slim. An x-ray showed the bullet from Oscar Morgan's gun had broken into five pieces, and they feared one of the fragments had affected the area that

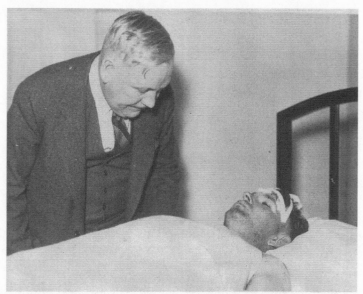

Chester Comer refused to tell authorities where the bodies of his five victims could be found. *(Courtesy: Oklahoma Historical Society)*

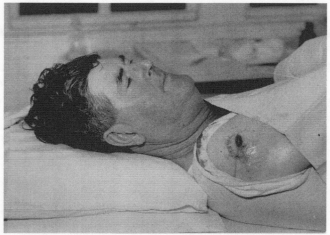

Marshal Oscar Morgan was shot once in his right arm, and then returned fire. *(Courtesy: Oklahoma Historical Society)*

Lester Simpson's Chevy Sedan, where Chester Comer shot it out with Oscar Morgan. Note the three bullet holes through the vent window.
(Courtesy: Oklahoma Historical Society)

controlled his speech. Shackles that were placed on him the day before were removed. With all the lawmen standing around, there was no need for them.

As police often do when a suspect is caught or killed, they tried to connect Chester to other murders. This included a connection between Chester and the disappearance of two vacationing couples in New Mexico earlier that year. George and Laura Lorius, and Albert and Tillie Heberer were on a summer-vacation tour of the southwest, where they were known to have stayed at the Vaughn Hotel in Vaughn, 100 miles east of Albuquerque, on May 21. They ate breakfast in the hotel café early the next day and after they departed, they were never seen again.[2]

Although a filling station attendant, who had cashed forged traveler's checks for a man using the Lorius name, later said that

---

[2] The Lorius-Heberer mystery is still one of the biggest mysteries in New Mexico history. The bodies have never been found, and the case is unsolved to this day.

the man looked similar to Chester, Chester did not have a forearm tattoo like the suspect in the Lorius case.

"It could have been a grease spot," investigators replied, hoping to explain the absence of a tattoo. But it wasn't.

Investigators that Tuesday also pieced together a few more facts, including verification that the clothing Chester gave his second wife had actually belonged to his missing first wife, Elizabeth. Her grandmother identified the clothing as belonging to her granddaughter.

"Yes, those were Elizabeth's," Grace Childers said, before breaking into loud sobs.

At 4:00 p.m., Chester was given a blood transfusion which seemed to rally his strength—enough so that by 5:15 p.m. he was given a "truth serum" injection which yielded nothing because he couldn't talk anymore. After Chester tried to cop a feel from a nurse who was attending to him, state crime agent Jack Roberts believed Chester was playing a game with everyone in the room. Roberts played a game of his own when he handed Chester a nickel-plated revolver with an empty chamber. Chester looked at him with surprise, grabbed it, and pulled the trigger three times.

"He could talk if he wanted to," Roberts told a reporter outside in the hallway. "He's just holding out on us. I stood by him for hours, watched him. He's just smart."

But he wouldn't be smart for very long. Late the next day on Wednesday, November 27, he developed pneumonia. Doctors and nurses wrapped his bed in an oxygen tent but it wasn't enough to save him. Chester Comer died at 11:13 p.m.

He never did tell investigators what they wanted to know.

The first of Chester's murders to be verified resulted from the positive identification of the Kansas mystery woman as that of Chester's first wife, Elizabeth Childers, the day after he died. A friend of hers made the connection and told police, who checked on the lead and then notified the family.

"Yes, that girl up there must be our baby," said Elizabeth's grandfather, James Childers, after he was furnished with a detailed description. "They both had the same kind of scar just above the right ankle." His identification was supported by his wife, Elizabeth's uncle, and her younger brother, Jack. The .38-caliber slugs removed from her body were later matched to a gun that was in Chester's possession when he was captured. The *Daily Oklahoman* reported that the Childers family was going to have Elizabeth's body moved to Oklahoma City.

Elizabeth Childers, Chester Comer's first wife. *(Courtesy: Oklahoma Historical Society)*

For the next three weeks, hundreds to thousands of volunteers searched every day for the bodies of Lucille Stevens, Ray Evans, and the Simpsons. The governor of Oklahoma offered a reward of $125 to anyone who found them. Ray Evans's nude body was discovered in a field three miles north of Lindsay on December 11. He was nowhere near Fittstown or Ada, the locations Chester had told investigators.

Two thousand mourners attended his funeral in Shawnee, the largest in the city's history at that time. One year after his funeral services, civic groups erected a three-foot-high concrete memorial and placed it on the lonely country road where his body was found. Below a photograph of Ray Evans, the engraved inscription read:

Sept. 27, 1895 – November 19, 1935 – Ray
Evans, Attorney, Shawnee, Okla.
Martyr to Hitchhiking

On December 15, the charred, skeletal remains of a young woman were found in a field near Edmond, fifteen miles north of Oklahoma City. She was identified, by her teeth, hair, and a belt buckle, as Lucille Stevens, Chester's second wife. Eight days later, on December 23, three young men hunting rabbits in a sagebrush field ten miles west of Sapulpa discovered the bodies of Lester Simpson and his son, Warren. The location, nearly one hundred miles from where the Simpsons were kidnapped, surprised investigators. The funeral for Lucille Stevens was held in Maysville, and the Simpsons were buried in Piedmont. Large crowds attended both.

Two days after Chester Comer died, one hundred curious onlookers attended his funeral held at the Watts and McAtee Funeral Home in Oklahoma City on November 30. Most of them were Bible-carrying, sympathetic, old ladies who sought out Chester's family members to comfort them, an Oklahoma City newspaper reported.

Also in attendance were three young girls of junior-high-school age, ". . . pushing back long bobs with fingers on which bright nail polish was slightly cracked."

Chester would have liked that.

Chapter Six: The Bizarre Tahlequah Coed Case, 1935

ON THE AFTERNOON of March 27, 1935, a bizarre scene was unfolding on the campus of Northeastern State Teachers College in Tahlequah, Oklahoma. A Chinese student was sprinting from the library to the campus exit. Behind him was an attractive nineteen-year-old coed firing a .32-caliber pistol at him.

"I know he's one of them and I'm going to kill him!" Lois Thompson screamed. The young Chinese man was screaming too. He'd already been hit once in the wrist, the bullet exiting near his elbow.

Despite a wounded right arm, twenty-seven-year-old Daniel Shaw was running as fast as he could for the campus gates when Lois came to a stop, took careful aim, and squeezed off three more rounds, one of which passed through Shaw's lung. Too scared to stop, Shaw kept on running and made it about two blocks away to the Gilbreath Auto Garage, where he tried to hide in a run-down Chevy that was missing an engine.

Lois was less than half-a-block away from her target when another student caught up with her near Garner's Grocery, not far from the auto garage.

"Give me that gun before you hurt someone," student Jack Horn ordered Lois. "I've only got one shot left and I want to make it good. I am not a good shot anyhow, but I know he is one of them," Lois replied.[1]

---

[1] Reports differ as to whether she fired four or five shots from the six-shot revolver.

But Horn persisted and Lois told him to call the police as she handed him the gun. Other students and bystanders came running up to see what in tarnation was going on and a small crowd began forming. Horn and another man loaded Shaw into a bystander's car and took him to the small hospital that served the city of twenty-five hundred people. Tahlequah was once the capitol of the Cherokee Nation of Indian Territory back in the old days, before Oklahoma became a state in 1907.

At the hospital, doctors gave Shaw a fifty-fifty chance to live that first night.

Lois was immediately arrested and taken to the small, limestone jail that was once the Cherokee Nation's prison. There, she refused to answer Sheriff Grover Bishop's and County Attorney Sanford Martin's questions. But Sheriff Bishop was already familiar with Lois Thompson, and the events that led to her being in jail were even more bizarre than an attractive young coed shooting a foreign student in broad daylight on a college campus.

THE STORY OF HOW THESE two students collided began on February 14, 1935, when Daniel Shaw enrolled in Northeastern State Teachers College to further his cultural studies of American Indians. He arrived in the United States in 1931 from Hong Kong, where he had worked for British and American missionaries. Prior to his missionary work, Shaw had studied at a seminary in Singapore. Over the last four years, before he arrived on the campus of Northeastern State Teachers College, he had attended several different academic institutions around the United States to study American culture and American Indians. He was described by others as a patient and exceedingly polite young man with respectful manners.

Like many of the other students on campus, sophomore Lois Thompson was of Indian heritage herself. She attended school with her older sisters, Clarice and Ruby, who were seniors, and her sister Lela, who was a junior. A local newspaper described

Lois as a quiet and reserved girl who was "far from the 'modern' or 'flapper' type." Despite being described as attractive, she hardly ever dated and never got much attention from the boys—or anyone else, for that matter.

Extortion Notes

Three days after Shaw enrolled on campus, Lois's troubles began when she mysteriously started receiving notes demanding money. At first, the notes only insisted on small amounts of a few hundred dollars or else harm would come to her. All of them had instructions for her to bring money to some meeting place at night and were signed, "The N.S.T.C. gang." The notes had been covertly slipped into her books, her locker, on a drinking fountain, or through the mail. All total, she received thirteen notes that February and March, each one of them rapidly increasing to the ridiculous sum of $3,000, with an alternative that if she didn't pay, she would be murdered.

That was a problem. The Thompson family wasn't rich at all. If she was an heiress, or came from an important local family, the extortion notes might have made more sense to everyone. However, it was a well-known fact around town that her family didn't have much money. Her widowed mother lived in a modest farmhouse two miles outside of town. It didn't make sense why anyone, including some unimaginative group who used the initials of their school as the name of their gang, would find wisdom in trying to extort money from a poor country girl.

Even so, this was the 1930s. Kidnappers, gangsters, daring bank robbers, and racketeers were often in the major newspapers. Fifty miles away in Tulsa, a high-society murder had occurred the previous Thanksgiving with the killer claiming it was self-defense after he tried to put a stop to an alleged plot to extort $20,000 from one of the richest families in town. If the money wasn't paid, harm would come to the Tulsa family's beautiful daughter, Virginia Wilcox. It was Tulsa's crime of the century and the story was reported on in newspapers throughout the country and around the world. When Lois

Lois Thompson

began receiving the first few notes, the sensational murder trial had started that same week. The remarkably beautiful Wilcox girl was a star witness, and her name and photo appeared in newspapers throughout the country.

Maybe the N.S.T.C. gang had gotten the extortion idea from the Tulsa case? Perhaps they were confusing Lois Thompson as one of the children of Tahlequah's Mayor, James P. Thompson, who did have some money? However, this didn't seem likely since a few minutes of asking around in that small town would have clarified that Lois didn't come from *those* Thompsons.

The other problem, besides a lack of money, is that Lois acted as though she believed the extortion notes, and she was very convincing in her dramatic role as the heroine caught up in a mystery. As one observer would later write in a newspaper feature story: "A child, with ordinary common sense, would realize that such letters, under such circumstances, must be a clumsy joke, a silly college hoax, but, if Lois is to be believed, she took the notes in deadly earnest, and several times went to the appointed rendezvous to meet the gang, in fear and trembling, but hoping to convince them that she could not raise the ransom."

Although she was careful to follow the detailed instructions, each time Lois went to the proposed meeting site, the gang failed to keep the appointment. Soon after, the next extortion note would arrive under even more mysterious and intriguing circumstances and designate a new place and time, without bothering to explain why she was stood up the night before. At each of those points, a normal person might begin to wonder if the whole thing was a stupid joke or clumsy hoax, but not Lois Thompson. Instead, she kept on obeying each note, hoping she could talk her way out of the situation.

Supporting Cast

Since it was always impossible for her to communicate with the gang, she confided in others. Every good movie, and every good actress, needs supporting characters and Lois found hers in her siblings, school administrators, and the local police.

Lois's co-star was her sister, Lela, to whom she revealed everything, and together the two went to their protective and righteous-minded brother, Pitchford, who took the letters equally seriously. After some amateur detective work, the young man set his sights on John Cannon as the leader of the N.S.T.C. gang. In his mind, the boy had looked at his sister "with evil intentions," a feature writer later reported. At gunpoint,

Pitchford pulled John Cannon out of the library and marched him down to the sheriff's office where he was going to be made to confess to the death threats and extortion attempts he had made against Pitchford's innocent sister.

But when they got there, John Cannon did not confess. He had no idea what they were talking about and, after some detective work by professionals, it was clearly determined the student had nothing to do with the whole affair. This news came too late for Cannon who was too humiliated to return to school. He dropped out and went home to Checotah, Oklahoma.

Police, Enter Stage Left

By now, police and school officials were pulled into the melodrama by Lois and Lela Thompson, who were deathly afraid. As the notes kept coming in, always delivered in a clandestine manner, a student employee with the college was brought into the investigation and told to keep an eye on Lois, her books, and her dorm room. However, it was very important the student was told by the school, not to tell Lois.

The amount of money demanded by the gang increased with each message, and so did the deadly tone. Fortunately, deputies were with Lois as she carried out her instructions. As she stood by herself at each of the designated meeting sites, holding a package or envelope, officers were hiding nearby, ready to spring their trap on whoever picked up "the money."

But just like before, no one ever came.

Sheriff Bishop would later tell a newspaper reporter that each time he and his men waited, a car would drive by slowly. "We didn't chase the car because we hoped it would stop and pick up the money. Then we would have a good case against the man or men responsible for the notes." The sheriff also disclosed that in the beginning, one or two of his men working the case "thought she might have written the notes herself. But that idea was refuted by the fact that a car always went by the place they told her to leave the money."

Shoot the Wrong Man

The only ones who knew about the secret meeting locations were the police, the gang, and Lois—and her siblings, of course. The four times deputies accompanied Lois, nothing happened. The fifth time, they would have better luck.

Or bad luck.

Lois's eleventh note gave instructions for her to deliver a package containing money to a rendezvous point on the night of March 2. By an unfortunate coincidence, seven college boys were also in that same area that night doing what college boys often do—drinking and having fun as they drove around the countryside in a large sedan. As the slow-moving car rolled by, Lois walked up to it and "tried to give them a dummy package, which the boys knew nothing about and didn't want to take," a state official would later report.

After several dry runs, this was the moment the lawmen were waiting for. They popped up out of their hiding place and began shouting orders. Jack Christy, a college student and passenger in the car, was shot by officers as he tried to run away because "he looked suspicious." Christy later explained he didn't run because he was involved in an extortion plot, he ran because he didn't understand what was going on and was scared.

Following medical treatment for a flesh wound, Christy was questioned and released after deputies determined he had nothing to do with the case. The other boys were also let go after they were interrogated. None of them knew anything about an extortion plot by the N.S.T.C. gang—which they had never heard of.

More Notes

After the Jack Christy debacle, which was kept out of the local newspapers, Lois continued to receive more notes. On the one occasion when she says she failed to keep the date, she received a letter scolding her:

You did not meet me Thursday night. I thought you were going to disobey but I saw you when you got it from the office. Had another chance when you get this from office.

Go and get money immediately. Inform as before. Then meet me where county line divides Stilwell County line. Have money wrapped in white paper and stay by road on left side.

Have it there at 10 o'clock. When you drive up and stop, cough and come to car by side of road. Be prompt. Saturday night at 10 o'clock. You are marching to the tune of death. I am the one that is beating the drum. Watch step. Last chance. Be careful how you get there.

Lois made that appointment and like all the other times, no one from the gang showed up.

By now, a sensible person would realize the whole thing was probably a twisted college prank. At this point, it was entirely possible that whoever was doing it would have heard from the rumor mill of seven ambushed boys, one of them wounded, that Lois Thompson was the star of a mystery that involved the police. And if the police were involved in her case, it was time to stop playing a joke on her. Real or not, it was time to leave poor Lois Thompson alone.

But that's not what happened. Instead, Lois surreptitiously received yet another note, but this one was different. It sounded odd, as if it were written by a foreigner who would choose different words than Americans would.

You can not go to the office. You did not go yesterday. You are going to be killed today. We are not kidding. We mean it. You can have the whole U.S. police department with you but we will kill you if we knew the next minute we would die. The U.S. detectives can't catch us. You had better not have your family with you. This is no joke. We mean business. We are getting revenge for our buddy.

The language of this particular letter was also strange to investigators. *U.S. police department? U.S. detectives?* Do they mean federal justice department agents, or does the entire United

States have a police department, like Tahlequah, or Oklahoma City, or Tulsa have police departments?

We will kill you if we knew the next minute we would die. Why would they die? Are the U.S. detectives' police department going to kill the N.S.T.C gang? Or, do they know that Lois is now carrying a .32-caliber revolver around?

Getting revenge for our buddy? Who is that? Is it the wounded Jack Christy—or John Cannon, who was forced to leave school out of embarrassment? The same John Cannon whose roommate just happened to be Daniel Shaw?

In Lois's mind, *"our buddy"* must have been John Cannon, and in the mind of a movie heroine forced to play detective to defend herself, she set her sights on Daniel Shaw. A foreigner. A Chinaman. A "celestial" with few friends and no family on that side of the world. Shaw was a complete outsider for whom local residents would have little sympathy. This was, after all, the 1930s.

And if the foreigner Daniel Shaw were dead, he wouldn't be able to deny he was part of the N.S.T.C. gang that had persecuted Lois all these weeks. She would be the heroine and her melodrama would end with her name in the papers.

She would be famous.

Daniel Shaw's Version

Lois's version of what happened on the afternoon of March 27 wouldn't come until later that summer in front of a packed courtroom. Daniel Shaw was interviewed the day after he was shot, from his hospital bed, and gave the following account.

> I am Chinese student in America but quiet, good boy. All Chinese students have to be good boy because, if bad boy, they will be deported, but I am good boy anyhow.
>
> All this happen, quick, foolish, no sense, like nightmare. Lois is good girl. I only know her from sitting with her in religious classes, but she must be crazy. First, her brother get bad idea to pinch my roommate who is good American boy and doesn't do anything but so ashamed now, he go home.

Next day I go into library to read in book and Lois call me out and say she like talk with me on steps [a rock bannister leading to the library]. We sit down on steps and she ask if I know who write ransom notes. I say I don't know anything but I and John Cannon didn't write them.

Her sister, Clarice, look out of library and smile like nice girl and ask when Lois come back to library. Lois smile nice, too, and say 'pretty soon, about five minutes.' Then she stand up, and ask me to stand up and I think she going back to the library.

I get up, I bow and stand still, as gentleman should till lady leave. But I see she have now gun in hand and getting ready to shoot. So I do not wait. I go away. She shoot. I look back and see she is holding gun. I see I didn't have any gun. So I run. She run after and shout, 'Halt! Halt!'

She shoot four times and hit me in left arm and lung. I wish to halt and tell her that there is misunderstanding but I think she is crazy so I say nothing and run some more until I drop in garage.

From his hospital bed that day, Shaw told a Chinese official from nearby Muskogee, Oklahoma, who was connected with the Chinese Consulate in Houston, that he forgave Lois and wanted "to forget all about it." He made the forgiveness statement to fellow countryman, Albert Eng, who wanted to have Chinese consular officials get involved and stand behind Shaw, possibly in anticipation that race might play a factor.

Despite the fact that Shaw told him to wait a few days, Eng contacted consular officials in Houston anyway. Fortunately, Shaw's health was improving, and barring pneumonia or another secondary complication, he would live.

The extortion note case of tiny Tahlequah was now an international incident. News of the attractive young coed who shot a Chinese student over an alleged shakedown plot blew up the newswires from coast to coast. Her story appeared in all forty-eight states and even crossed the border into Canada. Lois's picture from her high school yearbook, or photographs of her gathered from family members, were transmitted from coast to coast.

Daniel Shaw

Lois Thompson was famous. Just like Virginia Wilcox in the Tulsa case.

Arrested and Bonded Out

Lois stayed in jail until March 29, when she waived her arraignment and was released on a $2,500 bond that was signed and paid by several local businessmen. Her attorney, William Miller, proudly told reporters that one hundred Tahlequah citizens had volunteered to post bond for his client.

On April 6, Lois got her fourteenth and final death threat from the N.S.T.C gang. The note was posted in the family outhouse by someone who had snuck onto the Thompson's property during the night. Although it seemed preposterous that a gang of college kids would still want to play their game now that newspapers throughout the country were covering the story, county, state, and federal officers renewed their search for the author. With Daniel Shaw still in the hospital recovering from his wounds, they were certain it was not him. They wouldn't find out who it was until later.

Lois's preliminary hearing was set for April 30 but was delayed by County Attorney Sanford Martin, who wanted to wait until Shaw was released from the hospital to tell his story. It was rescheduled for May 23.

Two months of waiting for Shaw to recover allowed Martin to carry out his investigation with the help of state and federal agents. Oklahoma's governor also deemed the international implications serious enough that he sent Assistant State Attorney General Owen Watts to support Martin in his prosecution of Lois.

A Surprise Announcement

On the night before the May 23 preliminary hearing, Watts and Martin released a bombshell statement to the press that a justice department handwriting expert had determined that Lela Thompson had written the notes, and since it was her sister who wrote them, Lois must have known about them too.

Lois and Lela were the "N.S.T.C. gang" all along.

But at the time, the prosecution team had no clear motive established. To them, the whole bizarre affair was still a mystery. "There's no rhyme or reason to it," Watts confided to a newspaper reporter the day of the announcement. "Certainly Lois knew her sister was writing the extortion notes on which she declared her assault against Shaw was based. We cannot, frankly, quite figure this case out. There is no explanation."

The explanation would come later.

At the preliminary hearing, Shaw and several others gave testimony of what had happened on March 27, and the events leading up to it. After it was over, Lois and her sister were charged, arraigned, and made to post a $500 bond each on a charge of assault with a deadly weapon for the shooting of Jack Christy. Although it was the cops who shot him, the girls' actions had led to the shooting. The charge was filed by a special investigator working for the governor who wanted backup charges in place in case Lois was declared not guilty at her first trial, which was set to begin June 17.

Newspaper Interview

The news that Lois and Lela were behind the notes all along made it into newspapers from California to New York. The negative publicity was a nightmare for the modest but proud Thompson family. Five days before the trial started, Lois and her mother granted an interview request with the local *Tahlequah Citizen* newspaper where Lois's brother, Haskell, worked as a linotype operator.

It was an odd interview with restrictive parameters for the reporter. It was an interview that obviously had an agenda. In the presence of her mother, the two spoke to a reporter from their home, where Clarice, Ruby, and Lois were staying after they had quit school following the shooting. The interview was granted with the condition that no questions were to be asked about the trial, and that the reporter, "keep the story as small as possible."

In her opening proclamation to the reporter, Lois said, "I would rather not make any statement concerning the case or myself. Already publicity on this case has been very distasteful. I know newspapers have to have their news, you see I have a brother working on a newspaper, but if you will study it a minute I know you can see my side, too. This being written up as though you had suddenly become public enemy number one is one of the most unpleasant things of my life."

Her only comment regarding her ordeal was, "I am sure that anyone who had been in my place and knew what I had gone through would have done the same thing."

After that, Lois and her mother answered softball questions about who she was, what her background was, whether she was a member of a local church, and what her hobbies were. Their motivation for giving the story was an obvious attempt to show she was a good person, and could not possibly be the mastermind of the whole affair, as the prosecutor alleged. By establishing the questions which could be asked, the interview was designed to be one-sided, and the local paper accepted it. If the resulting story also had a positive influence on the potential jury pool the following week, that was a possible motive.

The Trial

Jury selection began Monday morning, June 17, and lasted approximately two hours. All members of the eight-man jury were middle-aged farmers. Two of them told County Attorney Martin they were unable to read or write.

"It doesn't make any difference," District Judge Oliver Brewer interrupted. "They look like they have common sense and that is all that is needed."

The trial was held in the beautiful, red-brick, Cherokee Nation Tribal Courts building that was packed with the curious who wanted to see the most famous trial in Cherokee County for the last ten years. Three hundred young boys, old women, smartly dressed ladies wearing their Sunday best, and farmers with sunburned faces and white foreheads, all packed themselves into a too-small courtroom. They were there to watch Lois Thompson and her defense team of two attorneys battle for her innocence against a three-man prosecution team that included Martin, Owen, and special prosecutor, Henry Vance. Vance had been retained by the Chinese Consulate in Houston. The Oklahoma governor's office wasn't the only institution to send one of their minders to look after their interests. If the case against Lois Thompson went south, there could be important international consequences.

As the wrongly persecuted heroine, Lois was attired in a white cotton dress with matching hat that was tilted to one side and slanted forward. When a photographer snapped a picture before the trial began, Lois scowled at the cameraman.

The trial began at noon and in his opening argument, Prosecutor Martin told the jury, "The state will attempt to prove that several extortion notes, which Miss Thompson claims prompted her to shoot Shaw, were written by her sister,

Lela Thompson." The motive, he added, "was a desire for publicity."

There it was—the motive that escaped him in May. It was the only plausible explanation that tied together all the reasons why a young college student and her sister would concoct an intriguing plot that resembled a Mary Roberts Rinehart mystery novel.

Defense attorney Miller's opening statement was unimaginative and merely restated what their argument had been all along. "Miss Thompson will plead self-defense," Miller declared. "She shot because she felt her life depended on it. We expect an acquittal. The trial shouldn't take more than two days."

Daniel Shaw was the first witness called to the stand. He denied any knowledge of the notes, writing the notes, or delivery of the notes. He related the events that took place on March 27 in a statement very similar to the one he gave from his hospital bed the day after the shooting. The one point he did add, however, was that his feelings were hurt when Lois accused him of writing the notes. To be accused of something so horrible was difficult for the humble boy to endure.

The next two witnesses called to the stand were students Ruth Holopeter and Dick Kisner, who had seen Lois talking with Shaw on the library bannister that day. They reported that Lois had appeared normal, and that there was no expression of fear on her face. Students Maggie May Hicks and Jessie Still also saw them talking and testified that they had overheard Shaw tell Lois, "I'm sorry," though they didn't know what was meant by it.

The prosecution's case was a *prima facie* one that presented the facts as they were. However, the trio of attorneys were holding back several rebuttal witnesses who they hoped would decimate the defense's case.

When Lois testified in her own defense the second day, her attorney led her through a series of questions in which she denied that she or her sisters had written the notes, or were behind them. Lois also testified that she spurned Shaw's romantic interest in her, a twist to the story that was news to Daniel Shaw. A short time after she rejected him, she started receiving the notes. The insinuation behind this claim supported the defense's theory that Shaw's motive was to get revenge on Lois. Lois continued her attack on Shaw by telling the jury she believed Shaw was a member of the N.S.T.C. gang that threatened to kill her unless she paid them off.

She then told her side of the story of the afternoon she shot Shaw and chased him across the campus. "I shot Shaw when he told me, 'You are coming with me and I am going to kill you,'" Lois proclaimed. "I knew I was shooting in self-defense."

This recollection of their conversation sounded ominous and not at all in line with what she told the jury next. As if she had already forgotten what she had just said, Lois quoted a more humble Shaw as saying: "'I'm very sorry about the notes and I would like to help you. If you will give me the notes I will get the person who wrote them.'"

"Then you know who wrote them? I asked."

"'Yes,' he replied."

"Did you write them?"

"'No,' he said."

"Did you deliver any of them? I asked him next."

"'Yes,' he said."

"How many of them? I asked."

"He said, 'Two.'"

"The two from the post office?"

"'Yes,'" Shaw replied, according to Lois.

She then told a strange story of how, on the morning of March 2, while she was at the drinking fountain, someone came up from behind and poked a gun in her back and asked her if she had been to the post office and gotten the note. No, she hadn't, she told the gun-wielding stranger. At that exact moment, someone was approaching from the other end of the hall and the man told her not to look around and to stand there and not talk to whoever passed if she knew them. After they walked by, he returned and handed her another note and then told her to remain there for one minute while he got away. She declared that she had never heard the voice before and did not look to see who it was.

It was the note that led to the shooting of Jack Christy later on that night.

In rebuttal testimony that would come later, the police chief, who was on the stakeout that night, said that he advised Lois to ignore the slow-moving car Christy was riding in because it was "just a bunch of drunks."

Then, the prosecution set Lois up for their key piece of scientific evidence. On cross-examination, special prosecutor Henry Vance asked Lois: "Are you acquainted with the handwriting of your sister Lela?"

"Yes."

"Are these notes in her handwriting?" Vance queried, displaying fourteen notes Lois claimed she received from the N.S.T.C. gang.

"No," she replied.

Now that Lois was locked into her testimony, the hinges of it were about to be blown off by the prosecution's rebuttal witnesses. Two students, including the one enlisted by the school to keep a watch on Lois, her books, and her locker, testified that the notes couldn't have been passed to her on the dates and locations she gave in court. Nor was a mysterious stranger seen talking to her. They knew. They'd been watching her.

Furthermore, Special Agent Charles Appel, a respected handwriting expert for the justice department, testified that a "scientific examination of the extortion notes and specimens of Lela's handwriting examined by him were compared and his expert opinion was the notes were written by the same person," the Associated Press reported.

Agent Appel told the jury that he had examined forty specimens of handwriting in connection with the case and selected Lela's as the same as the writer of the extortion notes.

"The reversed ? mark found in both Lela's handwriting specimen and the extortion notes was the first time I'd ever seen it," Appel declared. He also noted that the division in the words "**can not**" and "**any one**," which normally would be written as one word, were unique to Lela's handwriting sample.

The defense then called Lela to the stand. She testified that when she was instructed to give her handwriting sample, she was directed to misspell the words "can not" and "any one." She emphatically denied writing the extortion notes.

In rebuttal, the prosecution recalled Appel, as well as a state handwriting expert, who both reported that it was against their departments' policies to tell a suspect how to write a handwriting specimen. They also reported that samples are dictated orally to suspects from a typewritten statement.

Lela had just been caught in lie.

Another contradiction made by Lois was revealed when she testified from the stand earlier that Shaw "came looking for her" the day of the shooting. Justice department Agent Paul Hutchens reported that during his investigation after the shooting, Lois told him: "She decided she was going to find out if Shaw wrote the notes—got a gun and went to school March 27 with the idea of talking to Shaw about the matter."

She went looking for him, not the other way around.

Testimony on the second day of trial was completed by 9:45 p.m. and the court battle was all but wrapped up. On the last day, June 19, the defense's closing argument rambled on with an outrageous insinuation designed to incite racial prejudice.

"Japan is not friendly to the United States but the Japanese do not send members of their own race here to spy but instead send Chinese," asserted co-counsel, W.B. Wall. "I think less of a man who would sell out to another country than anybody," Wall added with righteous indignation that seemed buffoonish.

To backtrack over the slanderous comment he'd just made, Wall qualified his statement by saying he knew nothing about Shaw except that he was a quiet, unassuming student of American Indian culture.

"All I know is that Lois was acting in good faith and that she shot Shaw in self-defense at a time when she feared for her own life."

With an eye-roll to the defense attorney, Assistant Attorney General Owen Watts began by saying, "The whole affair was a hoax and a conspiracy from the beginning. Lois knew her sister, Lela, wrote those notes all the time."

Watts recapped the findings made by his expert witnesses, and pointed out the contradictions and discrepancies made by Lois and Lela during their testimonies.

The jury was dismissed and then met after lunch to deliberate the case. The debate they faced was not whether Lois was guilty—they were sure of that—but how to fix her punishment. After six hours of deliberation, the jury declared Lois Thompson guilty of shooting Daniel Shaw and recommended a jail sentence of thirty days.

"The dark-haired, dark-eyed part-Indian girl listened to the verdict with the same stoicism she had shown throughout her trial, but when members of her family gathered about her tears welled up in her eyes and she sobbed softly," the Associated Press reported.

The *Tahlequah Citizen* reported one week after the trial that the pending charge against Lois and Lela would be dropped if Lois completed her thirty-day term to the satisfaction of the prosecutor. Her sentence began on Monday, June 24.

For many people living outside of Tahlequah, the thirty-day jail sentence seemed absurd in relation to the shooting and the hoax. But the real absurdity manifested when local citizens rallied for one of their own with a petition of one thousand signatures demanding the prosecutor recommend a suspended sentence.

Resisting immense political pressure to intervene on behalf of the girl he had just prosecuted, County Attorney Martin said, "In my opinion, Miss Thompson has been well represented. The jury has found her guilty and if she is guilty, no one could be more guilty."

But jail wasn't that bad for Lois and she passed her time constructively. Sheriff Grover said the limestone building had never been cleaner after "she took to it."

Although she never did get the kind of national, sympathetic publicity she wanted, Lois did receive more than eight hundred visitors while she was in jail, "every one of whom was properly sympathetic," a newspaper feature writer wrote a few months later.

Immediately after the verdict was read, Daniel Shaw traveled to Hawaii to continue his studies.

Epilogue

A psychiatrist who was consulted about this case by a third party said that, in his opinion, Lois's desire for publicity, while steadfastly denying she was behind the entire charade, was likely a case of a "factitious victimization."

Above, the flat iron cell inside the limestone jail, below, where Lois Thompson served her 30 day sentence for shooting Daniel Shaw. The jail is now the **Cherokee National Prison Museum.** *(Photos by Author)*

Chapter Seven: The Wife Who Lost Her Head, 1946

ON THE MORNING of January 2, 1946, two motorists driving up the steep grade of Waterman Canyon in the San Bernardino Mountains pulled over into a wide turn-out to refill the radiator. The winding road is known as the Rim of the World Highway[1] and they had climbed three thousand feet in four miles. The engine was already overheating. As the two men waited for the motor to cool, they stood near a rock-ramparted ledge to take in the panoramic view of the valley below. When one of the travelers happened to look down into a ravine directly below him, he got another breathtaking view: a woman's legs protruding out from underneath a green and white blanket that was wrapped around her and tied with a rope.

The sheriff, the coroner, and eight deputies from the San Bernardino County Sheriff's Office responded, and with the aid of ropes and mountaineering equipment, they retrieved the torso of a middle-aged woman. Although her legs and arms were still attached, her head and hands were gone—sawed off, by the looks of it.

At mid-center of her chest, police could plainly see a bullet hole. Another one was found on her left side, below her armpit. Besides an old scar on her leg, the only other identifying feature on the woman were bunions on her feet so severe that they would have required medical treatment sometime in the past. The police estimated her age to be approximately thirty-five.

---

[1] Officially, it is California State Route 18.

Other than a few sketchy footprints, the killer left behind no clues that he was even there. It appeared as if he had driven into the turn-out, carried the woman's body from his car to the cliff, and simply thrown her into the ravine sometime within the last twenty-four hours. But the location of the woman's body did give investigators one clue: the killer was not from the area. Anyone who lived around there would have known plenty of other places in the San Bernardino Mountains to hide a body that would never be found.

As dumping grounds go, this particular area was a bad choice.

The story of the headless woman found in Waterman Canyon made it to the front pages of area newspapers later that afternoon. Radio stations interrupted their normal broadcasting to report on the grisly discovery. Within just a few hours, the San Bernardino Sheriff's Office received more than one hundred telephone calls from people requesting more details or to view the body. By the following morning, the calls, tips, and inquiries coming in from all across the western United States were too numerous to count.

Within an hour or two of the first radio broadcast, fifty-two-year-old Arthur Eggers reported his wife missing at the Temple City substation of the Los Angeles County Sheriff's Department where he worked as a clerk. Arthur was a shy, unassuming man who wore gold-rimmed glasses and had a receding hairline. His wife, Dorothy, was a forty-two-year-old, vivacious, restless woman who dominated her smaller, diminutive husband. The sheriff's deputies who had worked with Arthur for the last fourteen years knew the couple had a rocky marriage. When he filed the report, Arthur speculated that his wife had run off with another man. The last time he saw her was three days before, on December 29, around nine o'clock in the morning.

As part of their routine investigation into the identity of the headless woman, lawmen throughout California reviewed their missing persons files for any identifying features that would match the torso found in Waterman Canyon. Despite her missing head, the coroner measured the unknown female from her shoulders to her feet and estimated her height at five foot seven or five-foot eight-inches.

When Los Angeles County deputies assigned to Temple City reviewed Arthur's report of his missing wife, they noted something odd: he had listed Dorothy as being five-foot two-inches tall. The Temple City lawmen who were friends with the couple and had danced with Dorothy at department social functions, knew for a fact that she was five foot seven, the same height as the woman found in Waterman Canyon. They politely asked Arthur if he believed his wife could be the unidentified woman in San Bernardino.

"Yes, I thought of that," Arthur replied to a deputy. "That's why I filed the official report, for the record. I went over there last night and took a look at her, but it isn't Dorothy, thank God."

But the lawmen soon discovered Arthur was lying. While he did go to the San Bernardino's coroner's office, Arthur never actually looked at the body. He just sort of milled around and then left. The height discrepancy—and lying about viewing the woman's body—raised their suspicions, and the deputies began a secretive investigation of their coworker. When they were in the office, they treated Arthur Eggers as they always had, but outside, they were digging into the couple's private life.

From her friends, county investigators learned Dorothy had grown tired of her husband of eighteen years. She was running around with other men and was promiscuous. She didn't care if Arthur knew. They also learned Dorothy hadn't been seen or heard from since December 29, which was also the last day Arthur claimed he had seen his wife. Her relatives also confirmed that she was five foot seven inches tall, weighed about 145 pounds, and had recently had surgery on one of her bunions. She had also received treatment by a local chiropractor for a spinal condition. With these two discernible features, both the doctor and the chiropractor were called in, and they positively identified the body as that of Dorothy Eggers.

Dorothy Eggers

The forensic connection between Arthur and his wife's death came on January 19, when a new deputy to the substation told his colleagues he had recently purchased a 1940 Plymouth sedan from Eggers for $800. Although he didn't know Arthur and his wife personally, the other deputies knew that was Dorothy's car, not Arthur's. When the title was transferred to the new owner at the courthouse, Arthur told the deputy his wife was outside in the sedan. However, the woman the deputy saw was much younger and more slender. She turned out to be the couple's nineteen-year-old niece, Marie. She lived with the Eggers along with her younger sister, eleven-year-old Lorraine.

When crime scene technicians examined the six-year-old Plymouth, they found that the trunk had recently been cleaned. However, it wasn't clean enough, and in little nooks and crannies authorities found Type-A blood—the same blood-type as Dorothy's. A search of gun records turned up a registration document showing that Arthur owned a .38-caliber revolver—the same caliber of rounds found in the woman's body. When Arthur was at work, investigators searched his house where they found more Type-A bloodstains in the couple's bathroom.

Arthur Eggers, son of the former sheriff of San Francisco County,[2] was arrested on January 22 on suspicion of murder. He was interrogated over the next five days in the Los Angeles County Sheriff's Office. Arthur confessed to forging Dorothy's signature on the title in order to sell the car, but he denied killing his wife. He also admitted he had given her clothes away to charity but only because he believed at the time that she wasn't coming back. Deputies also discovered that on January 4, Arthur had sold his wife's engagement and wedding rings to a jeweler for $10, under a false name and fictitious address.

When forced to view her body, he admitted that it had to be her, and that he never actually saw it before when he said he did. While observing his dead wife's headless body, deputies noted that he displayed no emotion, and he was surprisingly calm when he discussed it with them.

"I'd say that was her," Arthur said coolly. "I'll claim the body."

When asked why he didn't claim the body the first time he said he viewed it, Arthur had an excuse ready for them: "I lied for the benefit of my wife's aged mother. I wanted to put her mind at ease."

His theory of her murder, he told the lawmen, was that she was murdered by one of her lovers. "I wouldn't hurt a hair on her head," Arthur told deputies. "I wouldn't kill her. I wanted her to raise the children."

While Arthur brooded in a holding cell, he was confronted by the older niece about the quilt that was wrapped and tied around her aunt's body.

---

[2] Sheriff Frederick Eggers, 1912-1915

"That quilt was on the bed," Marie calmly stated.

"Whose bed?" he fired back.

"It was on my bed for a while, then I saw it on your bed."

Arthur stared at her a little too long as he thought over his reply. "The girl is lying," he finally said, with a shrug of his shoulders to the officer next to her.

Arthur was held in jail on charges of grand theft in connection with the fraudulent sale of his wife's car. Without a murder confession, it was the only way they could keep him in jail. On January 27, detectives subjected Arthur to a four-hour lie detector examination, but he was too nervous and jumpy to give detectives anything more than inconclusive results.

Arthur continued to hold out until Robert Jones, a retired deputy sheriff, was brought in to talk to him. The two had worked together a long time and Arthur respected the man.

"Art, I believe you are guilty. I believe you will have a better chance if you confess. Get it off your chest and lay it on the line," Jones said flatly.

"Okay, Bob," Arthur sighed. "All right, I did it. I'll tell you anything you want to know."

In his confession to detectives, Arthur said he returned home from work around one o'clock in the morning on December 30. As he approached, he heard the front door slam and saw a man leave the house, walking away at a fast pace. Suspicious, Eggers entered his home through the back door, turned on the lights, and found his wife in their bedroom, naked.

"'I am going to leave you and go with Bob,'" Arthur claimed his wife told him. "It was always 'Bob this' and 'Bob that.' I had suspected her for a number of years. I started to boil over. She called me an 'insect' and 'cheapskate.' She said, 'What are you going to do about it, you little insect?'"

What he did about it was grab his gun from his dresser. He was set to chase after the man, when he got into a physical fight with his wife, who tried to stop him from going after "Bob."

The struggle spilled over to the bathroom where they both slipped and fell to the floor, and when they did, Arthur claimed, his gun accidentally went off. After that, he put her in the bathtub, dismembered her with his rip saw, wrapped her in the blanket, put her in the trunk, cleaned up the mess, and dumped her out in Waterman Canyon.

Despite being a cuckold, Arthur insisted he still loved his wife. "I'm sorry. I didn't mean to kill her. I will always love her."

The morning after he confessed, Arthur led investigators up the mountain road. Newspaper reporters tagged along and took a dramatic picture of him showing detectives how he threw the headless body of his wife into the ravine. He also drew a map directing them to where he had disposed of his .38 caliber revolver and ripsaw. When the report of their findings eventually made it into court documents, the details were gruesome. Stuck to the flat steel of the saw "was a fatty, greasy substance and human blood. There were also numerous bits of tissue, bone and fatty debris" which adhered to the teeth. One large fragment of human bone was also forcibly wedged into part of the saw. Test bullets fired from the gun were later matched to those found in the body.

During the five days he was interrogated, Arthur Eggers told investigators lie after lie after lie. When he finally confessed, he continued lying in order to mitigate his level of guilt. His story of where he concealed Dorothy's head and hands changed frequently, and he played a cat-and-mouse game when it came to leading officers to where he tossed them.

After the detectives and a large troop of four hundred Boy Scouts had consumed several hours tromping and plodding through the difficult brush twenty miles from where Dorothy's body was found, Eggers changed his story. It was an extremely cold day, and investigators later speculated that Arthur just wanted to get somewhere warm.

"Well, it's almost too horrifying to tell, but here's the truth," he said with an aw-shucks grin. "I burned Dorothy's head and hands in the incinerator at home."

However, when investigators went to his house and collected the ashes for testing, they didn't find any bones or teeth. Like the deputies, he knew teeth could survive a fire, and he had a story to cover his latest lie.

"Dorothy had plastic dentures and I guess they must have melted completely," he said. As they sifted through the ashes looking for charred bones, detectives asked Arthur when he had burned the head and hands. "Why, in the morning of course. It's against the law to burn anything in your incinerator after noon," he replied.

The day after his first confession, Arthur changed his story completely, including the time and manner of how Dorothy was killed.

"He has lied so much that we are going to get his story straight once and for all," Captain Gordon Bowers declared to reporters. He was the sheriff department's chief homicide detective. "He has told some truths, but most of his details are self-preserving lies in his attempt to escape a first-degree murder charge. He is trying to show there is no premeditation on his part."

When asked about the veracity of Eggers's confession, Captain Bowers told reporters that his story, like most of Arthur's stories, was fictitious. "If the slaying took place as Eggers said it did, that meant the couple's adoptive children and a roomer,[3] slept through the fight and the shooting in the small bungalow."

Despite Arthur's confession, and all the discrepancies which conflicted with the known facts investigators compiled during their investigation, he pleaded not guilty and not guilty by reason of insanity. Although this dual plea was extremely

---

[3] Lester Loomis, 41, rented a bedroom from the couple.

common in California murder cases at that time, it was a strange one to make. It was the legal equivalent of saying: "I didn't do it—but if I did do it, I was crazy at the time."

By the time of his grand jury indictment in late February, Arthur had already reversed his story: he had never killed his wife, and the body found in Waterman Canyon wasn't even Dorothy. She was still alive and her disappearance was part of her master plan to persecute him. When the funeral director with Mater & Simone Mortuary sought him out to proceed with giving Dorothy a proper burial, Arthur refused to pay for the funeral expenses because he had no relation to the dead woman found in the San Bernardino Mountains.

This story conflicted with a slip of the tongue he had made five days after he confessed, in which he announced he would never reveal the location of Dorothy's head. "I swear by these upraised hands," Arthur dramatically proclaimed from his jail cell, "that no one will ever know what I did with them!"

When asked about going to trial without the head or hands, Captain Bowers wasn't concerned. "We no longer need to establish *corpus delicti*. We have practically given up searching for them."

Arthur did manage to do one thing right in those early days after his arrest: he hired an aggressive attorney. James Starritt was a chubby-faced little man who wore fashionable ties and had a mop of curly hair. During his client's grand jury indictment, Starritt attacked the prosecution with bold new claims. He argued the confession was inadmissible because it was secondary and hearsay evidence. Arthur's confession was never put in writing. The defense attorney also condemned the indictment itself, which failed to mention that Dorothy Eggers was even missing.

"That body may be the headless horseman of Sleepy Hollow, for all this transcript shows," Starritt protested.

When Judge William McKay denied his petition to block the indictment, Starritt appealed to a higher court with a writ to stop the proceedings against his client. His Sleepy Hollow argument contended that Dorothy was not missing, and without a head and hands to conclusively identify her, the state had no case.

Although bold, Starritt's legal claims were drowned out by the forensic evidence, and it only postponed his client's trial to May. However, the defense attorney did manage to get the confession set aside when Judge McKay declared police had gone too far in their tactics to get it. His ruling cast doubt on its admissibility at trial because "[It] was given under circumstances not in accord with ethics or pure principles."

Dorothy Eggers's torso may have been found in San Bernardino County, but the evidence showed she was likely killed in her Temple City home at 202 North Rosemead Boulevard. When Arthur's confession was thrown out, Los Angeles County prosecutors turned to the sheriff department's criminologist to piece together the forensic evidence. Amassed together, it was overwhelming: the blood-type match from the trunk and the bathroom, the ballistics comparison with Eggers's .38 pistol, the fatty tissue and bone fragments found in the ripsaw marked with the initials "A E," the green and white family blanket that was wrapped around the body, hairs from the torso which matched those found in Dorothy's hairbrush, and the positive identification of her body by her doctor and chiropractor.

The murder trial of Arthur Eggers began on May 6, 1947, with the prosecution approving potential jurors based on their responses to questions about the death penalty. As he listened to this, Arthur's mousy face, with his darting blue eyes and constant handwringing, signaled to reporters his high anxiety.

The state's case in Superior Court Judge Clement Nye's courtroom was as strong as trial watchers had predicted. The criminologist parsed out the forensic evidence to the jurors efficiently and effectively. Dorothy's nieces, also described by newspapers as the couple's adoptive daughters, were the primary witnesses. Marie described how Arthur made her practice signing Dorothy's signature so he could deceptively transfer the title to her car during the sale to a deputy. She also identified the blanket as one that was on her bed the year before. Boarder Lester Loomis denied he was ever intimate with Dorothy, and he told the jury that Arthur claimed he had viewed the Waterman Canyon torso and told him it was not Dorothy. And finally, a neighbor testified that on January 3, she had seen Arthur Eggers vigorously cleaning the trunk of his wife's car.

In his opening arguments, defense attorney Starritt condemned Dorothy Eggers as a harlot who violated the sanctity of the Eggers home, and that she was accidentally shot during an argument. His legal strategy was simple. Blame the victim, and build sympathy for his client who had to endure a wife who was an unfaithful shrew.

"Our evidence will prove Mrs. Eggers was a domineering, forceful woman who was not averse to attending dances alone and picking up strange men," Starritt told the jurors. "For a long time Eggers heard rumors of his wife's unfaithfulness. When he saw with his own eyes the truth of these rumors there was a blinding flash in his mind and he grabbed a gun to defend the sanctity of his home. In the struggle, Mrs. Eggers, who was strong physically, was accidentally shot."

Starritt also told the jury that the female torso in Waterman Canyon was not Dorothy Eggers. He was prepared to call a witness to the stand whose testimony would point away from Arthur as the one who had dumped that unknown woman in the ravine.

While his attorney outlined his case in his opening remarks, Arthur maintained his bizarre behavior by sitting in his chair with his eyes closed, giving the impression that he was dozing off into a light sleep. If he later said something from the stand that contradicted what his attorney had just said, he needed plausible deniability.

With little to go on, and no expert witnesses of their own, the defense's star witness was a tense Arthur Eggers. But James

Starritt saw this as the smart move because if anyone could prove to the jury his client was crazy, it was his crazy client himself. With his attorney guiding him, Arthur told the jury their marriage had been a happy one until one or two years before her death. Around that time, Eggers declared, Dorothy had informed him she was beginning "the change of life," and she had become difficult to get along with ever since. He heard rumors that she started going to dances while he worked late at the substation, and that she was picking up men. He said he never believed these rumors because he trusted her and "didn't give it much thought."

James Starritt, left, in the courtroom with his client, Arthur Eggers, right.

Just prior to her disappearance, Eggers and his wife had an argument about Christmas presents. She ridiculed him for not getting a present for their boarder, Lester Loomis, and called him a "cheapskate."

Questioned by his attorney, Arthur said he was returning home from work during the early morning hours of Sunday,

December 30, when he heard the front door slam and saw a tall man, who resembled a family friend, run off down the street.

"I went into the house and found my wife in the bedroom. She was nude," Eggers testified. "I told her I was going to stop such goings-on and got my gun from the dresser drawer. Dorothy grabbed me and we struggled in the bedroom. She pushed me into the bathroom and we both fell down. The gun went off. Next thing I knew, I was crying and then I heard these voices.

"[I was] sitting on the toilet seat, crying and scared, and then I know I got in the car, and somebody else was in that car and kept saying, *'She is in back, she is in back.'* I found myself driving along the water front, but I kept hearing these voices. *'She is in back, she is in back.'* I stopped the car and looked in the trunk but it was empty. I thought it was all a bad dream, but when I went back to the house, Dorothy wasn't there."

According to his testimony, Eggers only remembers one shot, and he could not identify the other person in the car who was talking to him.

"Did you intend to harm your wife?" Starritt asked his client.

With dramatic posturing that bordered on overacting, Eggers rose from the witness stand, raised his hand as if taking an oath, and righteously declared: "No! As God is my judge, I never had any thought of killing my wife. I loved her."

Lack of intent meant second-degree murder and no death penalty.

"Do you know where she is today?" Starritt asked.

"Sometimes I think she is dead. Sometimes I think she is alive and laughing at my predicament," the slim defendant sighed. "But that body I saw in San Bernardino WAS NOT my Dorothy!"

Following his client's cross-examination by Deputy District Attorney Barnes, Starritt called his surprise witness, who testified that someone else threw that body into the ravine. Lloyd Wayne Cuthbert explained to the jury of ten women and two men how on the night in question, he came to the aid of an unidentified man with bloody hands changing a tire not far from where Dorothy's body was found.

While the courtroom buzzed with excitement over this new development, Barnes calmly called his own surprise witness to the stand to refute the defense's insinuation. It was ex-Marine Fred Matuskey, who professed he was the mystery man that night. He admitted his hands were bloodstained while he was changing a tire on the Rim of the World Highway. He explained that he was on his honeymoon following a wedding four hours earlier, and he had cut his hands when removing the traditional tin cans tied to the back of his car.

After his alternate suspect scenario blew up in his face, Starritt rested his case. The jury's verdict of guilt came as no surprise to anyone but Arthur Eggers. As the bailiff was reading the verdict, mousy little Arthur blinked rapidly behind his gold-framed glasses but showed no other emotion. A few minutes later, he was overheard to say to his attorney, "How could they? It wasn't Dorothy's body. I know it isn't Dorothy's body. This is absolutely unfair."

Although the jury declared his guilt, a legal snag began to unravel during deliberations when the foreman sent a note to Judge Nye asking if they could set his punishment at life in prison without parole. No, Nye wrote back. It was a first degree murder charge and that meant the death penalty.

But the jury didn't want to send Arthur Eggers to the gas chamber. They returned the guilty verdict without a recommendation for punishment. Judge Nye then ordered them to decide the defendant's sanity. However, before that hearing could begin, one of the jurors declared she had "a closed mind" on the sanity question, and the foreman wrote the judge: " . . . that if the same jury were retained, it would be a hung jury."

Judge Nye dismissed the jury and was forced to call for a new one. It was a huge blow to the defense, since a new jury did not have the experience of witnessing the cracked eggshell that was Arthur Eggers. Starritt vigorously attacked these moves and called for a mistrial, which was eventually overruled.

On June 4, Arthur made the news again when he formally resigned from his job with the Los Angeles County Sheriff's Department. In his letter to Sheriff Eugene Biscailuz, Eggers wrote, "I will always hold the highest regard for you and your department." He ended with a request that all accrued sick leave and vacation pay be forwarded to his account at the county jail.

Arthur's sanity hearing began on June 11 and lasted two weeks. Three psychiatrists testified that he was sane, and Arthur himself was put on the stand to answer that question.

"Do you think you're sane?" Starritt asked.

"Of course I'm sane!" Arthur fired back.

One of Arthur's two sisters, Etta Williams from San Francisco, gave jurors the impression that insanity ran in the family. "Their father, Frederick Eggers, former Sheriff of San Francisco County, had hallucinations that the late Gov. Friend Richardson was about to appoint him Warden of San Quentin Prison," the *Los Angeles Times* reported.

When he heard this, Arthur jumped to his feet, pointed a finger to the sky, and shouted, "Let his spirit rest!"

After he was ordered to sit back down and keep his mouth shut, Arthur's sister then told how her brother had suffered several bad falls as a child, one of them leaving him unconscious for seven or eight hours. Brain damage was the implication.

The new jury disagreed. On June 29, the jury of eleven women and one man decided the defendant was sane when he murdered his wife Dorothy and butchered her body.

Arthur Eggers was not *crazy insane*, he was *crazy weird*.

His only reply to the verdict was, "That still isn't her body." For some strange reason, he still clung to an errant belief that if the woman's torso found in a Waterman Canyon ravine wasn't Dorothy, then he was innocent—even though he admitted on the stand he shot her and indicated he had put her in the trunk of his car. It didn't matter to him that expert witnesses relying on forensic evidence, and Dorothy's own doctor and chiropractor, had declared the torso was that of his dead wife. If he said it wasn't her, then it wasn't her, and everyone should just take his word on it.

Judge Nye sentenced fifty-two-year-old Arthur Eggers to die in the gas chamber. As he was being led back to the county jail, he continued to deny the body was that of his dead wife.

Arthur Eggers, San Quentin mug shot. *(Courtesy: California State Archives)*

"Someday, somewhere, she'll show up and make fools of all the prosecutors," he declared. "She's probably waiting to hear what happens to me."

But that was never going to happen, and one month later, the Mater & Simone Mortuary buried what was left of Dorothy Rosmond Eggers in Valhalla Cemetery in North Hollywood.

Over the next two years, Arthur's new attorney, Berwyn Rice, fought for his client with new trial motions, an appeal, and postponements. Arthur Eggers was scheduled to be executed on February 6, 1948, along with Admiral Dewey Adamson,[4] but nine hours before the cyanide gas pellets would drop, both men were granted a stay of execution while federal judges considered constitutional issues in Adamson's case. The judgment in that case did not alter Arthur's death sentence, it only postponed it by ten months.

Rice continued to fight in vain for his client that summer, and a last ditch clemency request to Governor Earl Warren was denied. On Friday morning, October 15, at ten o'clock, Arthur Eggers was strapped into the steel chair inside San Quentin's apple-green-painted gas chamber. Fifteen minutes later, he was pronounced dead. Until the last moments of his life, he continued to profess it was not Dorothy's body found in a ravine off the Rim of the World Highway.

Epilogue

Fourteen months after his death, Arthur Eggers's will pledging his entire estate of $258.18 to the Salvation Army was filed in probate court. Eggers also stated in his will, "I forgive all those who tried to harm me."

On the scrap of paper penned in his death-row cell two months before he was executed, Eggers called Warden Clinton T. Duffy "a great humanitarian." In the years ahead, Warden Duffy would become the most famous warden in America with his book, *The San Quentin Story,* recounting his time as the warden of San Quentin. Duffy later gained more fame when he passionately argued against the death penalty in his book, *88 Men, 2 Women.* A short passage relating a conversation about the death penalty Duffy said he had with Arthur was included in the book.

Two months after Eggers was executed, a bullet-riddled human skull was discovered one mile away from where Dorothy's body was found. Initial hopes that it belonged to Mrs. Eggers were quickly dismissed.

---

[4] Admiral was his name, not a military rank.

On August 29, 1954, two fifteen-year-old twins, Peter and Paul Gaeta, found a human skull while hunting in Eaton Canyon near Pasadena, California—sixty-five miles away. Three weeks later, police announced that a photographic layover comparison between the skull and Dorothy Eggers "proved beyond doubt that the skull was not that of Mrs. Eggers," the *Los Angeles Times* reported.

During his trial, Sheriff Biscailuz of Los Angeles County, and Sheriff Emmett Shay of San Bernardino County, both testified to the search they conducted based on Eggers's first confession. "Both men said Eggers 'admitted' wrapping the missing parts in a newspaper and tossing the package over the cliff near Panorama Point," the *Los Angeles Times* reported at the time. After deputies and four hundred Boy Scouts searched the area for several hours, Eggers told them it was all a hoax, and her head and hands were burned in the incinerator behind his house. This was later proven to be false after the ashes were examined. Lawmen speculated that Arthur's first claim, that he tossed them near Panorama Point, was likely the truth.

Panorama Point overlooks a ravine above the bottom of Waterman Canyon, and is located on State Route 18, between Inspiration Point and the Wayne A. Thomas Memorial Cross Foundation. It can be found on Google Maps.

To this day, Dorothy Eggers's head and hands have never been found.

Note: For those who are interested, a gruesome photograph of Dorothy's torso can be found with Google Image Search.

Chapter Eight: The York Family Massacre, 1947

ON SUNDAY MORNING of May 25, 1947, Willard York and his family piled into his late-model Buick sedan dressed in their best clothes. The prominent San Antonio, Texas, investment advisor knew that it was important to look the part of a successful securities trader. Church wasn't just a place to get closer to God; it was also a place for the ambitious thirty-six-year-old to make connections.

Next to him sat his wife, Gertrude. In the spacious back seat were his two children, Ann, 13, John, 9, and his sixty-seven-year-old mother, Mary. In Willard's rear view mirror was his beautiful ranch-style home located on 1,600 acres of rolling hills near Bulverde, on the western edge of Comal County. Although it was a forty-minute commute to his San Antonio office, living on the ranch in the peaceful countryside was worth the daily commute. It was a scenic area that was home to many notable families and it was right where Willard York thought he should be.

As the Buick slowly made its way down the family's long private road, Willard rounded a sharp corner and spotted a black car blocking the junction to the county road which led to the Methodist Church in New Braunfels. As he got within fifteen feet, Willard recognized the car. He also recognized the man getting out of the car and it was the last person he wanted to see.

It would also be the last person he ever saw. The tall, well-dressed man walked to the driver's side of York's car, raised a rifle to his shoulder and took aim.

"Don't shoot, Lloyd, please don't shoot," Willard pleaded.

A half-second later, a bullet passed through the open window and bored into Willard's chest, killing him instantly. Lloyd put two more bullets in Willard and then swung the rifle toward his wife.

"Please, Lloyd, don't shoot!" the mother of two screamed. Lloyd shot her anyway.

Frightened, young John had pushed open the back door, and had just gotten his feet planted on the ground when Lloyd shot and killed him. The boy's small body dropped back inside the car, then rolled out the open door onto the gravel road. A bouquet of wildflowers he had picked that morning to take to church was still gripped tightly in his right hand.

Mary York leaped out of the back seat on the other side and started running. She made it about twelve feet back up the private road before she felt a hot, burning sledgehammer knock her to the ground. Then, another bullet slammed into her.

In the middle of the shooting, Ann York exited the back seat on the opposite side of Lloyd and was looking for a place to run when she caught sight of him pointing the rifle at her. When he pulled the trigger, they both heard a "click."

"Then as he began to reload his gun, I saw my chance," she would later tell police. "I ran toward the woods but a bullet hit me before I was able to get away." She had been shot in the right hip. Lloyd fired several more times at the fleeing girl but missed. During the massacre, the shooter's glasses fell off and were crushed when he accidentally stepped on them. His vision was so poor he could barely see Ann as she ran into the woods. Giving up, he dashed to his car and sped off.

It didn't take long for neighbors to reach the junction of the county road and the lane which led to the York ranch. Peter Avilla, the owner of the ranch next to the York's, ran as fast as he could in the direction of the gunfire. When he got close to the Buick, other neighbors and a passing motorist were already there. Avilla could see the shock and horror on their faces, and as his eyes took in the horrific scene of four murdered people, he understood why. But as he counted the bodies, he realized one person was missing.

Ann had kept on running and never looked back. She pushed her way through a high-brush area and then a line of trees to make her way to the home of neighbor Otto Voges. With a bullet wound in the young girl's hip, it had taken her thirty minutes to reach his house.

Comal County Sheriff Walter "Doc" Scholl and Justice of the Peace H.R. Voges, a relative of Otto's, were the first local authorities to arrive at the scene. Sheriff Scholl took witness statements from a crew of men who were cutting down cedar trees nearby. They reported seeing a black car parked at the junction an hour before they heard the gunfire. He also spoke with neighbors who arrived shortly after hearing the shots. On the driver's side of the Buick, the sheriff found eleven .300-caliber shell casings and the broken eyeglasses.

The four bodies were eventually taken to a New Braunfels Funeral Home, while the family's last surviving member was brought to a hospital in that same city. Ann's attending physician told the sheriff that her condition was not critical. He was more worried about her state of shock. He had given her a sedative and told the lawman she could be interviewed in a few hours after she slept.

It didn't take long for local radio stations to report the news that the Willard York family had been gunned down.

"News of the massacre spread like wildfire," crime reporter Burton Leeds would later write in a magazine article. "Talk of lynching began to be heard among the tight little groups of citizens who gathered on the streets of New Braunfels and San Antonio, the two cities where the York family was so well known."

State-level crime-scene technicians from Austin drove the fifty miles to the funeral home in New Braunfels, where they examined the bodies. Bullets would have to be carefully removed in case they found the rifle to match them with. Later, they met up with Sheriff Scholl at the crime scene and looked in vain for tire tracks belonging to the mysterious black car. Scholl also ordered his deputies to spread out and interview friends of the York family. However, none of them could shed light on a motive strong enough to send a crazy man to massacre an entire family.

By two o'clock that afternoon, word reached Sheriff Scholl that Ann was alert enough to talk. He rushed to the hospital with a deputy, and the two lawmen cautiously sidled up to the bedside of a somber little girl who was now an orphan.

"Do you know the man who did this terrible thing?" he asked her gently, holding his hat between his two weathered hands.

She told him who it was.

Sheriff Scholl straightened his body and turned to see the shocked expression on his deputy's face.

After a moment of silence, he asked the girl again. "Are you sure about that?"

"I'm positive," Ann said. "We all recognized him."

As the deputy stayed with the girl, Sheriff Scholl walked briskly to a telephone at the nurses' station and called the name into his office, which then notified law enforcement in San Antonio with a pick-up order.

Thirty minutes later and thirty miles away, a well-dressed man walked into the San Antonio Police Headquarters and with the smooth, casual gait of a gentleman accustomed to respect, made his way to Watch Commander Lt. Ferdinand Fest.

"Who's in charge?" Dr. Lloyd I. Ross asked.

"I am," Fest replied.

"I think I killed a man," Dr. Ross stated.

"Did you?"

"There's a rifle in my car. I think it's been fired."

Fest picked up the telephone and called in Detective Sergeant Joe Hester in his office to come to the front desk and question the doctor.

"There's a rifle in my car that has been fired," Dr. Ross told the detective when he walked up. Almost as an afterthought, the doctor said he didn't remember killing anyone.

Ross was no ordinary doctor. The forty-two-year-old was a Harvard-educated surgeon who was popular and well known in San Antonio social circles. Until recently, he had been the York family doctor and close friend. His wife, Gladys Ross, was active in the local garden club and had been close friends with Gertrude York.

Detective Hester retrieved the rifle and then had to play a guessing game with the evasive doctor as to the meaning of it all. During the interview, the doctor said he had "woke up" while driving, and had then come to the police station.

Comal County officials arrived a short time later to question their chief suspect. Dr. Ross told them that the only statement he was willing to make was that he could not remember a single thing that happened that morning. He insisted over and over that his "mind was blank" and he "didn't remember shooting anyone."

Back at the Comal County Jail in New Braunfels, Dr. Ross stuck to his story even though his interrogators persisted. They would have to take his word for it, he told them, that he was not malingering about his lapse of memory.

Dr. Ross was no fool, and he knew exactly what he was doing, they would later come to realize. He was laying the groundwork for his future defense.

By the next morning, Ross's attorneys had come to his aid and Sheriff Scholl knew he wasn't going to get anything more out him. If Ross thought he could outsmart him, he underestimated the sheriff's determination. He'd have to dig deep into the personal lives of both the Ross and York families to get to the truth. Already, wild rumors were flying around New Braunfels and San Antonio that an inappropriate love triangle had led to the shootings. It was true that the two families had once been close friends.

Sheriff Scholl returned to the hospital to make inquiries with Ann York. He asked her if she knew what had come between her father and Dr. Ross. She told him that she knew the two had quarreled, but she didn't know why.

Reporters for the *San Antonio Express* daily newspaper were also digging into the story and had come up with the "why." As it turned out, the motive wasn't love or sex, it was money and justice, which they reported on in a story published the day after the murders. Willard York, the newspaper learned, had allegedly been playing a shell game with his client's money.

Earlier that year on March 19, Dr. Ross filed a complaint against York with the Securities and Exchange Commission office in San Antonio. The complaint charged that the Willard York Investment Company had been doing business while insolvent, and had used customers' securities without their consent. On that date, Federal Judge Ben H. Rice Jr. issued a temporary restraining order prohibiting the York Company from doing business.

On the same day he filed a complaint with the SEC, Dr. Ross filed a civil suit asking judgment in district court against York, alleging that the investment advisor was indebted to him in securities, stocks, and bonds amounting to $80,279.67.[1]

The suit also claimed that at least part of Dr. Ross's stock portfolio was wrongfully used as collateral by York to secure multiple loans totaling $41,000. That money was then used by York to finance "get-rich-quick schemes" in a failed attempt to recoup earlier losses York had incurred.

In his suit, Dr. Ross explained in great detail the various investments the broker had made for him over the years. When Dr. Ross tried to liquidate his account, York disputed the amount of money Ross had invested with him. An independent audit of Dr. Ross's investment account was undertaken on his behalf. That investigation revealed York had diverted $80,279

---

[1] The equivalent of $840,000 in 2014.

of Dr. Ross's money to his own personal use, with most of it going toward the purchase of his 1,600-acre ranch.

On March 24, York filed a voluntary bankruptcy petition in federal court, a move that would have prevented Ross from recovering any of his funds. York listed his indebtedness at $182,197.38. His assets came to $115,570.91 which included a $64,000 life insurance policy payable to his wife.

To dig into Dr. Ross's life, Sheriff Scholl spoke frequently with the press. He was trying to get a message out to those who might shed more light on the case.

"He knows the score and we haven't anything from him in writing," the sheriff told a reporter for the *San Antonio Express*. "He is a very cool and composed man."

A preliminary hearing, scheduled the day after the murders, was cancelled by agreement between the defense and the state—but not before an enormous, overflowing crowd had gathered at the New Braunfels Courthouse. A photograph published in the *San Antonio Light* newspaper the next day reveals that a throng of curious spectators, with nothing better to do that Monday, had crowded the judge's courtroom with a large overflow that consumed the entire lobby. Although rumors of mob violence persisted, the crowd of men, women, and children, which consisted of farmers, soldiers, businessmen, and housewives, just wanted to get a look at the man who had committed the bloodiest crime in Comal County history.

Reporters for the local newspapers cajoled Sheriff Scholl into allowing them to conduct a jail-cell interview. To the sheriff's surprise, Dr. Ross consented. However, it wasn't a very productive interview because the doctor's amnesia persisted, and he "remembered nothing about the fatal shooting," the *San Antonio Light* reported. When asked if he could tell them what happened that Sunday morning, Ross replied, "If I could, I'd be glad to."

But Dr. Ross had no problems remembering his financial history with Willard York. He first met York when he came to San Antonio twelve years before. When asked about his financial dealings with York, Ross replied, "There never was a partnership, silent or otherwise."

A partnership agreement, as opposed to an advisor-client relationship, could have been legally interpreted in such a way that it left Dr. Ross equally responsible for the fiasco created by Willard York. Still feeling wronged by York and reflecting his belief that he was owed something, Dr. Ross told reporters that he didn't think the civil suit between them "had been cleared up."

Meanwhile, the wire services had carried the story of the York family ambush by a respected surgeon to newspapers throughout the country from Albany, New York, to San Mateo, California. The story was heavily covered by most daily papers in Texas. The drama was also front-page news in Ross's home state of Ohio. By mid-summer, the Ross-York story had settled down and was crowded out by reports of "flying discs," and the theft of atomic secrets. But that didn't stop the flood of mail Dr. Ross received from all across the country and as far away as England, Sheriff Scholl would later report.

Charged with four murders, Ross was held without bail. His defense team consisted of former district attorney, Fred Blundell, and well-known San Antonio attorney, Jack Ball. The cancelled preliminary hearing was postponed until Ann could convalesce from her wounds and appear. She was unable to attend her family's funeral services held a few days after they were killed.

As Ross awaited court action in his case, he was held on the third floor of the Comal County Jail, where his snobbish behavior was noted. "He moved around the jail with an attitude of aloofness that did not endear him to the other prisoners," Burton Leeds described in his article. "Heedless of their scorn of him because of his horrible deed, he would sit on his bunk for hours, reading from a tattered Bible, endlessly tying and untying surgical knots, or staring into space with his head in his hand."

By July 7, Ann had recovered enough to testify during a grand jury hearing. It was an emotional moment for her and others in the courtroom as she faced the man who had shot her and gunned down her family in cold blood. His indictment on four murder charges and one attempted murder charge was a forgone conclusion.

A trial date was set for later that month but then postponed until September 9 by a defense motion. Blundell and Ball wanted more time to assemble witnesses who would support their defense that their client was insane. Ross would not be tried on whether he did it or not, but rather, on whether he was actually insane on the day he mowed down the York family.

When the trial finally got underway in September, District Court Judge J.R. Fuchs halted the proceedings and ordered a change of venue, announcing that he had become convinced it would be impossible to find a local jury with unbiased views on the case.

The trial was moved to La Grange, in Fayette County, and rescheduled for October 13. Comal County District Attorney J. Lee Dittert chose to only try Ross for the murder of Gertrude York, with the other three murder charges held in reserve.

Ann York was the second person called to testify in the prosecution's case, and reporters were sure to note every aspect of her appearance, every gesture she made, and every word she spoke. "Twisting a handkerchief in her nervous hands as she spoke," the Associated Press reported to readers nationwide, "the brown-eyed school girl described the Sunday morning slayings of which she was the lone survivor."

When asked to point out her mother's killer, "The frail girl stood-up and pointed the forefinger of her left hand. . . . She looked him in the eye and repeated: 'That's him, Dr. Ross, the defendant.'"

Like Ann, Dr. Ross was carefully scrutinized by reporters, who noted how he sat, his facial expressions, his apparent lack of interest in the case, his groomed appearance—and even the double-breasted blue suit he wore.

Inside the courthouse built in 1891, the courtroom was packed with those who needed to be there, and those who wanted to be there. Two hundred people sat in the bottom chamber, while another one hundred crowded the balcony. The collective packing of so many people raised the temperature and the room became stagnant with hot, dry air that eventually forced the bailiffs to open the windows.

Among District Attorney Dittert's array of witnesses were those who testified to hearing the shots or observing the defendant's black car at the crime scene. Ballistic experts also testified that the bullets and shell casings matched Ross's .300-caliber rifle.

Dittert's other star witness in the case was Sergeant Hester, who testified that when he played his guessing game with the defendant, Dr. Ross made statements that he had "entrusted cash and securities" with Willard York and that "they were lost."

This was the motive, Dittert told the jury.

The case he presented was short and simple. Following jury selection, it had lasted only a day and half. It was, Dittert said before the trial, an open-and-shut case.

Ross's defense team wasted no time in trying to establish their client's insanity. The first witness called to the stand was a doctor who knew Ross back in Ohio in the mid-1930s and had diagnosed him then as having "rheumatic brain fever." Such a condition could lead to "all sorts of strange behavior."

A nurse from his office testified that Dr. Ross had been "acting weird" for two weeks before the murders. She said he would change his socks often during the day and was constantly washing his face. Three other doctors who worked with Ross also stated that they believed he had gone insane shortly before the shooting and was insane the day of the shooting. One of them made a colorful comparison that Ross's mental condition "was breaking down like a bad battery in your automobile." However, when cross-examined, all three admitted they never saw Ross on Sunday, May 25, and had no direct knowledge of his behavior that day.

According to the published memoirs of his professional colleague, Dr. Elmer Cooper, as a doctor, Ross was a rigid, obsessive perfectionist in his work. He was a top-tier surgeon who was loved, trusted, and respected by all at the Catholic hospital where he worked. When Ross lost most of his life savings with York, it was a tremendous blow to his ego.

> He was devastated by the fact that he had been swindled by this man who had become his best friend. With his zeal for perfection, his obsessive, overly compulsive nature, he could not accept this evidence of his own fallibility in so grossly misjudging York's character.
>
> He brooded over the situation, becoming increasingly disturbed and frustrated. As the weeks passed, before the shooting, Dr. Ross became more and more upset and paranoid about the situation. His work began to deteriorate and he refused to undertake difficult surgical procedures, electing instead to sit in his darkened study at home, brooding. Gladys Ross and those of us who were his friends tried to ease his depression by reminding him that with his superb surgical skills, he could soon recoup his loss and go forward in his career. Heedless of our advice, he continued to recriminate himself for being so unperceptive—for not recognizing the 'con' man in Willard York.

Cooper was as close to Willard York's financial improprieties as anyone could get. He too had lost money with the "con man"— over $12,000.[2] But where Ross couldn't cope with the loss, Cooper passed the incident off as a life lesson.

On Tuesday, October 21, psychiatrist Dr. W.J. Johnson recounted that during an interview, the defendant told him, "'God wanted me to do it.' He said that he prayed to God to tell him the details of the crime and say that if he did kill out of revenge, that he should be punished and sent to the electric

---

[2] $128,000 in 2014.

chair; or to tell him that he was an instrument of God and carrying out an infinite purpose. He said he prayed to St. Jude to go to God and explain it all to him."

On cross-examination, the prosecutor asked Dr. Johnson if any one of the single acts of the defendant could be considered as insanity.

"Yes," he replied. "A man charged with an offense like this who tells his wife when she visits him for the first time in jail that he wants to see the funny papers to find out how *Li'l Abner*, *Orphan Annie*, and *Terry and the Pirates* are getting along is definitely crazy."

Closing arguments were made on Thursday, October 23, and the jury received the case at 6:25 p.m. The attorneys from both sides had burned through most of the day reviewing and debating the judge's nine pages of instructions to the jury. It was a document which took longer to read than the fifteen minutes the jury of ten farmers and two craftsmen needed. They brushed aside all the insanity claims and voted Dr. Ross guilty of murder with malice, and recommended the death penalty.

"Ross's wife, Gladys, and his sister, Miss Renna Ross, of Alliance, Ohio, wept as the verdict was read. The defendant remained [stoic], but after he had had a brief, private meeting with his wife, tears glinted in his eyes," Leeds wrote in article.

Defense attorneys announced the following day that they would file a motion for a new trial—standard procedure when a defendant loses a murder trial. Nearly eight weeks later, Judge Fuchs listened to arguments on December 15. By now, Ross's defense team had swelled to four attorneys, who argued there were seventy errors in the trial. When Fuchs rejected the new trial motion, the all-star team of defense lawyers appealed to the criminal court of appeals. Oral arguments were scheduled for June 9, 1948.

During the course of the October trial, a new report had surfaced which stated that Dr. Ross had actually lost closer to

$120,000. The recovery of those misappropriated funds was blocked when Willard filed for bankruptcy. In April 1948, attorneys and relatives, working on behalf of Ann York, filed a wrongful-death civil suit against Ross for approximately the same amount, $120,500. Insane or not, it's doubtful that Ross missed the irony.

When June 9 came, his defense attorneys reviewed the case through their 163-page appellate brief, specifically citing testimony from their eighteen defense witnesses who testified to Ross's insanity.

"To rebut that testimony, the state offered no doctors, no psychiatrists," defense lawyer Leonard Brown told the panel of judges. "They had only seven witnesses—two newspaper reporters, a lawyer, officers of Bexar County, and two deputy sheriffs of Comal County."

Five of those seven witnesses, Brown reported, hadn't even collectively spent the same amount of time with the defendant that Dr. W.J. Johnson had in one visit. "The evidence of the defense was too strong to be swept aside by non-expert testimony," Brown insisted. To support his argument, he cited an earlier opinion from the criminal court of appeals themselves, who held it was reversible error to allow a non-expert witness to testify in an insanity case unless he has had the opportunity to observe the defendant closely.

"To permit that testimony would be a travesty upon the law," the appeals judges had written in the summary opinion of their prior ruling.

Although Brown made a good argument, one that might have been successful in other states, it wasn't good enough for Texas justice. In their eleven-page opinion, the appeals court also made a strong argument that was highlighted in newspapers throughout the Lone Star State on November 3, 1948.

> Particular attention is directed to the fact that following the shooting, he returned to San Antonio, went to the police station and surrendered himself to be imprisoned for this crime. It

would be singular that a man should do this in the absence of any realization of wrong-doing.

The strongest conclusion which might be reached from the testimony of the great majority of witnesses was that he committed the offense under an irresistible impulse. It was not that he could not understand, but that he could not control his action. Under such facts he should be made to pay the penalty of the law since the jury so decreed.

In other words, Dr. Ross still had to be executed.

Even though they were down 0-3 in the courtroom, his defense team wasn't going to give up. On December 9, they filed an eighty-four-page request for a rehearing with the same appeals court. This time, their petition held that there were nineteen errors in the appeals case.

Six months later, on May 11, 1949, the Texas Criminal Court of Appeals denied Ross's motion for a rehearing. It was one of the longest intervals for the criminal appeals court in Texas history at that time. Motions to rehear cases were common and often ruled upon in one to three weeks.

During his appeals, Ross was moved to a jail that could accommodate a long-term, high profile prisoner more adequately than the meager Fayette County facilities. Wharton County Sheriff T.W. "Buckshot" Lane gave reporters insight into Ross's mental state after the doctor was transferred to his jail.

"That won't make a darn bit of difference to Dr. Ross," Buckshot told reporters after he was asked his opinion of how his star prisoner would take the appeals court's denial to rehear his case. "I think he'll burn, and I think he thinks so too, if he thinks at all. He really looks terrible."

Lloyd's older sister, Renna, had moved from Ohio to Texas to be near her brother. She contributed $30,000 of her own money toward her brother's legal fees and to support his wife and daughter. She burst into tears when she heard the high court's ruling.

"I guess Miss Ross will give him the news," Sheriff Lane said. "It's her privilege. She may want me to tell him. She has been very loyal to him—never misses seeing him on visiting days—Tuesday and Friday. His wife comes down to see him, too, from San Antonio. She visits about every two weeks.

"He sure looks bad. . .very drawn and he's aged considerably. He's puffy under the eyes. He never shows any kind of emotion. He never discusses the case or anything else with anybody. The only thing he's ever shown any interest in is playing checkers with other prisoners. But he doesn't play checkers much anymore. Just clams up and keeps to himself."

Newspapers throughout Texas declared that the denial to rehear his motion for a new hearing before the appeals court was Ross's last recourse. Unless the governor commuted his sentence, he was going to die in the electric chair. But those same newspapers underestimated his defense team. With four losses to their record, it seemed as if they would keep fighting until the switch was thrown.

Their next recourse was a Hail Mary pass two weeks later on a motion for a stay of execution pending a new sanity trial. Even if he wasn't insane at the time of the murders, his lawyers argued, he was insane now, and the state of Texas couldn't execute an insane man.

The motion was filed back in Judge Fuchs's Comal County Courthouse where it was easily granted, but this wasn't necessarily a win in the defense team's column. State law mandated that if two doctors provided affidavits that a prisoner was *currently* insane, a sanity hearing, with a jury, had to be called.

Dr. Ross had four affidavits in his motion.

Judge Fuchs scheduled the hearing for June 14 in Fayette County's Victorian-era-style courthouse, where the original trial had taken place. He also enlightened them on one important fact: according to state law, no appeal could be filed after a jury rendered its verdict in a sanity hearing. Sane or not, they were playing for all the marbles this time, even if Dr. Ross had lost his.

They had twenty days to prepare.

During that time, Ross had been moved from his Wharton County jail cell back to Sheriff J.T. Flournoy's facilities in Fayette County. A week before his sanity hearing, Ross's appearance began to decline even more. He stooped more when he walked and he had stopped shaving. A black, scraggly beard began to grow and in 1949 America, nothing said "crazy" like an educated white man with a beard.

When June 14 came, Ross's attorneys requested the hearing be moved back to Comal County. Their argument was based on a belief that a sanity hearing over the current status of a prisoner had to be tried in the county in which he was indicted. But Judge Fuchs could find no precedent for this argument of the state sanity law passed in 1931. They were going to hear this out in La Grange, the seat of Fayette County, he ordered.

Jury selection took up all of the next day and spilled over into the morning hours of Thursday, June 16. Judge Fuchs, impatient with its slow progression, became the first judge in Texas history to take complete control of the jury selection process.

"He assumed a man-to-man tone with the jurors, spoke in the language of a layman and paused frequently to ask if he was understood," the *San Antonio Light* reported later that day. By now, the public's fascination with the Ross's legal saga had dwindled to only a sparsely filled gallery for the jury selection.

Both the defense and the state attorneys protested. Judge Fuchs terse reply to them was: "You have been antagonizing the jurors."

Later that day, in a hot courtroom now packed with more trial watchers, the defense opened with two doctors who testified to their colleague's sanity. Unlike his trial nearly two years before, Ross's sanity on the day of the murders was not the issue, but his current sanity was. One of those expert witnesses was the superintendent of the state mental hospital in Austin. On cross-examination, prosecutor Dittert seemed to be feeding the defense's argument, when he asked the doctor his medical opinion of Ross's mental condition.

"He is . . . hopelessly and legally insane," the doctor answered.

When called to report on Ross's mental health, another doctor said, "He is out of touch with reality. He is in a world of his own. He is in an irreparable state."

In the courtroom that day, with everything at stake, Dr. Ross never looked crazier in his life. Before the hearing, he had taken off his socks and stuffed them in his pockets. His trousers were baggy. His shirt was pulled out in the back and was unbuttoned too low in the front. His hair was greasy—and then there was that wild beard he kept stroking. When he walked into the courtroom, Ross seemingly failed to recognize his family sitting just a few feet away.

But his appearance wasn't even the most shocking thing in the courtroom that day. Following the testimony of the two doctors, a clearly affected Dittert stood up and addressed the judge. "If your honor please," he began, "it is my recommendation that the jury be instructed to find the doctor insane."

A collective and audible gasp rumbled through the courtroom.

"I believe the ends of justice and the rights of society are amply protected in this case. I know I will probably heap condemnation upon myself for this request. I am not convinced he is insane, but the state of Texas is too big to send a man to the chair if there is any doubt."

With a pause to swallow, a clearly emotional Dittert added, "After all, I have to live with my conscience."

The jury agreed, and Dr. Lloyd I. Ross, the man who co-wrote, "Hyperinsulinemia Secondary to an Adenoma of the Pancreas with Operative Cure," for the medical journal, *Archives of Surgery*, was slated to be the newest resident of the Austin

State Hospital for the Insane. Before he personally transported Ross to the state capitol the following day, Sheriff Flournoy wasn't shy about speaking his mind.

"The doctor really put on an act in that courtroom—that's my opinion," the sheriff said in an interview arranged by an Associated Press reporter who knew he was displeased with the verdict. "There was all the difference in the world in the way Ross acted in that courtroom and the way he acted in jail.

"In the courtroom, Ross didn't pay any attention to anyone, not even his own family. He didn't say a word to his family or anyone else. He just sat there, staring at the floor or reading the Bible. This was certainly funny to me, because in the cell with the other prisoners, he acted absolutely normal. He chatted with prisoners, washed his clothes, and shaved. Whenever he wanted something, he asked for it.

"That's another thing, that beard he wore in court. Last Sunday he started refusing to shave—before that he had shaved regularly except for his mustache which he kept trimmed. So when he came to court, he had a beard.

"And then this business about him not recognizing people. Well, he knew and talked freely with all the people that came to see him in jail.

"I was mighty surprised the way that trial turned out, and I think a lot of other people were too. To stay out of that chair, Dr. Ross will have to play crazy for the rest of his life."

The reporter let the sheriff spill his guts and struggled to keep up with his notes so he could get an accurate quote. The verdict, many believed, had been scandalous, an insult to the York family survivors.

But there was one person who was convinced that Dr. Ross wasn't faking anything. "And then the truth of the tragedy dawned on me," Dr. Cooper would later write in his memoir. "Lloyd Ross typified the psychologically unwavering perfected individual whose family background and precise professional technical training denied him the acceptance of imperfections, errors, variances or disappointments. Like honed steel, this ramrod precise personality could not flex, or give with tension, or exigency, but instead must break, and break he did."

Sheriff Flournoy was right about one thing: if the psychiatrists at the hospital ever found Dr. Ross sane, he could be sent back to death row.

Epilogue

Ross was first an inmate-patient at the Austin hospital, and then in 1957 he was transferred to the Rusk State Hospital for the criminally insane. His sister, Renna Ross, moved from her Ohio home to be closer to her brother whom she had always adored.

On July 21, a little more than a month after his 1948 sanity hearing, the jury in Ann York's wrongful death suit awarded her $39,375. The jury, which sat through ten days of testimony, also awarded Willard York's father, Ewart York, $3,619 for the death of his wife. The York's original claim for $120,000 had been reduced to asking $94,000 at the start of the trial.

She would see none of that money. That verdict was appealed, and the plaintiff's claim was lowered again, this time to $26,000. The wrongful-death suit dragged on and in May 1958, ten years and one month after it was filed, the case "was dismissed for lack of prosecution," the *San Antonio Light* reported. The paper's five-sentence story did not explain how the judge came to that decision, but hinted that the case was dismissed because Ross was ultimately declared insane.

During his time in the Austin and Rusk hospitals, Dr. Ross refused counseling and treatment. Just as Sheriff Flournoy said, Ross had to stay insane in order to stay out of the electric chair. A 1957 Associated Press story covered his unusual predicament.

> Meanwhile, Dr. Ross is continually aware of the death sentence, Dr. Charles W. Castner, superintendent of the Rusk State Hospital, said in a letter [to the parole board]:
> ...this knowledge is seriously interfering with the mental improvement of this patient. In all of our interviews with him,

he eventually goes into an episode of extreme anxiety and usually terminates the interview by stating 'what's the use of trying to help you doctors help me get well when death awaits me should I recover.'

At that time, Ross's attorneys were trying to get his death sentence commuted. However, his death sentence was never officially declared in court. The two years of appeals by his lawyers prevented Judge Fuchs from passing sentence. When he was declared insane at his final sanity hearing, he was immediately sent to the state hospital in Austin. By 1958, his lawyers couldn't get his death sentence commuted because Ross had never been officially sentenced. Since there was nothing to commute, the doctor was caught in a legal limbo.

According to the book *When Darkness Falls - Tales of San Antonio Ghosts and Hauntings,* by Docia Schultz Williams, Dr. Ross was finally paroled after serving thirty-five years as a patient-inmate. Since his trial was held in La Grange, he was required to live there when he was released. The sheriff at the time, Charlie Prilop, took pity on the old doctor and accepted him into his home. During his incarceration, Gladys Ross reportedly never visited or wrote her husband, yet she didn't divorce him either. She lived alone in their San Antonio home as a recluse for most of her life. The couple's daughter, Mary Ann, reportedly disowned both her parents and moved to California where she got married and raised children of her own.

In his book, Dr. Cooper wrote that he, along with the Sisters from the hospital, visited with Dr. Ross as much as they could after he was sent to an insane asylum. "I . . . found him totally unrepentant, convinced that his act was justified by the heavenly voices that commanded him to eradicate the York family from the earth."

Dr. Ross died in a La Grange nursing home on May 11, 1992. He is buried in Alliance, Ohio.

Chapter Nine: Blind Man's Bluff, 1955

EXTORTION LETTERS NEVER make sense the first time they are read. The threatening messages they convey are too foreign to be immediately understood. It takes several readings before the danger they promise is accepted with clarity. But shortly after two o'clock on the afternoon of April 15, 1955, the owner and president of Portland, Oregon's largest department store, Meier and Frank, only got about halfway through his first extortion letter when he felt a gigantic explosion rock the twelve-story building which occupied an entire city block. The bomb had gone off in the men's bathroom on the third floor, and the blast sent glass, bricks, tile, fragmented porcelain, faucets, pipe, and pieces of wood flying one hundred feet out across Morrison Street in a 180-degree zone, while the sound wave rolled through the man-made canyons of the downtown business district.

Outside, Dorothy Ostrow was slightly injured when she was hit by flying glass as she walked up the steps of the Pioneer branch post office. As she instinctively ducked down, blast debris fell down around her. If she had happened to be looking up at that moment, she would have seen a wash basin flying by, which landed a half-block away from the third-floor window of the department store. She required fifteen stitches to her face and would carry a scar for the rest of her life.

Inside, janitor Emil Hanson had just opened the restroom door when the blast blew him backward. As the sixty-two-year-old was being treated by the company nurse in the infirmary, store owner Aaron Frank walked in to check on casualties.

"I don't know what happened, Mr. Frank," the dazed janitor reportedly told him. "I went in to wash the windows and everything blew up."

Incredibly, Hanson and Mrs. Ostrow were the only two injuries from the explosion, which sent hundreds of patrons out into the streets. They were surprisingly calm as store security and employees ushered them out of the building. Newsmen would later quote some of them as saying the blast they felt was small, while others said it was "like an earthquake."

Firemen climb to the third floor men's restroom of the Meier & Frank Department Store in Portland, Oregon, after it was blown to pieces by dynamite on April 15, 1955.

As firemen made their way up the truck ladder to the third floor, police turned away those same reporters who were now pleading to get inside the building. One of the more resourceful correspondents was able to sneak in. He eventually made his way to the third floor, where he saw for himself the powder-burned walls of the bathroom and overheard a female clerk talking about "the smell of firecrackers."

The bomb blast was so disturbing to local residents that Portland Police Chief Jim Purcell and Captain of Detectives Bill Browne took personal command of the investigation. Aaron Frank led the senior lawmen and other investigators back up to his office, where he showed them the extortion note he was reading when the blast occurred. The two-page letter was tucked inside a business envelope addressed to Aaron Frank with the word IMPORTANT! calling attention to itself in the corner.

> About the time you receive this, a bomb will explode in your store. This is only a warning. A second and more powerful charge of explosives has been hidden and set by an accurate timing device to explode some time in the 12 hours ending at noon, April 16.

The extortionist demanded $50,000 and in return, he would inform Frank how to dismantle the bomb before it went off. The author promised never to bother the store's owner again if the money was delivered safely. He ordered Frank to place $50,000 in $5, $10, and $20 bills in a light-colored suitcase just large enough to hold the money. No more than half the money was to be in $20 bills. A store representative was instructed to take the briefcase and stand in front of the Imperial Hotel between 6:30 and 7:00 p.m. and wait there for five to ten minutes. He was told to wear a white carnation in his lapel to mark his identity for the extortionist who would be watching from a distance. Then, he was to proceed to a telephone booth two blocks north, where he would receive a call with further instructions.

The note emphasized one important point: the man with the carnation must not be a policeman.

Since the store did far more in business each day than $50,000, Frank agreed to the demands and within two hours had the money in the briefcase ready to go. Rookie police officer Paul Leines volunteered to be the bagman. Since he was new to the job, Chief Purcell and Captain Browne thought

Leines was a smart choice. If the extortionist was an experienced criminal who was familiar with many of the officers on the Portland police force, then he may not recognize Leines as a policeman himself.

Not taking any chances, Frank ordered the large department store—where Clark Gable once had a job selling neckties before he became famous—to be closed on Saturday. Meanwhile, Lt. Dean Blackwood from the department's bomb squad combed every square inch of the bathroom, looking for clues. Every bit of debris and broken material was carefully examined. Since no clock pieces or other commonly used bomb parts were found, Blackwood concluded that the explosive device was just several sticks of dynamite taped together and set off with a slow-burning fuse. If this was any indication of the extortionist's bomb-making skills, detectives were skeptical there was another one with "an accurate timing device," as the note claimed. But even if the bomber was bluffing, they weren't going to take any chances.

Nearly five hours after the explosion, Officer Leines, wearing a business suit with a white carnation and carrying a cream-colored briefcase with $50,000 inside, waited as instructed in front of the Imperial Hotel for five minutes. The hotel was just four blocks from the department store, and it was thought the extortionist might be watching as Leines walked the short route. Plainclothes officers on the streets, in unmarked cars, and peering through high-rise windows scanned the crowd for anyone seen trailing their man. When the five minutes were up, Leines walked two blocks further to a curbside pay phone, where he was told to wait for further instructions.

At 7:08 p.m. the phone rang. A man with a "nervous, medium-high and rather soft voice" gave Officer Leines the prearranged password and instructed him to return to the Imperial Hotel and feel under the seat of the third phone booth in the lobby. Leines agreed and hung up the phone. Before he left, he quickly wrote where he was going, crumpled up the note, and dropped it on the ground.

"No onlooker would have suspected Leines was leaving the first of a series of notes to be left to keep detectives informed of the next step ordered by the extortionist," wrote Don Whitcomb for a crime magazine article. Whitcomb was a reporter for a Portland newspaper and covered the Meier and Frank bombing from beginning to end. He was the journalist who snuck into the department store after police had sealed off the building.

Sitting inside the hotel's oak-wood telephone booth, Leines opened the envelope, found a key inside, and read the note.

> Go to the Union Station. There, go to baggage locker 1037. In the locker find a brown manila envelope. Inside is another envelope with a note for further instructions.

He scribbled out another message and dropped it outside the booth. A detective would come along soon, pick it up, and then radio to his counterparts its contents. Since the typewritten instructions he found were now evidence, Leines carefully folded the letter, put it back in the envelope, and placed it inside his coat for safekeeping.

At the railroad station baggage locker, he found yet another note. This one instructed him to hire a Yellow Cab Company taxi that did not have a two-way radio. The cab was to cross the Willamette River and take Highway 99E to Eugene, Oregon. During the 125-mile trip to Eugene, the cabbie was ordered to drive no faster than twenty-five miles per hour. Somewhere between the two large cities, a car would pull up behind the cab and flash its lights three times. This was the signal for the cab to " . . . pull to the side of the road. The right rear door is to be opened, and the bag set down outside without anybody getting out," his instructions read.

After the drop, the taxi was ordered to drive five more miles before turning around. If no contact was made between Portland and Eugene, then the cab was to turn around at the

Eugene city limits, and drive no faster than twenty-five mph back to Portland.

Twenty-five mph? Did the extortionist know what he was doing? Highway 99E was a two-lane road. Anyone driving twenty-five mph there would back up traffic in the northbound lane for miles. If the extortionist needed to pass other cars to get behind him, it would be difficult if the southbound lane was busy.

Fortunately, Chief Purcell and Capt. Browne had correctly assumed that a car would be involved somehow in the payoff. In the hours leading up to the 7:08 p.m. phone call, Browne's men worked quickly to outfit several private cars with two-way FM band radios which at the time, could not be heard on the known police wavelength. They had already been using the FM band to notify detectives who followed Leines as he went from point to point. Because of Aaron Frank's stature in Oregon as the head of a major department store chain that extended throughout the Northwest, as well as being one of the richest men in America, Chief Purcell and Portland Mayor Fred Peterson's own personal cars were outfitted with radios, and would be used in the leap-frog trailing of the taxi.

It took some time before Leines could get a taxi without a two-way radio. He finally found one driven by Donald Halfman, who had to stop at a company station and call his boss for the fare. Leines paid the station cashier and the two took off on their slow trip to Eugene. At twenty-five mph, it would take five hours to reach the city. Since it was already past eight o'clock and dark outside, Leines wondered if the drop would go through or not.

Behind him, the unmarked police cars trailed behind the taxi at a safe distance. They scouted out suspicious-looking vehicles and kept tabs on them as they plodded along on their journey. Whitcomb would later detail the problems created by the bomber's snail-pace demand.

"The tail was not hard because a king-sized traffic jam quickly built up behind the dawdling taxi. At one point, cars had been blocked back for a two-mile stretch. One irate truck driver passed and cut in so sharply that Leines recalled afterward: 'If the taxi driver hadn't seen him coming and slammed on the brakes, the story would have ended there.'"

Sometime after midnight, the cab reached the outskirts of Eugene, where it turned around, and in the same, slow manner as before, drove back to Portland.

The extortionist never popped his head up. Had they spooked him off? Did he figure out he was being followed? Was he blocked by the traffic jam he inadvertently created?

Nobody knew and investigators didn't know what to expect next. In newspapers the following day, reporters who worked the story all day and night didn't know what to tell their readers. "A hood of secrecy continued to shroud the investigation," reported the morning edition of an Associated Press story. "Investigators have withheld all details in connection with the blast."

Their silence would continue for a few more hours that Saturday as they waited in vain for the extortionist to contact them in some manner. Meanwhile, fifty detectives were tasked to cover every inch of the twelve-story building which was the flagship store of the Meier and Frank department store chain. With eleven acres of shopping space, it was one of the largest retail stores in America. Although they didn't find a bomb, the store was kept closed all day Saturday in fear they may have missed something. There was no explosion as the note promised. Lieutenant Blackwood's hunch was right: they were dealing with a novice. There was no second bomb and it was only a bluff.

That didn't stop police from checking the whereabouts of all the known bomb extortionists throughout the West Coast who had the skills to build a sophisticated bomb. One of them was in prison in Mexico, and another was serving time in San

Quentin. All the others were nowhere near Portland when the blast occurred.

Store employees were questioned thoroughly, especially those working on the third floor. One clerk told investigators she remembered seeing a woman and a man with a shopping bag walk into the third-floor stairwell before the explosion. The man's slow, careful movements indicated to her that he might be elderly, and the young-looking woman was helping him. When other employees working near the stairwell were questioned, they also remembered the couple, who were seen leaving shortly before 2:00 p.m. She said the slow-moving man wore dark glasses and appeared to be in his thirties.

Before the letter reached store president Aaron Frank, it was first picked up at a first-floor customer service counter, where a long-time store employee said she thought she saw a woman drop it off.

On Monday, April 17, the store reopened with uniformed police officers stationed outside and throughout the entire store. Frank offered a $25,000 reward for information leading to the apprehension of the bomber. Now that the tide had turned against the unknown blackmailer, Frank and the police wanted him to feel the heat. Several hours after his announcement, a consortium of five Portland banks chipped in another $3,000 in reward money.

Frank confidently told police, and then later Portland newspaper reporters, that it couldn't be a store employee who was behind it all. "We have a perfect relationship [with our employees]. We have no labor troubles and no disgruntled employee has recently been discharged."

He was right about that. Police were already going over the company's records looking for any terminated employee with a criminal record of violence. None were found.

Five days after the explosion, chemical tests on the blast residue would confirm it was probably dynamite. Blackwood's men began the slow task of interviewing outlets where dynamite was sold. With the excitement of Friday's explosion settling down, Captain Browne was put in charge of the investigation. To help him in what would be one of the city's most important investigations in years, Browne hand-picked seasoned detectives Lt. Bard Purcell, Jim Quinn, and Prescott Hutchins to assist him. Bard Purcell was the chief's brother.

Browne was a tall, heavyset man whose large stature could be intimidating to most criminals. In an era where third-degree methods were often employed to get confessions, Browne didn't believe in physically harming a suspect.

"There's no excuse for using the third-degree on a man," Browne later told writer Don Whitcomb. "Even if it were right, third-degree doesn't work as well as scientific methods." His approach was to get the suspect to talk about anything. "It doesn't matter what. Ask him about the weather, his favorite food, anything. If you get him to say something, you can pry the truth out of him eventually."

The fifty-seven-year-old promised not to retire until the Meier and Frank extortionist was captured.

The call Leines received at 7:08 p.m. was traced back to a downtown phone booth. No fingerprints were found. An interview with a Yellow Cab call dispatcher uncovered a telephone inquiry a week before from a man asking how many of their cars had two-way radios, and what the fare to Eugene would cost. That incoming call was also traced back to a public pay phone.

Assessing their evidence, Browne and his men had very little to go on. A mock-up of the men's restroom was constructed in a rural testing field and then blown up several times with dynamite. Judging by the amount of damage caused, Lt. Blackwood told Browne he estimated the bomber had used eight to ten sticks of ordinary-grade dynamite. At the time, dynamite was in common use by farmers and building contractors. A check of state-mandated purchase records in Oregon and Washington did not uncover any buyers that warranted further scrutiny.

When it came down to it, the only physical evidence Browne and his team had was residue from the blast that told them it was dynamite, and the typewritten notes. Since the keystrokes of every single typewriter ever made left its own unique, identifiable marks, police departments all across the country kept typewriter records as if they were fingerprint records. Browne knew this was the best chance he had of solving this case, and more than three hundred photostatic copies of the extortionist's notes were produced and circulated to law enforcement agencies of all types and sizes throughout the Northwest. If that typewriter could be identified, it could lead the chief detective right to the bomber.

Experts later informed Browne and his men that the extortion notes were typed on a Royal Standard typewriter, of which there were nearly three million in circulation. They estimated thousands of them were being used in Portland by high schools, colleges, business secretaries, and professional offices, not to mention those privately owned. With that daunting task facing them, Browne divided the city of more than 370,000 people into four sections, and assigned each of his men to check all the Royal Standard typewriters in each quadrant.

News of the Meier and Frank department store explosion inspired nearly two dozen copycats to call in phony bomb threats all over the city. Four high schools in the Portland area received early-morning telephone calls warning them that a bomb was in the building and set to go off. Thousands of youngsters were evacuated, and each school was thoroughly searched. No bombs were found, and a quick investigation led to two high school boys who thought it was all a big joke. They were arrested and told to laugh about it in jail. At every school, administrators announced that for each bomb threat the school received, one day would be added to the end of the school year. The threats to Portland High Schools stopped after that announcement, but there would be others up and down the West Coast.

Although the bomb threats at the high schools stopped, the Sylvan School,[1] where the young children of Chief Purcell, David Meier, and Richard Frank attended, received a bomb threat and a demand for $20,000. No device was found there either. Police officers were assigned to protect one school official, as well as the Meier, Frank, and Purcell families. Phone lines were monitored but no more calls came in.

A few weeks later, Abernethy Elementary School received a bomb threat at ten in the morning, which forced the evacuation of six hundred frightened school children. They knew it wasn't a drill when police and firemen arrived, and were all allowed to go home early that day.

The copycat trend became deadly when a car bomb killed a thirty-five-year-old Portland attorney after he left a country club stag party. Browne's detectives soon arrested the attorney's handyman, Victor Wolf, who was attracted to the lawyer's beautiful wife. She was also implicated in her husband's murder. Wolf later told police he got the idea from the store bombing, and assumed the police would believe it was the extortionist who killed the attorney. He was sentenced to life in prison.

Wolf's arrest didn't stop more crackpots from making threats in other cities. That spring and summer, bomb threats were made in Houston, Pittsburgh, Spokane, and Radio City Music Hall in New York City. The Houston and Pittsburgh cases were made against American Federation of Labor union offices.

Two were made in Spokane: one to a hotel, and the other in a high school, where a fifteen-year-old chemistry student went so far as to actually build a bomb, leaving it in a sack under a desk where it was later found by a very surprised janitor.

After studying all the local bomb threats, Browne and his men observed that none of them were made on paper. They

---

[1] It is now West Sylvan Middle School.

were all telephoned in. That got them to thinking that if the extortionist used his typewriter in this case, perhaps he used it for other criminal purposes. Since the Portland Better Business Bureau handled mail-order scams, business swindles, and other rackets, they kept a record of typewritten documents by known con artists from the Portland area.

To help in his investigation, Browne brought in two postal inspectors who could spot, with the naked eye, similarities in keystroke type. After examining the extortion notes, they could go through the BBB's records and set aside documents with keystroke identifiers. Close matches would then be sent to the FBI laboratory in Washington, DC, for comparison.

In October, the two inspectors came across the file of a well-known Portland resident named Clarence Peddicord. When they examined the typed letters made on the stationery of a business he ran out of his home, they finally found the match they were looking for all these months. Samples were sent to the FBI for verification. As excited as they were, there was just one small problem with their suspect that might rule him out as the Meier and Frank extortionist: Clarence was blind.

Thirty-eight-year-old Clarence Peddicord possessed a curious combination of personal courage, optimism, flair for publicity, and criminal cunning.

Clarence was born a healthy, normal boy in 1917 in New Mexico, where he was the youngest of five children. His mother died when he was sixteen years old. Three years later, while working on a refrigeration unit near Vancouver, Washington, a coil burst—spewing sulfur dioxide into his eyes.

"A doctor was called by friends but while Peddicord lay writhing in pain, the doctor prescribed only plenty of sunshine and fresh air," Whitcomb wrote. "It was Peddicord himself who called an ambulance, but even as he was rushed to the hospital he realized it was too late. The last clear view of the world he had was inside of that ambulance."

From the beginning, Clarence was determined not to let his disability hold him back. An aid agency for the blind gave him a Seeing Eye dog named Duke and in 1938, with Duke's help, he climbed to the top of Beacon Rock in the Columbia River Gorge in Washington. Twice. His name got into the local newspaper and all of Vancouver was proud of him. Later that year, another charity organization helped him establish a candy machine vending business throughout Vancouver.

One year later, in August of 1939, wire services ran a tongue-in-cheek feature story that the executioner at Sing Sing Prison in New York had taken ill, and there was a job opening for his replacement. With a newfound talent for attracting publicity, Clarence applied for the job, and a photograph of him standing with Duke was featured in newspapers across the country. He was turned down for the position.

"I hate to think what I would do if I got the job," he later admitted to reporters, "but I've tried everything else in my search for work."

Not long afterward, Clarence married his high school sweetheart, Lucy Dillabaugh. The couple had one child but the union ended after just one year.

By 1941, his candy-vending business had grown to the point where he needed a driver to help him manage all his machines. An attractive young girl named Dorothy May McCourtney applied for the job, got it, and later married the handsome young Peddicord.

With World War II, government rationing of sugar hit the candy companies hard, and Clarence's business quickly failed. After that, the couple ran a lunch stand near a Portland shipyard. They were able to make a modest living, but when an unknown employee poisoned his dog Duke, Clarence closed down his lunch stand and quit in disgust. The murder of his beloved dog changed him.

"He got it in his mind that if he could see again, he could get a job in a war plant and make some money," his wife Dorothy would later say. "But he couldn't get a job and after the death of his dog, he began to get bitter."

Peddicord's plan to see again was to receive a cornea transplant from a doctor who had operated on his eyes before. However, his quest for money to pay for the operation would set him on a path to his first illegal scheme that would get him into trouble with authorities.

While living in California briefly in 1945, Clarence rented the same house a lot of times to different people, then tried to run away with the security deposits. Police found him back in Vancouver, Washington, and he was returned to California where the authorities proposed a deal to his wife.

"I'd left him before that, but they charged me too, and told me if I would plead guilty, he would not have to do any time. I pleaded guilty and they turned us both loose," Dorothy said.

Failure followed failure. Clarence ventured into the popcorn business, which didn't work out. Then he tried to sell a battery restorative called Nu Charge, but when the battery companies found out about it, they made trouble for Clarence and he was forced to close down that operation as well.

In September of 1948, Clarence had a new plan. He would hitchhike from Portland to New York City to raise money for a cornea transplant. The tale of a blind man walking across the country to get back his sight was a human-interest story the wire services couldn't ignore. His venture was reported on in newspapers throughout the United States—which is exactly what Clarence wanted. When he talked to reporters, he knew how to harvest sympathy with his down-on-my-luck story that emphasized his gallant spirit to save his wife and children from the poorhouse. It was all true, but Clarence knew exactly what to say to get the reaction he wanted.

By the time he reached Detroit, a Chicago radio program called *We the People* asked him to be a guest on the show. As a result of this appearance, a businessman in Saratoga Springs,

New York, offered to pay for Peddicord's operation and train fare to New York City.

Clarence Peddicord after he was featured on *We the People*.

After a single cornea transplant by Dr. Raymon Castroviejo, an early pioneer in corneal transplants, his bandages were ready to come off by mid-December. When they were removed, Clarence could see out of the eye.

"It was wonderful for a minute," he later told reporters. "The doctor took the bandages off. I opened my eyes. The miracle I had been waiting twelve long years for had happened. I could see. Sunlight was streaming across the ceiling.

"But before I could adjust myself, I suddenly saw the points of scissors coming right at my eye. The doctor was only going to cut the stitches but I didn't know that and I jerked my head back. That jarred my eye. It began bleeding inside and I was blind again."

His eyesight never returned. After that debacle, Castroviejo promised to operate again on him in six months, but forbade Clarence or newspapers from publishing his name. Peddicord would never again be able to raise the money, and the second operation never took place.

After he returned to Portland, Clarence attempted to earn a living with one fraudulent scheme after another. By then, he just didn't care anymore. The world had been unfair to him, and he saw nothing wrong with a little reciprocation—especially if it meant supporting his family. At first, it was an ill-fated guide dog association for the blind. Then, it was a company called Metro Chemical Laboratories which advertised distributorships for a soap that could extend the life of women's nylons. Then, Metro Chemical tried to sell distributorships for a product that could extend the life of batteries. It was a variation of his old Nu Charge business.

Despite being blind, Clarence had taught himself how to type, and by all accounts, he was good at it.

In total, Peddicord's Metro Chemical Laboratories Company led to the accumulation of eighty to one hundred complaints against him with the Portland Better Business Bureau, who investigated the operation, which led to its being shut down. By early April of 1955, Clarence went back to selling pencils in public venues, and receiving state aid for the blind. But it wasn't enough to support his wife and their five children.

Desperate, that's when he came up with the idea to extort money from Aaron Meier by setting off dynamite in the men's bathroom, with a promise that if he didn't pay, there would be a bigger, more powerful bomb the following day.

When the two postal inspectors compared the photostatic copies of the extortion note with letters typed on stationery for the ill-fated Metro Chemical Company, they recognized the typeface immediately. Although they were 100-percent positive,

Browne sent the letters off to the FBI in Washington, DC, for comparison. Their opinion concurred with the postal inspectors and by December 15, eight months after the bombing, Browne and his men were ready to arrest Clarence Peddicord. Since the money exchange required a taxi to make the drop for a car that would follow behind, the Portland lawmen assumed he had an accomplice. Whitcomb would later describe the moment Clarence was arrested in his magazine article.

> It was a sad faced group of detectives and postal inspectors who made their way out to the flimsy little dwelling in a temporary war housing unit to talk to the man. All of them knew Peddicord. He had been a familiar and tragic figure on the streets of Portland for many years, peddling his wares and showing, each year, more and more of the strain that came from trying to live with the accident that had scarred him in youth. The grim purpose of their visit was not lightened by the concerned look of the woman who opened the door, nor by the questioning faces of the five little Peddicords, ranging in age from two to 12. And it was almost more than the authorities could do to go ahead with their mission when they saw the pathetic little Christmas tree with its handful of tinsel and the few cheap gifts set out under a window.

Captain Browne would later admit to Whitcomb that it was the most heartbreaking arrest of his career. In the presence of his wife and children, Browne told Peddicord about the connection they had made between the typewriters. Knowing it was all over, Clarence gave his family a heartfelt goodbye.

As they made their way back to the Portland police headquarters, Browne decided the best way to get Peddicord to tell who his accomplice was would be to catch him off-guard with a direct question in a stern voice. It worked. Clarence replied without thinking: it was Joyce Keller, his sister-in-law. She had been in trouble with the law before and Clarence knew she could keep her mouth shut. His wife had no idea her husband and sister were involved in the Meier and Frank store bombing.

When he realized what he had done, Clarence immediately retracted that statement and said it was someone else. The two had made an agreement to keep quiet if they were caught and he had just gone back on his promise. He tried to repair the damage by dodging the question, or mentioning her first name only, or not using any name at all.

It didn't matter anymore. The twenty-eight-year-old divorcee was arrested at 1:30 the next morning at the rundown rooming house where she lived. Unlike Clarence, who had glibly talked to police about his involvement for more than three hours, Joyce Keller steadfastly denied she had anything to do with the case, and she hid her face from photographers who were waiting for her at the police station.

Later that morning, a clerk from the department store was brought in and positively identified the two as the woman and man with a shopping bag she had seen go into the third-floor stairwell on the day of the bombing.

During his confession to police, which was recorded, Clarence told investigators, "I did not mean to hurt anyone. I would not have planted a second bomb."

The threat of a second bomb was just a bluff.

Clarence then told police everything that had happened. One week before the bombing, he bought dynamite and slow-burning fuse cord from a farm supply store on the outskirts of Portland. The woman whose help he enlisted was to get $10,000, and he would take the rest. The day before the bombing, he went to the railroad station where he rented locker 1037 through a vending machine. He then put the key and the instructions in an envelope and taped them under the seat of the telephone booth.

Originally, he thought of collecting the ransom alone by having the store representative throw the money-filled suitcase off the back of a train. He discarded that plan as impractical when he imagined himself stumbling along the railroad tracks with a cane, trying to probe and prod for the suitcase.

No, he was going to need someone who could see. His accomplice assisted him with typing the note by helping him spell words correctly, and by reading it back to him. She also advised him on what to say and how to say it. They spent a lot of time on getting the words right to make it perfect. The dynamite and note together had to convince Aaron Frank that it was better to pay $50,000, or the second bomb would create more damage. Frank had to fall for his bluff.

Lieutenant Blackwood was almost right about the bomb, but it was twelve sticks of dynamite, not eight or ten as he had estimated. The dynamite was taped together and set with ten minutes of slow-burning fuse cord. Clarence then placed the dynamite inside a normal-looking shopping bag and taped the end of the fuse to the top of the bag.

On the day of the bombing, they dropped off the note at a customer service counter in the basement then took the elevator to the tenth floor. Inside the men's restroom, there were too many men, and too many people shopping close by. They next tried the men's room on the eighth floor but that room was too crowded as well. It was the same story with the second-floor men's room. He was just about to give up but decided to try the men's room on the third floor. The third floor was women's wear, and he only found one man inside, smoking a cigarette. With his glasses off to trick anyone there into thinking he wasn't blind, Clarence remarked out loud, "My, it's smoky in here."

It worked. The man snuffed out his cigarette and walked out. He would later recall the incident to police who interviewed him. "Come to think of it," the man said, "his eyes did seem to stare."

After the man left, Clarence went into the last stall and set the shopping bag down next to the toilet. Feeling around for the cord still taped to the top of the bag, he took a deep breath, and lit the fuse. "I prayed that nobody would be killed."

He and Joyce then left the store by walking slowly and calmly down the little-used stairs. After they made it outside,

206 · Jason Lucky Morrow

Clarence and Joyce walked south and were at the corner of 6th Avenue and Morrison Street when they heard the explosion. The detonation was much larger than either of them had anticipated.

"The blast scared us both," Peddicord was recorded telling detectives. They both decided to stick around and within a few minutes, police and fire trucks were on the scene.

"Joyce saw the firemen carrying things down the ladder and thought they were bodies. She got sore as well as scared and told me she had warned me against using too much dynamite. I hadn't meant the explosion to be so big either. We quarreled."

One hour later, the two were at a cocktail lounge, calming their nerves with alcohol. In a quiet corner, Joyce told him she wanted nothing more to do with the plot. She was out. Clarence was devastated. He tried to carry on alone. He then made his way to a public pay phone and made the 7:08 call. In desperation, he tried to find someone else to help him get the money-filled suitcase. Concluding he could get no one else to go along with his scheme, Clarence then said he stood by the side of the road where the taxi would pass, and listened for a slow-moving car with the hope he could flag it down and get a ride. But that didn't work either.

Although police still had a lot of questions for him, there was one curious point they wanted to clear up: why did he order the taxi to travel at only twenty-five mph?

"Joyce isn't a very good driver," he explained. "I was afraid she might get into an accident if he had to follow a car that was going faster."

When his accomplice pulled out of the plot, it was the best thing that could have happened to Clarence Peddicord. It gave him eight more months of freedom. "Had he made the trip, he would have been caught that night," Capt. Browne declared to reporters.

During the last week of December, while everyone else was enjoying the holidays, Clarence Peddicord and Joyce Keller were indicted by a Multnomah County grand jury which charged them with "causing injury to persons and property by unlawfully, purposefully and maliciously setting off a bomb." Their bond was set at $75,000 each.

Just prior to Christmas, before the indictment, Oregon papers carried a short news item with the announcement that Police Chief James Purcell was taking up a collection among officers and citizens to buy presents for the five Peddicord children. It would be the last Christmas they would all spend together for many years. The failed extortion plot, and Peddicord's arrest, literally broke his family apart. Later, his five children were made wards of the state. Overcome by her husband's involvement in the crime, Dorothy Peddicord voluntarily checked herself into a mental hospital.

During a January 1956 plea hearing, Clarence surprised the court and his own attorney when he pleaded guilty and demanded to be sentenced immediately. His lawyer's plan, which was told to prosecutors and the judge beforehand, was for his client to plead not-guilty by reason of insanity. The judge refused to accept Peddicord's guilty plea and, to his lawyer's relief, informed Clarence he would only accept an innocent-by-insanity plea. Two weeks before that hearing, he was examined by psychiatrists. The results of those examinations paved the way for his attorney's insanity defense.

In spite of his lawyer's attempts to take the case to a jury with a sanity hearing, Clarence was eventually able to plead guilty to the charges in April. It was what he wanted. However, his hope for leniency by pleading guilty backfired on him, and he was sentenced to twenty years in prison. "This comes as quite a shock to me," he said after his sentence was pronounced on April 20, 1956. "I've lost everything, my wife, my children, and my freedom."

Outside the courtroom, the deputy district attorney told reporters that the damage to the department store, the loss of one day's business, and the cost of the investigation for the police department totaled $200,000.[2]

Epilogue

On May 14, 1956, the day before he was subpoenaed to testify against his sister-in-law, Clarence Peddicord hanged himself in his cell with rope he had smuggled in. Jailors found him unconscious and were able to revive him. He was taken to the county hospital were doctors credited fast-thinking guards with saving his life.

The following day, Clarence denied ever having an accomplice and told the court he had acted alone during the entire plot. Circuit Judge Martin Hawkins had the blind man led into his private chambers for a discussion that included a sharp rebuke. When Peddicord was returned the courtroom, Judge Hawkins gave him one more chance. Clarence again refused and was held in contempt of court—a meaningless charge for someone sentenced to twenty years.

For a man who mostly knew bad luck his entire life, his attempt to keep his sister-in-law out of prison was successful. She was freed one week later on a directed verdict from the judge, who ruled there was only hearsay evidence against her. Without his testimony, the prosecution didn't have enough to convict Joyce Keller.

Dorothy Peddicord continued her downward slide after her husband's conviction. In July, while driving with an unnamed male companion, she was arrested for drunk driving. She was freed on $600 bond and later accused the arresting officer, a state patrolman, of inflicting bruises on her.

Her circumstances deteriorated further when she, Clarence, and another married couple, were indicted in federal court on mail-fraud charges stemming from their involvement in the Metro Chemical battery venture. In that scheme, Clarence and the others sold distributorships to unwitting buyers, who later learned the same products were commonly available in stores.

---

[2] $1.8 million in 2014.

The government's case dragged on for two years, and more people were added to the indictment. The charges against Dorothy were dropped when she divorced her husband and testified against him. On June 2, 1958, Clarence and five other men were found guilty. He received a five-year sentence that ran concurrent with his twenty-year sentence. One year later, his ex-wife remarried, to a man named Charles Brambora.

William Clarence Peddicord was paroled in April, 1966, after serving ten years of his sentence. He died on March 25, 1978, in the Whittier section of Los Angeles. He was cremated and buried in Portland. He was fifty-nine years old.

Despite the fact that they were police officers, detectives Jim Quinn and Prescott Hutchins, and the estate of Captain William Browne, fought in court unsuccessfully to receive the $28,000 reward.

Chapter Ten: The Orphan Maker of Route 66, 1961

TWELVE-YEAR-OLD Jimmy Welch was in shock. Something really bad had happened and he was still trying to comprehend it. On a lonely stretch of US Highway 66, thirteen miles west of Seligman, Arizona, he stood alone, waiting for a vehicle to stop and help him and his three brothers, Tommy, 9, Billy, 8, and Johnny, 5. Several cars had already passed by, ignoring him completely or misunderstanding his frantic waving as a greeting instead of what it really was—a signal to come to their rescue. The tall, lanky boy looked back at his brothers who, like him, couldn't believe their parents were dead. They were crying. Jimmy wanted to cry too, but he had a job to do. He had to get someone to stop.

Ten minutes earlier, his brother Johnny had awakened and untied the flap to the pup tent the boys were sleeping in, and had taken three steps to the family car to see if his mother was awake. She wasn't. Looking in the back seat, Johnny saw that his father was not awake either. He knocked on the window and called for his mother but she didn't move—and that's when he noticed something on her face. He turned back to the canvas tent, woke his brothers, and asked them, "What's on Mommy's face?"

It was an intriguing question that motivated Jimmy to pull on his cuffed Wranglers and Buster Brown's. When he opened the passenger door to look in on his mother, he saw that her face was covered in blood. Lots of blood. In the back seat, his father was in an awkward position, with his head down and his eyes slightly open, as if he were looking at the blood stains on his white t-shirt. Jimmy bravely reached in, tilted his father's head back to get a better look, and could clearly make out the bullet holes in his face and forehead.

When Jimmy and his brothers went to bed, they'd had parents. Now, they were orphans, and it would take decades to process the morning of Friday, June 9, 1961.

After the third vehicle had roared by, two salesmen heading west to their home office in Riverside, California, finally interpreted Jimmy's desperate waving as a cry for help. The salesmen pulled in behind the family's 1959 Oldsmobile 98, and all four boys ran to explain what had happened.

"Somebody shot Mommy and Daddy," Jimmy said through a flood of tears.

Don Cramer and Jere Eagle confirmed the boys' claim, then flagged down an eastbound car to notify authorities. It could take a while before help would reach them, so the salesmen decided it was best to stay with the boys. Yavapai County, Arizona, is one of the largest counties in the United States, with a land-mass almost the size of New Jersey. Prescott, the county seat, was nearly ninety miles away.

Highway Patrolman Dan Birdino was the first to arrive at the murder scene. He was quickly followed by Deputy Sheriff Perry Blankenship, who was stationed in Seligman. The driver had stopped at Johnson's Coffee Shop and reported the crime to Blankenship's wife, a waitress working the graveyard shift. After she called her husband, Deputy Blankenship then made two telephone calls of his own: one to his boss, Sheriff Jim Cramer in Prescott, and one to a local physician, Dr. A. J. Gungle.

At the desolate spot where the family had camped for the night, Blankenship and Birdino assessed the crime scene and talked to the boys while they waited for the cavalry to arrive. Thirty-one-year-old Utha Welch had been shot in the head multiple times with a small-caliber revolver while she slept in the front seat. Her husband, thirty-three-year-old James D. Welch, known as J. D., appeared to have been shot while rising up from the back seat after he was awakened by the gunfire that killed his wife.

Even though they slept in a Boy Scout pup tent just a few feet away, the boys told the officers they never heard the shots that killed their parents. Not long after they had settled down for the night, Jimmy said he heard his parents talking and called out to them but was told everything was all right and to go back to sleep. Approximately one hour before he was awakened by his little brother, Jimmy said he saw a bus park twenty feet behind their car, and two men got out to change a flat tire.

J. D. and Utha Welch

"Sometime before that," Jimmy continued, "I saw the lights go on in the car and I heard a door slam, but I thought it was Dad getting up and I didn't pay any attention to it."

He also told detectives he thought it could have been the trunk being slammed shut instead of a door. When officers looked there, it appeared as if the killer or killers had been there, looking for something else to steal.

Without moving the bodies, Dr. Gungle gave the Welches a cursory examination and estimated they had been dead for a few hours. When Sheriff Cramer arrived later that morning with County Attorney George Ireland, County Coroner Dr. Daniel Condon, Sheriff's Captain L. H. Johnson, and Undersheriff Sam Saum, they were briefed on the situation by Deputy Blankenship.

No empty shells were found in or around the car, and the father's wallet was missing. But the killer or killers had missed grabbing Mrs. Welch's purse, which contained $147, from underneath the pillow she was sleeping on. She was also still wearing her wedding band, diamond engagement ring, and an expensive watch.

Jimmy told the officers that the family had left their home in Spencer, a suburb of Oklahoma City, on Wednesday, June 6, for a summer vacation to visit their grandmother in Tulare, California. Their dad's mother was to undergo an operation the following week, and he wanted his family to be there while she was in the hospital. That first day, they drove as far as Amarillo, Texas, where they spent the night with relatives. Early the following morning, they continued their journey on Route 66 to Flagstaff, Arizona, where they stopped at eight o'clock in the evening. They visited with a friend of their father's for one hour, then continued on. Fifty miles down the road, they stopped in Ash Fork, Arizona, to buy gas. A service station employee later told officers that Mrs. Welch gave her husband $65 from her purse. Mr. Welch then used $5 to pay for the gas and put the rest in a leather billfold. The gas station attendant also told investigators that he had recommended a local motel to Mr. Welch.

When the lawmen questioned the motel owner, he confirmed that the family had been there but had decided not to rent a room. "He thought the price was too high so they didn't stay," the motel operator told them. He would turn out to be the last person, besides the boys, to see the couple alive.

The family then continued down the highway for another forty miles, passing through Seligman, until their headlights illuminated the only visible landmark for the last thirteen miles—two large piles of dirt and rocks that were a few feet taller than their Oldsmobile. Mr. Welch parked between the two mounds, and with the help of a flashlight and the car's headlights, he set up the tent for his sons, then settled down to get some sleep around midnight.

Sheriff Cramer looked around at the campsite the family had chosen. He knew his county well but had to admit to himself they had chosen a very desolate, eerie-looking place to stop for the night. A barbed-wire fence approximately thirty-five feet from the road separated the highway from a barren flatland that stretched for two to three miles until it met a long escarpment known as Aubrey Cliffs. Further north was the Coconino Plateau which led to the Havasupai Indian Reservation to the west, and Grand Canyon National Park slightly to the east. To the south, beyond the eastbound lane of one of America's first transcontinental highways, was a spearhead of flatlands that separated the foothills leading to the Juniper Mountains and Mohon Mountains to the west. The nearest piece of civilization, a ranch house, was more than five miles away.

Welch had parked the car twenty feet off the highway between the two large mounds. The terrain to the fence line was flat enough for the bus to pull off to the side with plenty of room for the two men to change a tire. The lawmen could find no tire tracks along the shoulder adjacent to the eastbound lane. The killer, Sheriff Cramer surmised, was likely traveling west when he found the Welches. Unfortunately, when the bus parked behind the Oldsmobile, it disturbed any other tire tracks that may have been there.

It was a sad end to a family vacation. The killer would be difficult to find. He could either be in California by now, or turned around and well on his way to New Mexico.

Doctor Condon concurred with Dr. Gungle that the Welches had been dead for a few hours and had probably been shot to death two hours before the bus stopped to change the flat tire. They also discovered something interesting about the bullet holes. Powder burns outlined the wounds to the mother, indicating that she was shot with the barrel pressed against her head while she slept. The father also had powder burns around one of the wounds, which told them that three bullets to the head and face wasn't enough for the killer, he had to make sure his victim was dead with a *coup de grâce*. It was about as cold-blooded as a killer could get.

But the strangest part was the math: three shots to kill Utha, and four shots to kill J. D. Since there were no shell casings to be found, Sheriff Cramer and his men were able to determine that the murder weapon had to be a revolver. If there was only one killer, and he never reloaded during his shooting spree, then the murder weapon was an unusual one: a small-caliber revolver with a chamber that held nine bullets. That would narrow down their search considerably—but only if there was one killer who used one revolver.

"It was a cheap gun . . . the kind any potential killer can order from a magazine for $12," Sheriff Cramer would later say. "It must have been a nine-shot revolver because that kind of gun is too hard to reload [in the dark]."

If the bus was there after the Welches were shot, then maybe one of the passengers or the driver saw something that would be of help. Sheriff Cramer sent his top investigator, Captain Johnson, to chase after it. He knew Greyhound drivers traveled at a relatively slow speed and there was a chance Johnson could catch up to it. He then turned to Deputy Blankenship and ordered him to take the children back to Seligman.

"See that they get some breakfast. Find someone to take care of them until we can drive them into Prescott later," the sheriff told him. He didn't want the boys around while their parents were being removed from the Oldsmobile and loaded into the coroner's station wagon.

Deputy Blankenship took the boys back to the coffee shop where his wife worked. She had stayed past the time her shift regularly ended. Bertie Blankenship had something to tell her husband about the night before, but it would have to wait. After a hot breakfast, the children were placed in the care of Mae Gibson, the Seligman correspondent for the *Prescott Evening-Courier*.

Back at the murder scene, Deputy Blankenship joined Sheriff Cramer, Undersheriff Saum, and County Attorney Ireland in searching the immediate area for clues. If the Welches had thought that parking between the two mounds would provide them with any kind of protection, they had been sadly wrong.

"Those two piles of rubble constitute the only cover for miles around," Sheriff Cramer was overheard to say by a newspaper reporter. "They could conceal someone sneaking up and also prevent the drivers on the highway from seeing him, too."

The sheriff theorized that the killer had likely pulled off the road, far behind the Welch car, and crept up to it while hiding behind one of the mounds, all without waking the boys' father. J. D. Welch was a large man who ironically made his living as a cross-country truck driver, sometimes traveling the same road on which he was murdered. His familiarity with the road may have fostered a false sense of security about his family's safety.

The hard-packed desert soil around the two mounds did not reveal the footprints the lawmen were hoping to find. They continued searching both sides of the highway for three more hours, but found nothing. Sheriff Cramer would have to return over the weekend with more men and volunteers to search up and down Highway 66 and the side roads that intersected it, and to trace the family's route all the way back to Spencer, Oklahoma.

NEWS OF THE UNEXPECTED, COLD-BLOODED slaying of a popular local couple was met with shock and disbelief in the tiny Oklahoma community. Newspapers throughout the Sooner state would cover the story and investigation for the next few weeks. Although they had only lived in Spencer for one year, the Welches were heavily involved in local activities. Utha volunteered her time with church, civic, and school organizations that benefited children in the community. She was the sixth-grade homeroom mother for her son Jimmy's class at the local elementary school. She was also a den mother for the Cub Scout den in which her younger sons participated. J. D. Welch volunteered his time with the Boy Scout troop and took Jimmy and other boys his son's age on camping trips. He was known to go out of his way to make sure a local boy in foster care attended those Boy Scout meetings alongside his son. To make sure the foster boy made it to the meetings, the Welches allowed him to spend the night at their house.

Nearly everyone in the family's circle of friends knew about the trip the Welches had been planning for weeks. It was going to be the first vacation the family had taken in four years, and they had talked about it often before they left. After visiting with J. D's mother in Tulare, the family was going to return to Oklahoma through Colorado Springs, where they would stop and visit with Utha's mother. The family's Oldsmobile 98 was a proud purchase they had made two weeks before they left on June 6.

"The whole community is upset about it, because they were such nice people," reported Mrs. J.W. Stowe to a reporter for an Oklahoma City newspaper. She, along with her husband, ran the local grocery store. "They were highly respected people, the kind that would do anything for anybody."

Mrs. Stowe added that before the family left, Utha Welch had stopped at her store to buy lunch meat and bread, and had casually mentioned to her that the boys insisted on bringing their Boy Scout tent so they could camp along the way.

"The family decided they would alternate by camping out one night and staying in a motel the next," Stowe explained.

"I have never heard of anything so bad," said a neighbor of the Welches, in the same article. "We are worried about the little boys."

So were the rest of the couple's family. Utha was an only child, but J. D. had three sisters and four brothers. Six of his seven siblings lived in California near their mother in Tulare. On Saturday, the day after the tragedy, eleven family members in two cars drove from California to Prescott to take the boys and the Oldsmobile back to Oklahoma, where a funeral would be held the following week. While they were en route to Arizona, the medical examiner was performing an autopsy, which confirmed that seven shots were fired from a .22-caliber revolver. Although the lead bullets were badly distorted, they appeared to be from the same manufacturer and were sent to the FBI office in Phoenix for further examination.

After taking custody of the boys from a county welfare office, the Welch family caravan continued its journey and arrived in Spencer early Sunday morning. Their grandmother and another uncle flew from Los Angeles Saturday evening and landed in Oklahoma City later that night. The grandmother had postponed her surgery in order to attend the funeral for her son and daughter-in-law. Utha's family also traveled to Oklahoma that weekend.

"You read about this happening in the papers, but you never think it will happen to you. When it does, it is a shock, it is just terrible," one of the boys' aunts stated to a reporter from the *Prescott Evening-Courier*. "The boys are taking it fairly well. The youngest ones don't understand what happened really and Jimmy, the oldest boy, doesn't want to talk about it."

But they did understand. They may have been young but they knew what death was. An Oklahoma City reporter caught up with the family at a relative's home on Sunday afternoon. The three youngest boys were playing outside when an argument erupted among them over who would get to ride a bicycle. The reporter could hear one of them crying loudly.

"That's Johnny," Jimmy said quietly. "He's afraid to go to sleep."

A little later in the day, his brother Tommy brought a lame bird into the house. Instead of letting it die, he wanted to try to save the poor creature.

Nearly one thousand people turned out for the funeral, held Tuesday morning, June 13, in an Oklahoma City funeral chapel. By noon, a large convoy of cars drove more than two hundred miles west to tiny Westville, Oklahoma, on the Arkansas border, where the couple was buried. For the Welch boys, their parents could just as well have been buried on Mars. After their belongings were packed up, they were going to live in southeast California with family members—sixteen hundred miles from the Westville Cemetery. Newspapers gave conflicting accounts of who the boys' guardian would be. The confusion was likely intentional since one of their aunts let it slip to a reporter that they would not say exactly where they would live, "for the boys' protection."

Sadly, they would have to leave their home, school, friends, and Scout clubs behind and go live far away, trying to start a new life without their mom and dad. In addition to losing their parents, there was a chance they might lose each other.

"We will try to keep the boys together—if it is possible," their grandmother told an Oklahoma City reporter.

OVER THE WEEKEND, SHERIFF CRAMER marshalled all his available resources to hunt for clues along the highway. Seventy-five volunteers and Yavapai County deputies, who comprised the Prescott Jeep Posse, and the Sheriff's Mounted Posse, searched both sides of the highway for the father's leather wallet or the murder weapon. In addition, thirty volunteers joined the hunt on foot, each of them walking miles in the desert sun, looking for anything that seemed out of place. The only item turned up by the entire group that weekend was a pack of cigarettes and a lighter that bore the name of a Tulsa company. Family members, however, reported that neither J. D. nor his wife smoked.

The night before their search, Captain Johnson reported back to the sheriff's office that he had caught up with the bus in Kingman, Arizona, eighty-five miles west of the murder site. The driver confirmed that between 4:45 and 5:15 that morning, he had parked approximately twenty feet behind an Oldsmobile sedan to change a flat tire. A female passenger reported that she'd had a clear view of the car from her seat and was confident that she had seen someone moving around inside. Her claim caused confusion about the time of death, until the medical examiner reported on Saturday that his autopsy proved the Welches were shot to death between two and three o'clock that morning—long before the bus arrived. The female passenger had to have been mistaken, Sheriff Cramer decided.

Besides the cigarette lighter that turned up, the sheriff's fingerprint examiner reported that he had discovered several partial prints on the car that did not belong to any of the family members. Although these could have come from the killer, Captain Johnson and his boss knew they could also have come from any one of the gas station attendants over the thousand miles the Welches had traveled on Wednesday and Thursday.

Added together, the physical clues didn't tell Sheriff Cramer very much. The severely damaged .22-caliber lead bullets and the partial prints would only be useful in confirming the killer's identity if a suspect was found—if the prints even belonged to the killer. But they first had to find a good suspect. Lawmen from the five northern Arizona counties that held US Highway 66 within their boundaries questioned employees at every business that catered to motorists. They were looking for any information they could find about someone acting suspiciously, or about the murder weapon or missing wallet. Their hopes were briefly raised then dashed that weekend over two separate reports about the same kinds of items they were hunting.

On Saturday, in Tucumcari, New Mexico, nearly six hundred miles east of Seligman, officers arrested a thirty-four-year-old transient motorcyclist who was trying to sell a nine-shot Harrington & Richardson .22-caliber revolver. After questioning him all weekend, they eventually let him go when it was determined that he had arrived in Tucumcari from Texas one and a half days behind the Welches. Not taking any chances, the police confiscated his revolver anyway and sent it to the FBI office in Phoenix for testing.

On Sunday in Peach Springs, Arizona, twenty-five miles west of the murder site, an Indian woman was detained after offering to sell a leather wallet to patrons in a local bar. She was questioned, and was then released after police decided she was exactly what she said she was—a leather craftswoman who had made the wallet herself.

The most interesting report Sheriff Cramer received that weekend came from Deputy Blankenship's wife, the waitress at Johnson's Coffee Shop in Seligman. On June 8, shortly before midnight, a rough-looking man in his early twenties walked into the diner and ordered coffee. As she was pouring him a cup, he stopped her.

"Wait a minute," he said. "How much does it cost?"

"Ten cents," Bertie told him.

"How about a nickel?" he countered. It was all he had. She took note of his thin face and icy expression. She had seen his type before and began to feel uneasy. He looked like the type who could pull out a gun and try to rob the place—even though there were several customers. She finished pouring the coffee and gently set it down in front of him.

"Here, I'm buying you a cup of coffee," she told him. It was her way of defusing any ill intentions the stranger may have had. He mumbled a "thanks," drank the coffee, and left without saying a word. A few hours later, he returned to the all-night diner.

"His attitude had suddenly changed," wrote Paul McClung in a crime magazine article published the following year. "This time, he was self-assured, almost arrogant. He ordered a full meal including tomato juice. He acted as though he didn't even recognize his coffee benefactress. He ate the hearty meal and paid for it with a $20 bill. She took the money and gave him his change without questioning him. She said she had never seen him before that night, and the man didn't look like the type who could get a midnight loan of a $20 bill."

To Sheriff Cramer and Undersheriff Saum, the coffee man was an intriguing suspect. The deputy's wife may have served a meal to their double-murderer. But like the other clues they had, it left them with nowhere to go and nothing to follow up on. Still, they thought it was important enough to keep her name and the man's description out of the newspapers. They didn't want him to return some night when she was working and tie up loose ends by killing Bertie Blankenship and anyone else who happened to be in the diner.

By Monday morning, June 12, the leads had already fizzled out and the Welches weren't even buried yet. In spite of this, the sheriff's office received hundreds of phone calls that weekend from all across the country from misguided but well-meaning citizens eager to help.

"Everyone thinks he knows who the murderer is," Sheriff Cramer told reporters, "but they don't know any more than we do, and at this point, all we know is that there are two dead people and four orphans."

The murder of a mom and dad during a trip to Grandma's house while traveling one of America's most popular highways became national news and terrorized thousands of families who were planning their own vacations that summer. It was a stranger-on-stranger murder by a human wolf who killed innocent people when they were most vulnerable—in the middle of the night, in their sleep, far from home, along a highway that cut through a miserable, God-forsaken wasteland where the nearest house was five miles away. Summer was just beginning and for the thousands of families preparing to hit the road, news of the Welch murder altered the mood of their own travel plans.

A few days after the Welch murder, both the Associated Press and United Press International ran stories featuring quotes from lawmen cautioning readers against the dangers of roadside camping and picking up hitchhikers. If you're going to sleep in your car, they warned readers, do so in a populated area. Or better yet, get a motel room. To drive home their point, the wire services reminded everyone that Highway 66 had a rich history of killers that preyed upon vulnerable travelers who often carried a large amount of cash with them.

"The Friday slaying of a vacationing Oklahoma couple on US 66 near Seligman, Arizona, as they slept in their car recalled scores of killings in similar circumstances along the nation's highways and served as a warning to the vacation bound," the AP reported in Sunday newspapers nationwide.

Between 1935 and 1961, nineteen people had been murdered or had vanished while traveling New Mexico highways, the same article disclosed. Fourteen of these cases happened on Route 66, and only eight them had been solved.

Oklahoma counted seven murders on the same highway in the same time period. Two of those had occurred in the last twelve months, both of them near Yukon, Oklahoma, just thirty miles away from the Welch home in Spencer.

The most famous of all US 66 murders was that of the five-member Carl Mosser family, who were hijacked near Luther, Oklahoma, on December 30, 1950, by ex-convict, Billy Cook. Later described in newspapers as a "mad-dog killer," Cook forced Carl Mosser at gunpoint to drive for three straight days. Their 2,100-mile journey of terror took them through Oklahoma, New Mexico, Texas, and Arkansas, finally ending in Cook's hometown of Joplin, Missouri. There, at two o'clock in the morning, he shot the entire family and dumped their bodies down an abandoned mine shaft.

Before his crime could be discovered, Cook returned to Blythe, California, where he had worked as a dishwasher before his murder spree. He then kidnapped a deputy and stole his police car. After he tied up the deputy and left him in a ditch forty miles outside of town, Cook drove ten miles farther south and used the police car's siren to stop and hijack motorist Robert Dewey. Nervous, Dewey asked to smoke a cigarette but accidentally dropped it between his seat and the door. When he reached down to pick it up, Cook thought he was reaching for a gun and shot him in the back. Dewey then struggled with Cook, who shot him one more time before dumping his body in the middle of the road.

Cook then drove Dewey's Buick across the border into Mexico. On a lonely road fifty miles south of Mexicali, the car broke down. With the hood up and a gas can nearby, Cook played the part of a stranded traveler. He then hijacked the first car to come to his aid, which was driven by Americans James Burke and Forrest Damron. Over the next eight days, the two men were held captive and forced to drive Cook five hundred miles south down the Baja Peninsula to Santa Rosalia, Mexico, where Cook was eventually captured by an alert Mexican police chief who had been hunting him for nearly a week.

During his three-week crime spree, Billy Cook traveled 5,000 miles, hijacked five cars, kidnapped ten people, and murdered six of them. He was executed on December 12, 1952, for the murder of Robert Dewey.[1]

In 1953, a camping couple were the victims of another Arizona crime. A recently released mental patient, carnival-ride operator Carl Folk, trailed Mr. and Mrs. Raymond Allen of Wattsburg, Pennsylvania, along US 66 from New Mexico into Arizona. When the couple camped for the night near Holbrook, the fifty-year-old Folk broke into their trailer, tied the two up, tortured the twenty-two-year-old woman with burning newspapers, then raped, choked, and killed her as her husband looked on. For this crime, Folk later paid with his life when he was executed in the Arizona gas chamber in 1955.

On February 10, 1960, the frozen body of Jacob Ray Krentz was recovered near Highway 66 just three miles farther west

---

[1] The author has spent the last three years researching Cook's crime spree for an upcoming book.

from where the Welches were murdered. While driving his own car, Krentz was shot in the back and killed by two intoxicated companions after an argument broke out. With the dead man still behind the wheel, the killers took control of the car, pulled onto the shoulder, and dragged Krentz's body all the way to the fence line. The shooter was later acquitted of murder, then tried and convicted of being an accessory to murder, for which he was sentenced to three to five years in prison. The other passenger in the car, who had testified against the killer, later went to trial, but the charges were dismissed after the jury in his case failed to reach a verdict.

On July 31, 1959, ninety miles east of the Welch site on US 66, a transient couple who made their living picking vegetable crops murdered a sixty-year-old Good Samaritan after he stopped to help them when their car broke down outside of Flagstaff. The common-law husband and wife claimed it was self-defense after the elderly man attacked the female. However, their story wasn't helped by their admission that they took $200 from their victim's wallet and drove off in his car.

AFTER HIS CLUES FIZZLED OUT, Sheriff Cramer employed a new strategy for hunting down the Welch killers. From now on, the perpetrators of any armed robbery or violent murder within a thousand-mile radius would be treated as suspects until they could be cleared.

"A hijacker seldom hits just once," Paul McClung wrote in his magazine article. "Sheriff Cramer knew all holdup men are repeaters, and once they've pulled that trigger they usually pull it again." Every armed robbery and hijacking case in the Southwest would have to be investigated for a possible connection to the Welch murders—and there was no shortage of deadly cases that summer. In what could only be described as separate but tragic coincidences, the narrative of cold-blooded killers on America's highways quickly intensified.

On Saturday, just one day after the Welch murders, a roadblock on US Highway 40 near Grantsville, Utah, put an end to a cross-country murder spree by two AWOL soldiers. On May 24, nineteen-year-old James D. Latham and eighteen-year-old George York deserted the military stockade at Fort Hood, Texas, where they were serving time as trustees for minor offenses.

Two days later, they were given a ride near Mix, Louisiana, by Edward Guidroz, a fish-market owner. With a wrench, they clubbed the forty-three-year-old so hard that they broke his skull. Believing he was dead, they threw his body out near a cemetery and drove off in his truck. Guidroz survived his attack and later described the pair to police.

On May 29, Latham and York caught up with two women near a Jacksonville, Florida, dog track where one of the women won $177 on a $2 bet with a number combination she had dreamed about the night before. Her companion was a twenty-five-year-old mother of four children. The clean-cut-looking boys strangled the two women and stole their flashy automobile, which held a .38-caliber pistol in the glove compartment.

One week later near Aiken, South Carolina, the duo tried to hijack another motorist who got away as they shot at him. The next day, the same day the Welches left for their vacation, Latham and York found easier prey in a seventy-one-year-old railroad porter near Tullahoma, Tennessee. Although John Whitaker begged for his life, they shot him to death and stole his 1956 sedan. The car took them as far as Illinois, where they killed two more men on Thursday, June 8, in separate incidents.

The deadly duo then passed through Missouri and entered Kansas, where they murdered another railroad employee, sixty-one-year-old Otto Ziegler, on Friday—the same day the Welches were murdered.

The boys continued driving until later that evening when they reached Craig, Colorado, where a carnival had set up for the weekend. There, they met Rachel Moyer, 18, who had dropped out of school to work as a maid in a hotel.

"She was both lonely and shy and yearned to go to California," a newspaper later reported. "York and Latham told her to come along. A fisherman found Rachel's body in a clump of trees outside Craig [the next day]. She had a bullet in the brain and Latham and York said they had [raped] her before they killed her."

Not long after Rachel's body was discovered, the boys were captured in Utah. Getting them to tell about their crimes wasn't difficult. They told police they hated the world, argued over which of them would get to die first in the electric chair, and claimed they had done their victims a favor.

"Hell, they're out of their misery in this damned world," one of them said. Both York and Latham seemed anxious to be executed and leave "this stinking, lousy world." They were sentenced to death for the Kansas murder and were hanged two months after Perry Smith and Richard Hickock, two killers made famous by Truman Capote's bestselling book, *In Cold Blood*.

Although it was soon determined that Latham and York had nothing to do with the Welch murders, their story, which shared copy space with the Route 66 slayings, only intensified the fear and apprehension travelers felt that summer.

On Thursday, June 22, two viable suspects with Arizona ties were made known to Sheriff Cramer and Captain Johnson when police arrested Fred Waldo, 23, for the armed robbery, kidnapping, and attempted murder of a Phoenix gas station attendant two days earlier. One hour before the Tuesday night robbery, Waldo and his partner in crime, James Abner Bentley, kidnapped four teenage boys at gunpoint and told them they were there to witness the shooting of two service station employees—"to prove their toughness," the boys later told police. By doing so, Waldo and Bentley hoped to build a reputation as a pair of cold-blooded killers.

However, when they couldn't find a filling station with two men suitable to murder, they settled on one at 67th Avenue and Buckeye, where twenty-year-old Edward Franklin Smith was working alone. After robbing Smith, Bentley shot him twice in the abdomen and forced the boys to load Smith into his car. Smith played dead, and when Waldo and Bentley stopped to dump the body, Smith fought back and disarmed Bentley. During the life-and-death struggle, Waldo stabbed Smith several times before he escaped. He survived his injuries and identified Waldo, then Bentley, as the men who had robbed him.

After Waldo was captured, he confessed when he learned that Smith had picked him out of a line-up. In a written statement, Waldo described his partner as "a trigger-happy guy who threatened to shoot me when he got mad. I was scared, but I managed to talk him out of shooting me."

During their kidnapping, Bentley bragged to his captives how he had murdered a liquor store owner one month earlier. Waldo confirmed this claim, and police were able to connect it to the May 22 murder of Fresno, California, liquor store owner, Homer Bryan. Although police would eventually learn otherwise, Waldo swore he knew nothing about the Fresno case. Waldo had a solid alibi for the day the Welches were killed, but he did not know where Bentley was that night.

When authorities dug into Bentley's past, they discovered he was a former mental patient with a long criminal career that stretched back to a 1952 arrest for auto theft and burglary in California. He had escaped several times from the California Youth Authority before he was committed to a state mental hospital in 1954. While there, he was diagnosed as a psychopathic personality who would kill in the future unless treated.

He went untreated by escaping seventeen times over a thirty-day period. Fed up with his behavior and with no legal claim to hold him any longer, hospital officials released him.

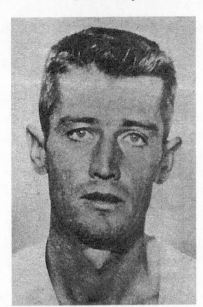

James Abner Bentley

In 1958, he served a jail term in Yuma, Arizona, for assault with a deadly weapon. He had never been arrested since that incident, although he was suspected of being involved in other crimes. Two years before his 1958 arrest, Bentley got married. The couple settled in the Phoenix suburb of Gilbert and eventually had two children. However, Bentley was too difficult to live with and his wife, Shirley, left him in late April 1961 to go reside with her mother in Fresno.

In 1961, the shortest route to Fresno from Gilbert was US Highway 66. James Abner Bentley became Arizona's most-wanted man and was quickly named the prime suspect in the Welch slayings.

"We have second and third hand information that these two subjects [Waldo and Bentley] were in the area west of Seligman on US 66 about the time Mr. and Mrs. James Welch were killed," Sheriff Cramer told a Prescott newspaper. "Our information is that both Waldo and Bentley are suspects in the killing of a liquor store clerk in Fresno, California, who was shot with a .22 caliber gun and a .38."

Although Waldo's alibi for June 8 and 9 was later confirmed, Sheriff Cramer knew what he was talking about when it came to the Fresno murder. Investigators there had done their homework and soon had confessions from two accomplices.

A reform-school pal, Billy Joe Chapple, confessed that he was the getaway driver for Waldo and Bentley on May 22 when the pair shot and killed the liquor store owner. A decorated World War II pilot, Bryan was locking up for the night when Bentley approached and shot him twice, once in the abdomen and once in the chest. When he fell to the ground, Waldo walked up and shot Bryan once in the head. The two then took the keys, unlocked the store, and stole $115 and some liquor. The night before, Waldo and Bentley had robbed another liquor store in Modesto, one hundred miles north.

For some inexplicable reason, Chapple brought his twenty-two-year-old wife and baby daughter along for the holdups. He and his wife were later arrested and charged.

Following Waldo's arrest on June 22, police in seven states hunted for James Abner Bentley over the next seven days. He was captured on June 29 in Fort Scott, Kansas, where he had traveled to intercept his wife, who had gone there with her mother to visit family. Shirley's grandparents tipped off police when they read in the newspapers that her husband was a wanted man. He was arrested just as he was about to leave town. Within hours of his arrest, Bentley showed the Kansas deputies why he was once a mental patient.

"He (Bentley) seems to be suffering from some kind of mental condition and is very nervous and excited," the local sheriff said at the time. "He's very difficult to question and we've been unable to get any real sense out of him."

In addition to his bizarre behavior, Bentley tried to commit suicide four times within hours of his arrest. He first tried to cut his wrists by rubbing them as hard as he could on a piece of angle iron used to construct the jailhouse bunk beds. The sheriff then handcuffed him to the bunk, but Bentley was able to slip his wrists out and was in the middle of hanging himself when the sheriff walked in on him. Another prisoner was put in his cell and told to watch him.

Bentley's third attempt that day was later described in newspapers and crime magazines as "creative." He had tried to choke himself to death by stuffing a large wad of toilet paper down his throat. The other prisoner, who was much larger, wrestled with Bentley and pulled the tissue out of his mouth. Bentley then tried to shove a sock down his throat but was again saved by his cellmate. With all means of an early demise taken away from him, the former mental patient then tried to go on a hunger strike but gave up after forty hours.

With his melodrama behind him, Fort Scott authorities were able to get Bentley to confess to the Phoenix robbery, as well as the Fresno murder which came about, he revealed, after he and Waldo had made a $15 bet over who would kill the liquor store owner.

Bentley denied having anything to do with the Welch murders but mumbled something to the effect that he may have been in the Seligman area at the time.

"In the course of the interview," a crime reporter later revealed, "he dropped a few inadvertent remarks which led [a Fort Scott deputy] to believe that the suspect could have been in the Seligman area at the time the Welches were slain."

Although Bentley had stuck his neck out, his wife and mother-in-law tried to save it when they told *The Fort Scott Tribune* and the sheriff that James "was in their Fresno home on June 9."

The two women, who enjoyed good reputations both in Kansas and Fresno, were believed. Sheriff Cramer's heart sank when he heard the news. When Bentley was returned to Arizona, he and Captain Johnson eventually got the chance to question their suspect but discovered, much like the Kansas lawmen, that Bentley's bizarre behavior made it difficult to get any information out of him.

And they didn't believe the alibi provided by his wife and mother. Sheriff Cramer spoke with Bentley's employer and learned he had shown up to bale hay at two in the morning, June 8, and had left three hours later. He next showed up at a friend's house to eat breakfast and then left Gilbert, Arizona, around noon, driving a 1949 Chevrolet. If he did leave town for Fresno to see his wife, his most likely route would have taken him through Seligman.

The statements from the Arizona witnesses left enough room for Bentley to squeak by on the alibi. If he drove to Fresno on June 8, he could have been in the Seligman area around the time of the murders—depending on what time he left. If he did leave Gilbert around noon, it was also possible that he was arriving at his wife's house early the next morning, around the same time the Welches were slain. Without more information, Sheriff Cramer and Captain Johnson didn't know what to think. Strangely, it did not occur to them to show Bertie Blankenship a mug shot of James Abner Bentley to verify if he was the coffee man or not. Instead, Waldo and Bentley were extradited back to Fresno where authorities had a rock-solid case against them.

But Cramer and his men didn't have to wait very long for more suspects to appear on their radar. Another highway killer was on the loose in the Utah Badlands. On July 4, a trio from Connecticut on a cross-country tour of the United States stopped at a scenic overlook known as Dead Horse Point, seventeen miles west of Moab. There, they met a short, stocky, dark-skinned man who struck up a conversation with them. He was familiar with the area and gave Charles Boothroyd, 55, Jeannette Sullivan, 41, and her daughter Denise, 14, an impromptu history and geography lesson.

The friendly man then left without mentioning his name. When the Connecticut travelers got back on the highway they saw the same man parked on the side of the road with the hood up. He appeared to be having engine trouble. Since he had been so nice to them, Boothroyd pulled his Volkswagen Beetle in behind him and got out to help.

The stranger asked for a flashlight, tinkered under the hood of his car and then started the vehicle. Suddenly, his mood changed and he angrily told Boothroyd and Jeannette, "I want money" as he climbed from the vehicle with a .22-caliber rifle in his hands.

Boothroyd laid his wallet on the road, but an angry Jeannette Sullivan picked it up, threw the cash down on the road, and turned to walk away. When she did, the man shot her in the back of the head, killing her instantly. He then shot Boothroyd in the face, twice, with the second shot passing through his hands as he covered his face.

While the killer was dragging Mrs. Sullivan and Boothroyd out of the road, Denise Sullivan got behind the steering wheel, started the Volkswagen, and tried to drive away. The killer chased after her in his own car, forced her to crash less than a mile away, and then kidnapped the young girl.

Boothroyd survived his wounds and alerted authorities, who launched an extensive search by land and air. Since it was a kidnapping case, FBI agents were flown in to join the manhunt. They were looking for a 1955 ivory-colored Plymouth with a license plate that began with "CJ."

On July 7, FBI agents found the car near Crescent Junction, Utah, with thirty-five-year-old Abel Aragon behind the wheel. When agents identified themselves, Aragon locked the doors, rolled up the window, and said, "FBI? Prove it!" He then shot himself in the head with a pistol. Aragon was rushed to a hospital but died two hours later without saying a word. Until July 4, Aragon was an upstanding citizen and the father of five children. He was a former marine who received the Navy Cross for heroism during the Battle of Guam in 1944. He had lost his coal mining job in December, however, and had grown increasingly depressed.

Five hours after he kidnapped Denise, Aragon stopped a truck driver and gave him a letter to mail to his wife. It was a goodbye message in which he professed his love to her and the children.

Aragon's .22-caliber rifle and a short-handled shovel were found three days later near a Polar Mesa mining camp the ex-marine was known to visit often. Although the search for Denise continued for several more weeks, her body has never been found.

Before Aragon was identified in the July 4 attack and his whereabouts on June 9 were learned, Yavapai County authorities looked upon the incident near Dead Horse Point with great interest. They also took an interest in any armed-robbery suspects from the Mississippi River to Los Angeles that summer, especially those in Arizona. When two young men robbed an auto parts store in a suburb near Tulsa later that July, investigators learned one of them had ties to Seligman. He was soon arrested in Arizona and held for extradition. The Oklahoma-Seligman connection was enough of a coincidence for Sheriff Cramer and Captain Johnson to consider it. They were still looking for the owner of the cigarette lighter they had found.

"We consider them both suspects, of course," Sheriff Cramer told a newspaper reporter. "Anyone who was in this area could be called a suspect."

His comment was revealing. If they considered anyone in the Seligman area on June 9 a suspect, it showed how far they were willing to go to solve the Welch case. They were lifting every stone and exploring every lead—hot or cold. But like their other hot leads, this latest one proved to be a dead end.

Crime stories that make the national news, like the Welch murders, have a short lifespan as sensational new cases eventually take their place. By the time Jimmy, Tommy, Billy, and Johnny began school in a strange new place, the murder of their parents was all but forgotten, except by those with a connection to the case.

"The summer passed and with it the memory of the Welch tragedy from most minds," crime writer D. L. Champion wrote in a 1962 issue of *True Detective* magazine, "but not from the mind of Sheriff Cramer, nor from the minds of any residents of northwestern Arizona who lived in the area of US Highway 66."

Eleven more pages of the calendar would be torn away until another hot lead surfaced in May 1962—and this one had a familiar name attached to it.

When they had considered the overwhelming evidence against them, Billy Chapple and Fred Waldo pleaded guilty and were sentenced to life in prison by separate juries. James Bentley also pled guilty, but additionally pleaded not guilty by reason of insanity. A sanity trial was held and a jury ruled against him. Another jury called to determine his penalty sentenced him to death on December 12, 1961.

Soon after he was sent to San Quentin, Bentley bragged to a fellow convict that sometime during the summer of 1961, he had murdered a vacationing couple in Arizona, just off Route 66, as the couple's children slept in a tent nearby. "The murderer had stated with some pride that he had not [killed] the children," the *True Detective* article reported.

Although this convict was released from San Quentin soon after he heard the inmate's story, he was arrested again in Berkeley, California, on burglary charges. Looking to cut a deal, the small-time crook told Berkeley detectives about the San Quentin prisoner who had bragged about committing a double murder in Arizona the year before. However, since he had never bothered to learn the killer's name, he could only provide them with a description. The Berkeley officers took him seriously, though, and after checking with authorities at nearby San Quentin, they were able to put the clues together and come up with a mug shot that the informant identified.

It was James Abner Bentley.

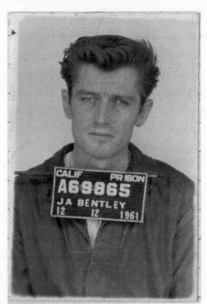

James Abner Bentley, San Quentin mug shot. *(Courtesy: California State Archives)*

The Berkeley officers then passed this information on to Sheriff Cramer. Although excited that their one-time prime suspect was now back in the picture, County Attorney George Ireland reminded them they would need more than the word of a jailhouse informant. When Sheriff Cramer and Captain Johnson considered the problem, they decided to have one hundred copies of Bentley's mug shot printed and shown to all the businesses along Arizona's Route 66 that catered to travelers.

At three o'clock in the afternoon on June 9, exactly one year to the day that the Welches were murdered, Undersheriff Sam Saum walked into Johnson's Coffee Shop in Seligman. Saum, like the others, had forgotten all about the coffee man Bertie Blankenship had described to them the year before. When she saw Bentley's photograph, she recognized him immediately. He was the guy she was afraid was going to rob the place. He was the one who only had five cents to his name, but then came back a few hours later with a $20 bill to pay for a big breakfast.

Bertie was driven back to Prescott, where she repeated her story to Saum's boss. It all tied in with the early morning hours in which the Welches were murdered just thirteen miles away, and her memory of the coffee man was too detailed and sharp for it not to be true. She even remembered that Bentley had ordered tomato juice with his breakfast.

Later that night, Sheriff Cramer, Saum, Captain Johnson, and County Attorney Ireland held a press conference in which they revealed that they had identified the Welches' killer. Their twelve-month investigation, which had included three hundred interviews, was officially over.

"He always has been a suspect of ours from the start," Sheriff Cramer told an Oklahoma City newspaper reporter the following day. "We based our suspicions on his evident admission and his other activities in this area about the time of the Oklahoma couple's murder."

The murder weapon was never recovered, and no mention was made of the partial fingerprints found on the Welches' Oldsmobile. Two months after the slayings, J. D.'s leather wallet was found by the side of the road two miles east of Seligman. The location gave away Bentley's movements that night.

After stopping at the coffee shop, Bentley continued west on Route 66 for thirteen miles until he found the Welches' car. At that moment, he was halfway to his wife's house in Fresno with only a nickel to his name. Ever since she'd taken the kids and left him in April, he had been in a downward spiral—robbing two liquor stores and shooting one of the owners.

To get to California, he was going to need more money, and he had no problem gunning down a mother and father in their car while they slept and stealing the wallet—which held an estimated $40 to $60. What he did for the next few hours is a mystery, but Bertie Blankenship claimed he was back in her diner between 2:30 and 3 a.m. to order a big breakfast with tomato juice.

The location of the wallet indicated that he drove back to Gilbert that night. With money in his pocket, he had changed his mind about visiting Shirley and the kids. He was not, as his wife and mother-in-law said, in Fresno at the time of the murders, Sheriff Cramer told reporters.

When J. D.'s family in California heard the news, they were very relieved. They had lived in fear for the boys' safety all that time.

"The children are adjusting quite well," one of their aunts told a reporter. "All of our family is relieved that the man who did this has been identified."

While on death row in San Quentin, Bentley's behavior "had been as strange as when he had attempted to swallow a roll of toilet paper at Fort Scott," Champion wrote. In April, two months before he was identified, Bentley was sent to a prison mental hospital in Vacaville, California, for further observation. He was still there when Yavapai County lawmen learned his identity. Fearful that he would somehow wiggle out of his death sentence, County Attorney Ireland filed first-degree murder charges against Bentley two days after the press conference. Phoenix police already had charges pending against him and Waldo for the armed robbery, attempted murder, and kidnapping of the gas station attendant.

Ireland's concern was well founded. The governor of California at the time was democrat Edmund Gerald "Pat" Brown, Sr. He was a vocal opponent of the death penalty and had recently asked the 1963 state legislature for a four-year moratorium on executions. On January 16 of that year, Governor Brown held a well-publicized meeting in his office to consider a clemency appeal for Bentley, who was scheduled to be executed in six days. The meeting was an opportunity for Brown to connect the condemned man's fate with a top political objective. To drive home his point, Brown latched onto arguments made by Bentley's attorney.

Recalling his client's 1954 commitment to a state mental hospital in Napa, J. Montgomery Carter told Governor Brown in his office, "It does not seem basically fair that a man whose future was predicted by the state should now have his life taken by the state for doing exactly what the state said he would do."

The lawyer's skillful repetition of the word "state" three times in a single sentence gave it an eloquent ring, but it was also an attempt to shift blame for his client's behavior elsewhere. Carter also ignored the fact that his client escaped from that hospital seventeen times during his thirty-day hold—which led to his dismissal and lack of treatment.

After he was sentenced to death, Bentley had spent much of the last nine months away from death row in the prison mental hospital where doctors said he was "mentally ill, but legally sane." Turning to Bentley's parents who drove from their home in Ripon, California, to attend the meeting in Sacramento, Brown asked them if they believed their son was dangerous.

"No!" Mrs. Bentley sobbed, as her husband, unable to speak, nodded his head in agreement.

Before the meeting ended, Brown gave them hope when he said, "I'm sincerely disturbed that under the law a man that all the doctors say is sick should be executed."

The next day, Brown held another meeting in his office to consider the cases of two more death-row inmates—one of them scheduled to die the same day as Bentley, and the other, two days later. At that meeting, however, Brown indicated he would not grant any reprieve for the three men while the legislature considered his moratorium.

That news was apparently enough to cause Bentley to have another one of his breakdowns, and on Saturday, January 19, he was back in a prison mental hospital where he was treated "because of a nervous condition."

On Monday, Brown's position that no reprieve would be granted while the moratorium legislation was being considered was confirmed in a statement he released to the press. He then left California to go on vacation, leaving his lieutenant governor behind, who was forced to turn down another last-minute plea from Bentley's attorney. The following day, Bentley was transferred from the hospital to a holding cell strategically placed thirteen steps away from the gas chamber. He spent his last night alive talking about the afterlife, with both a Catholic priest and a Protestant minister, before dozing off for four hours. In the morning, officials reported that he "ate a hearty breakfast." They did not say whether he had tomato juice or not.

At 10:04 on Wednesday morning, January 23, 1961, James Abner Bentley was strapped to a metal chair inside the all-steel, octagon-shaped gas chamber—alone. Eight minutes later, he was dead.

The man who was to die alongside him received a stay of execution from the United States Supreme Court. There would not be another execution in California for four more years— just as Governor Brown requested.

Did You Enjoy These Stories?
If you enjoyed this book, I would be grateful if you could post a short review on Amazon and/or GoodReads.com. Your support really does make a difference. As an independent researcher and writer, reviews and word of mouth are my only sources of advertising. By telling others, these stories can reach more people who find them just as fascinating as you do.

Also Available:

The DC Dead Girls Club: A Vintage True Crime Story of Four Unsolved Murders in Washington D.C. – Kindle only on Amazon.com

Deadly Hero: The High Society Murder that Created Hysteria in the Heartland
(Coming in 2015)

Visit: HistoricalCrimeDetective.com/forgotten/ to view more images about the cases presented in this book.

Acknowledgments

A book like this cannot be written alone and I would like to identify some very special people who helped me along the way.

I end this work with a warm and special appreciation for my editor, Gloria Boyer, who did an outstanding and thorough job while offering kind words of encouragement. To Judith and Clint Richmond, who edited early drafts of several chapters. They also dug into the work with great tenacity and came up with many helpful suggestions to smooth out the rough spots and improve the content.

My research brought me into contact with many helpful people who volunteered their time and energy—people like Patterson Smith, who owns the largest collection of crime magazines. I also want to thank the men and women who look after the records at the California State Archives, the Oregon State Archives, and the Oklahoma Historical Society.

I would also like to thank all of the dedicated fans who follow my blog, HistoricalCrimeDetective.com. It was their enthusiasm in the early stages of my journey into the historical true crime genre that encouraged me to continue on with what was then just a hobby.

Last but never least, I would like to thank my wife who believed in me and told me to go where my passion takes me. She is the love of my life, a better person than me, and in the end, the one whose tenderness speaks louder than any words I could ever write.

Sources

Chapter One: Denver's "Capitol Hill Thug"

Untitled, posted under "Denver" column, *Svenska Korrespondenten*, September 27, 1900, page 8. [Denver's Swedish community newspaper, translated with the help of Google Translate.]

"News Topics from Denver, Carnival of Crime Appears to Have Reached a Climax, Unmolested by Police," *Colorado Springs Gazette*, October 12, 1900, page 7.

"Colorado Notes," *Colorado Transcript*, Golden, Colorado, October 17, 1900, page 7.

"Miss McAtee Improving," *Daily Journal*, Telluride, Colorado, October 23, 1900, page 1.

"Miss McAtee Improving, *Durango Wage Earner*, Durango, Colorado, October 25, 1900, page 1.

"Colorado Notes," *Longmont Ledger*, Longmont, Colorado, October 26, 1900, page 1.

"David Pace, Thought to be Capitol Hill Thug," *Aspen Daily Times*, November 22, 1900, page 1.

"Capitol Hill Thug," *Aspen Tribune*, January 9, 1901, page 1.

"Colorado Notes," *Yuma Pioneer*, Yuma, Colorado, January 11, 1901, page 4.

"May Be a Fake," *Aspen Tribune*, January 12, 1901, page 2.

Untitled, "The Denver police have again…" *Aspen Tribune*, January 23, 1901, page 3.

"Assaulter of Women Abroad," *Aspen Democrat*, February 17, 1901, page 1.

"The Capitol Hill Thug, The Police Are Hot on the Trail of Alleged Terror," *Aspen Daily Times*, February 21, 1900, page 1.

"Three More Denver Women are Sandbagged," *Daily Journal*, Telluride, Colorado, February 23, 1901, page 1.

"Denver Thug at Work," *Aspen Tribune*, February 23, 1901, page1.

"The Denver Thug," *Aspen Weekly Times*, February 23, 1901, page 1.

"The Denver Thug," *Aspen Daily Times*, February 24, 1901, page 1.

"Round up the Thug," *The Denver Post*, February 24, 1901, page 1.

"Police Phased, Denver Thug Escapes All Traps Set," *Boston Globe*, February 24, 1901, page 8.

"Police of Denver Will Suspect Every Person on Capitol Hill," *Aspen Tribune*, February 25, page 1.

"Women Struck Down in the Dark; Terror in the City of Denver," *The Daily Gazette*, Janesville, Wisconsin, February 25, 1901, page 1.

"The Thug Perhaps," *Aspen Tribune*, February 26, 1901, page 1.

"Police Capture Denver Slugger," *The Daily Republican News*, Hamilton, Ohio, February 26, 1901, page 1.

"Three Denver Women Attacked," *Colorado Transcript*, Golden, Colorado, February 27, 1901, page 7.

"Colorado Notes," *Colorado Transcript*, Golden, Colorado, February 27, 1901, page 2.

"The Denver Thug is Arrested," *The Lyons Recorder*, Lyon, Colorado, February 27, 1901, page 1.

"The Thug is Recognized," *Aspen Daily Tribune*, February 27, 1901, page 1.

"Murderer of Woman," *Salt Lake Tribune*, February 27, 1901, page 1.

"Denies It," *Aspen Tribune*, February 27, 1901, page 1.

"Denver Capitol Hill Slugger Arrested," *The Lyons Recorder*, February 28, 1901, page 1.

"Denver Capitol Hill Slugger Arrested," *Yuma Pioneer*, February 28, 1901, page 1.

"Circle Grows Small," *Aspen Tribune*, February 28, 1901, page 1.

"Three Denver Women Attacked," *Eagle County Blade*, Red Cliff, Colorado, February 28, 1901, page 1.

"Hates All Womankind," *The Norfolk Weekly News-Journal*, Norfolk, Nebraska, March 1, 1901, page 4.

"Morphine Fiend, Fredericks Testimony is Not Reliable," *Aspen Daily Times*, March 1, 1901, page 1.

"Denver Capitol Hill Slugger Arrested," *Longmont Ledger*, March 1, 1901, page 1.

"Denver Women are Struck Down by Desperate Thug," *The San Francisco Call*, March 2, 1901, page 2.

"Maniac Cowan, The Denver Woman Killer, Once Resided in New Mexico," *El Paso Daily Herald*, March 2, 1901, page 1.

"Denver Murderer Known as 'Bug House Davis,'" *Albuquerque Daily Citizen*, March 2, 1901, page 1.

"Ten Women Attacked by Thug," *Corona Courier*, Corona, California, March 2, 1901, page 7.

"No Good, Fredericks Wanted Reward for Free Meals and Testimony," *Aspen Tribune*, March 2, 1901, page 1.

"Said That He Was No Negro," *Aspen Daily Times*, March 28, 1901, page 1.

"Cowan's Trial," *Aspen Weekly Times*, March 20, 1901, page 1.

"A Test of Telepathy," *Cedar Rapids Evening Gazette*, Cedar Rapids, Iowa, March 25, 1901, page 1.

"Fredericks is Cut to Pieces," *Aspen Daily Times*, March 29, 1901, page 1.

"Subdued, Fredericks is Not So Positive as He Was on the Other Trial," *Aspen Tribune*, March 30, 1901, page 1.

"Cowan Made Good Witness," *Aspen Daily Times*, March 30, 1901, page 1.

"Makes a Good Impression, Cowan a Good Witness and Proves Alibi," *Aspen Democrat*, March 31, 1901, page 1.

"Discredit is Cast on Frederick's Testimony by Two Witnesses," *Aspen Tribune*, April 1, 1901, page 1.

Untitled Editorial Snippet, *Aspen Tribune*, April 1, 1901, page 2.

"Still Jailed, Cowan Remanded to Prison for Another Day," *Aspen Daily Times*, April 2, 1901, page 1.

"Cowan Tried Again," *Aspen Tribune*, April 4, 1901, page 1.

"Is Cowan Insane?" *Aspen Daily Times*, April 6, 1901, page 2.

"Still Jailed," *Aspen Weekly Times*, April 6, 1901, page 1.

"Denver's Alleged Thug Discharged," *Colorado Transcript*, April 10, 1901, page 1.

"Al Cowan Released," *Colorado Springs Gazette*, April 14, 1901, page 1.

"Colorado Notes," *Colorado Transcript*, April 17, 1901, page 1.

"Capitol Hill Thug Again at Work," *Colorado Springs Gazette*, April 21, 1901, page 9.

"Assaults Another Woman on Capitol Hill, Cowan Not Suspected," *Durango Democrat*, April 21, 1901, page 1.

"Denver's Stupid Police Force," *Aspen Democrat*, April 21, 1901, page 1.

"Denver Fiend Appears Again," *Aspen Daily Times*, April 21, 1901, page 1.

"Cowan Looks for Work," *Aspen Daily Times*, April 27, 1901, page 1.

---###---

Chapter Two: The Murder of Father Kaspar Vartarian

"Robbery Moved Murder of Priest Whose Body Was Found in Trunk," *The New York Evening-World*, May 27, 1907, pages 1 and 2.

"Priest's Body in Box, Trunk Left in Room, *New York Tribune*, May 27, 1935, pages 1 and 2.

"Hunting for Priest's Slayers," *New York Evening-Post*, May 27, 1907, page 3.

"Now Think Priest Slain for Money," *The Evening-Star*, Washington D.C., May 28, 1907, Part Two, page 17.

"Armenian Priest Murdered for a Bag of Money," *The New York Evening-World*, May 28, 1907, page 2.

"Detectives Search for Murderers," *Los Angeles Herald*, May 28, 1907, page 1.

"Chicago Arrest False, Trunk Murder Mystery," *New York Tribune*, May 28, 1907, pages 1 and 2.

"Victim of Trunk Mystery," *The Evening-Statesman*, Walla Walla, Washington, May 28, 1907, page 1.

"Suspect in Chicago, Priest had Fortune and Feared for Life," *The Evening-Telegram*, New York City, May 28, 1907, page 2.

"Seek Place of Murder, Trunk Case Still in Dark," *New York Tribune*, May 29, 1907, page 3.

"Slayers of Priest are Hiding Here," *The Evening Telegram*, New York City, May 29, 1907, page 1.

"Ghost of Priest Haunts Lady," *Syracuse Journal*, Syracuse, New York, May 30, 1907, page 1.

"Armenians to Make Search," *Red Cloud Chief*, Red Cloud, Nebraska, May 31, 1907, page 7.

"Murdered Priest Buried," *New York Tribune*, June 3, 1907, page 4.

"Suspect in the Priest Murder Caught," *New York Evening-World*, June 18, 1907, page 1.

"Priest's Murder Caught?" *New York Sun*, June 30, page 1.

"Police to Bring Farkain Here," *The New York Times*, July 1, page 16.

"Sarkasian Knew of Murder," *New York Sun*, July 4, 1907, page 1.

"Third-degree By Cable," *New York Sun*, July 6, 1907, page 1.

"Wants Alleged Murderer Compelled to Confess," Associated Press, *Los Angeles Herald*, July 7, 1907, page 3.

"Police Refuse to Take Father Kaspar's Slayer," *New York Evening-World*, August 26, 1907, page 1.

"Murderers May Go Free, No Evidence to Convict in Killing of Father Kaspar," *New York Tribune*, August 27, 1907, page 2.

"Catch Man Wanted in Priest's Murder," *The New York Times*, December 21, 1907, page 2.

"Sarkasian Arraigned and Remanded," *New York Tribune*, December 22, 1907, page 7.

"Murders Famous in Police Annals of America," *The Post-Star*, Glen Falls, New York, June 28, 1909, page 1.

---###---

Chapter Three: The Carver Family Hatchet Murders

"Shoots Negro Who Slew his Wife and Baby," Associated Press, *The Logansport Press*, Logansport, Indiana, April 3, 1930, page 1.

"Husband Held in Deaths of Wife and Son," Associated Press, *Sarasota Herald-Tribune*, April 4, 1930, page 1.

"Florida Death Story Doubted," Associated Press, *Pittsburg Post-Gazette*, April 4, 1930, page 2.

"Carver Arrested in Florida Axe Murders, To Be Quizzed in Deaths of Wife and Son," Associated Press, *Cumberland Evening-Times*, Cumberland, Maryland, April 4, 1930, page 1.

"Triple Murder Plot Scented," United News, *Pittsburg Post-Gazette*, April 5, 1930, page 2.

"Jury Reverses First Verdict," Associated Press, *The Bradford Era*, Bradford, Pennsylvania, April 5, 1930, page 1.

"Probers Cite Him in Death of 3 in Home," *Sarasota Herald-Tribune*, April 6, 1930, page 1 and 2.

"Wife's Family Do Not Think Carver Guilty," Associated Press, *Sarasota Herald-Tribune*, April 7, 1930, page 1.

"Carver Seeks Release at Sebring," Associated Press, *The Evening-Independent*, St. Petersburg, Florida, April 9, 1930, page 9.

"His Lawyer Makes Plea for Action," Associated Press, *Sarasota Herald-Tribune*, April 14, 1930, page 1.

"Carver Jury Visits Site of Slaying," *The Evening Independent*, St. Petersburg, Florida, May 15, 1930, pages 1 and 4.

"Details of Triple Slaying at Sebring Are Told on Stand," Associated Press, *The Palm Beach Post*, May 15, 1930, page 1.

"State Rests Its Case in Carver Trial," Associated Press, *St. Petersburg Times*, May 15, 1930, page 1.

"Carver Case Defense Opens, 27 Persons Say He Has Good Name," *Sarasota Herald-Tribune*, May 16, 1907, pages 1 & 2.

"Nine Miamians Assist Carver in Murder Case," The Associated Press, *The Miami Daily News*, May 16, 1930, page 1.

"Sebring Death Case is Nearing End with Defense Data Heard," Associated Press, *The Palm Beach Post*, May 17, 1930, page 1.

"Carver Sobs Story on Stand, Court Crowded as Accused is Telling Story," by Ted Gill, Associated Press, *Sarasota Herald-Tribune*, May 18, 1930, pages 1 and 2.

"Defense Cites Carver's Grief over Tragedy," Associated Press, *The Miami Daily News*, May 17, 1930, pages 1 and 2.

"Landlord Bolsters Carver Defense in Wife Slaying Case," *The Evening Independent*, St. Petersburg, Florida, May 17, 1930, pages 1 and 19.

"Carver Takes Stand to Tell Details of Sebring Death Case," Associated Press, *The Palm Beach Post*, May 18, 1930, page 1.

"Final Arguments in Carver Trial are Opened Today," *The Evening Independent*, St. Petersburg, Florida, May 19, 1930, pages 1 and 12.

"Carver Guilty of Wife Murder, Jurors Decree," Associated Press, *The Miami Daily News,* May 21, 1930, page 1.

"Lawyer Pleads for Acquittal in Carver Case," Associated Press, *Sarasota Herald-Tribune*, May 20, 1930, pages 1 and 2.

"Carver Convicted of Murder, Jury Recommends Mercy in Verdict," Associated Press, *The Evening-Independent*, St. Petersburg, Florida, May 21, 1930, page 1 and 14.

"Carver Case Given to Jury after Nine Days of Testimony," Associated Press, *The Palm Beach Post*, May 21, 1930, page 1.

"Carver Held Guilty of Murdering Wife; New Trial is Asked," Associated Press, *The Palm Beach Post*, May 22, 1930, page 1.

"Carver Fight for New Trial is Dragging On," Associated Press, *Sarasota Herald-Tribune*, June 6, 1930, page 1.

"Carver, Convicted Wife Slayer, Gets Life Term," Associated Press, *Sarasota Herald-Tribune*, August 19, 1930, page 1.

"Carver Applies for Writ Pending Appeal of Trial," Associated Press, *The Evening-Independent*, St. Petersburg, Florida, September 9, 1930, page 1.

"New Carver Appeal to be Heard Today," Associated Press, *The Palm Beach Post*, June 19, 1931, page 1.

"The Inside Story of Florida's Celebrated Carver Case," by L. Grady Burton, 19th Judicial Circuit Prosecuting Attorney [case prosecutor] as told to Gene Plowden, *The Master Detective*, September, 1931.

"Screams of Woman Prove Big Issue in Carver's Trial, Associated Press, *The Palm Beach Post*, March 5, 1932, page 1.

"Carver Shouts His Plea of Innocence from Witness Stand," Associated Press, *The Palm Beach Post*, March 10, 1932, page 1.

"Alleged Slayer on Trial Second Time," International News Service, *Tyrone Daily Herald*, Tyrone, Pennsylvania, March 10, 1932, page 1.

"Carver's Trial Nears its End," Associated Press, *The Evening Independent*, March 11, 1932, page 1.

"Justice – And Florida's Carver Case," by John Field, *Official Detective Stories*, February 15, 1937.

Other

Interview with William Carver descendant, June, 2014. Anonymous by request.

1912 University of Pennsylvania College Yearbook, Profile William Raymond Carver.

World War II Draft Card retrieved from Ancestry.com on June 28, 2014.

Florida's Democrat Party nomination results for 1936 retrieved from: http://uselectionatlas.org/ on October 25, 2014.

---###---

Chapter Four: Mr. Secret Agent Man

"Escort Slain, Girl Declares," Associated Press, *The Morning Herald*, Gloversville and Johnston, New York, June 14, 1930, page 1.

"Girl's Murder Confession Rouses Detective's Doubt," *Brooklyn Standard-Union*, June 16, 1930, page 16.

"Insane Man Hunted in Second Killing," *The New York Times*, June 18, 1930, page 20.

"2,000 Police in Hunt for Maniac 'Petter Slayer' Who Threatens to Murder Third Victim Tonight," *Daily Star*, Queens, New York, June 18, pages 1 and 2.

"Short, Dark, Slender Foreigner is Sought as Insane Murder," *Daily Star*, Queens, New York, June 18, 1930, pages 1 and 2.

"Moisette Freed of Complicity in Mozynski Death," *Daily Star*, June 18, 1930, pages 1 and 2.

"Third Petter Dead, Maniac Boasts, Then Recants, Averring He Spared W.R.V-8, But Will Kill Seven More," *Daily Star*, June 19, 1930, page 1.

"Killer if Mad, is Paraphrenic, Doctor Believes," *Daily Star*, June 19, 1930, pages 1 and 5.

"1,000 Police Hunt Maniac Killer, Try to Block Threatened Third Murder," by Martin Sommers, *Buffalo Courier-Express*, June 19, 1930, page 1.

"Murder Fiend's Death Threats Followed, Third Killer Message Declared Counterfeit; Police Are Mystified," *Long Island Daily-Press*, June 19, 1930, pages 1 and 2.

"2,000 Police Patrol Queens in Hunt for Slayer of Two," *The New York Times*, June 20, 1930, page 1.

"Maniac Killer to Slay Brother of Mozynski Tonight, New Threat; Third Man Shot, Lunatic is Held," *Daily Star*, June 20, 1930, pages 1 and 2.

"Shriek for Helps Brings Flushing Hunt for Slayer," *Daily Star*, June 20, 1930, pages 1 and 2.

"Escaped Inmate of Asylum Held, Guilt is Doubted," *Daily Star*, June 20, 1930, pages 1 and 2.

"Artist Sketches Insane Slayer," by Cliff Miska, *Daily Star*, June 20, 1930, page 1.

"Maniac Gunman Suspect Held in Philadelphia," *Rome Daily News*, Rome, New York, June 20, 1930, pages 1 and 9.

"Mysterious Killer Shoots Third, Brooklyn Insurance Man, Putting up His Automobile, is Shot by Maniac Gunman," by David P. Senter, International News Service, *Olean Times*, Olean, New York, June 20, 1930, page 1.

"Police Round up Fiend Suspects, Girl Aids Search to Spot Killer, Maniac Cleared," *Long Island Daily-Press*, June 21, 1930, pages 1 and 3.

"Brooklyn Man Shot in Auto as Police Hunt Queens Slayer," *The New York Times*, June 21, 1930, page 1.

"Slayer Now Warns Brother of Victim," *The New York Times*, June 21, 1930, page 6.

"Maniac Says Slayings Over, Sorry for Murders; Claims to Belong to Red Secret Society," Associated Press, *Niagara Falls Gazette*, Niagara Falls, New York, June 21, 1930, page 1.

"Mission Ended, Murder Maniac Notifies Police," by Martin Sommers via Chicago Tribune Leased Wire, *Buffalo Courier-Express*, Buffalo, New York, June 22, 1930, page 1.

"Mad Slayer Reported to be on Watch," Special Dispatch, *Democrat Chronicle*, Rochester, New York, June 22, 1930, page 1.

"Man in Woman's Clothes Sought as Insane Slayer; New Threat to Kill Made," *Daily Star*, June 23, 1930, pages 1 and 2.

"Boston Suspect in Queens Maniac Killings Escapes," *Daily Star*, June 23, 1930, pages 1 and 2.

"Girls Fail to Identify Suspect as Mad Slayer," Special to Courier-Express, *Buffalo Courier-Express*, June 25, 1930, page 2.

"3-X Has Left Boro' Says Mulrooney, 200 Policeman Ordered from Petting Lanes," *Long Island Daily-Press*, July 8, 1930, page 1.

"Blattman Held in 3X Murder," *The New York Sun*, August 23, 1930, page 3.

"3-X Slayer Marks Two More for Death, Note Reveals Revenge as Motive," International News Service, *Syracuse Journal*, October 3, 1930, page 1.

"The 3-X Murders," by Jack G. Mauder, *American Mercury Magazine*, June, 1940, pages 222-227.

"The $1,000,000 Question: Does 3X Roam New York Today?" by Carl Sifakis, *Front Page Detective*, November, 1955.

---###---

Chapter Five: Spree Killer Chester Comer

United States Census

Year: 1910; Census Place: Center, Indiana, Pennsylvania, Roll: T624_1350; Page 13A; Enumeration District: 0065: FHL microfilm: 1375363

Year: 1920; Census Place: Buford, Baxter, Arkansas, Roll: T625_53; Page 13A; Enumeration District: 3: Image: 1011

Year: 1930; Census Place: Asher, Pottawatomie, Oklahoma; Roll: 1928; Page: 4B; Enumeration District: 0001; Image: 10.0; FHL microfilm: 2341662.

Arnold Comer

"Boy Broods over Murders," Associated Press, *Kansas City Star*, December 16, 1925, page 13.

"Fourteen Year-Old Boy Admits Three Murders: Arrest Ends Weekend of Wild Adventure," Associated Press, *Spokane Daily-Chronicle*, December 16, 1925, pages 1.

"Youthful Author of Series of Violent Deeds in Arkansas is Placed in Jail," Associated Press, *The Spartanburg Herald*, Spartanburg, South Carolina, December 17, 1925, page 12.

"Boy Who Murdered Three and Shot Other Trio On Trial," Associated Press, *The Evening-Independent*, St. Petersburg, Florida, January 28, 1926, pages 1 and 7.

"Boy Who Slew Three Awaits Sanity Verdict," Associated Press, *The Palm Beach Post*, January 29, 1926, page J30.

"Boy Desperado To Spend Long Time in Prison," Associated Press, *The Sarasota Herald-Tribune*, January 30, 1926, page 6.

"Boy Who Slew Three Sentenced," Associated Press, *Joplin Globe*, January 30, 1926, page 1.

"Arkansas Boy, Triple Slayer, Gets 21 Years," United Press, *The Miami News*, January 30, 1926, page F1.

"Mother Says Comer's Brother Placed in Arkansas Asylum after Killing Four: No Sign of Derangement is Shown, Kin Says," by Virginia Nelson, *The Daily Oklahoman*, Oklahoma City, November 26, 1935, page 5.

Chester Comer

"Attorney Sought," photo caption, AP wirephoto, *The Daily Oklahoman*, Oklahoma City, November 21, 1935, page 6.

"Hunt for Attorney Proves Fruitless," *The Daily Oklahoman*, November 22, 1935, page 1.

"Hunt Pushed for Shawnee Civic Leader," *The Daily Oklahoman*, November 23, 1935, page 10.

"Relatives of Hunted Oil Worker Quizzed in Evans Probe," *The Daily Oklahoman*, November 24, 1935, page 1.

"Two More Men Are Missing: Evans Search is Fruitless; Cases Linked," *The Daily Oklahoman*, November 25, 1935, page 1.

"Hitch-Hiker is Clue in Case," *The Daily Oklahoman*, November 25, 1935, page 1.

"Wife Waits, Worries, Prays, As Posses Search in Vain," by Eugene Dodson, *The Daily Oklahoman*, November 25, 1935, page 2.

"Evans Slayer is Near Death: Wounded Man Fails to Give Officers Clue," *The Daily Oklahoman*, November 26, 1935, pages 1 and 2.

"Cool Officer Shoots after Suspect Fires," by Eugene Dodson, *The Daily Oklahoman*, November 26, 1935, pages 1 and 4.

"Clues to Mystery Sought in Mumblings of Dying Man," *The Daily Oklahoman*, November 26, 1935, page 1.

"Young Oil Man Notes Number of Auto, Brings Comer's Capture: Mystery Car is Traced on Rural Road," by Bennie Turner, *The Daily Oklahoman*, November 26, 1935, page 4.

"Manhunt for Comer Ended, Case Goes On," *The Daily Oklahoman*, November 26, 1935, page 4.

"Mother Says Comer's Brother Placed in Arkansas Asylum after Killing Four: No Sign of Derangement is Shown, Kin Says," by Virginia Nelson, *The Daily Oklahoman*, November 26, 1935, page 5.

"Clothing Comer Gave Second Wife Identified as Other Mate's; Guard Joins Search Today," *The Daily Oklahoman*, November 27, 1935, page 1 and 2.

"Pasture May Hide Fate of Missing Pair, Brother of Simpson Brings New Word to City," *The Daily Oklahoman*, November 27, 1935, page 2.

"Comer's Life Not Known to His Families, Last Two Years Spent in Tangled Travels," *The Daily Oklahoman*, November 27, 1935, page 2.

"Notes May Link Mysteries," *The Daily Oklahoman*, November 27, 1935, page 2.

"Wife Missing," wire photo caption, *The Daily Oklahoman*, November 27, 1935, page 2.

"Comer Dies with His Story Untold, Wound Fatal, Hunt for Five Left to Fate," *The Daily Oklahoman*, November 28, 1935, page 1.

"Farmers Bare Story of Life in Blanchard, Jack Armstrong Name Used, Girl Court," by Leon Hatfield, *The Daily Oklahoman*, November 28, 1935, page 1 and 2.

"Blanchard Girl, 14, Finds Her 'First Beau' Madman," by Virginia Nelson, *The Daily Oklahoman*, November 28, 1935, page 1.

"Evans Was Army Lieutenant Who Didn't Even Cuss," *The Daily Oklahoman*, November 28, 1935, page 2.

"Deep Ravines Accessible to Nearby Roads," by Bennie Turner, *The Daily Oklahoman*, November 28, 1935, page 6.

"Woman Says Comer Given Ride in Car," *The Daily Oklahoman*, November 28, 1935, page 6.

"Search to Be Pushed Today," *The Daily Oklahoman*, November 28, 1935, page 6.

"Comer's Type of Insanity is Dangerous," *The Daily Oklahoman*, November 28, 1935, page 6. [Author's Note: Relevant to his immaturity and desire for underage girls.]

"Father of Second Wife Goes Home," *The Daily Oklahoman*, November 28, 1935, page 23.

"Comer's Wife May Rest in Kansas Grave," *The Daily Oklahoman*, November 28, 1935, page 1 and 2.

"State Offers Search Cash," *The Daily Oklahoman*, November 28, 1935, page 1 and 2.

"Small Crowd Attends Rites for Slain Man," by Virginia Nelson, *The Daily Oklahoman*, November 30, 1935, page 2.

"Comer Funeral Draws Gathering of 100," photo caption, *The Daily Oklahoman*, November 30, 1935, page 2.

"Investigating Daughter's Beau," Editorial Page, Edith Johnson's Column, *The Daily Oklahoman*, November 30, 1935, page 8.

"Search Again Fails to Reveal Missing," *The Daily Oklahoman*, December 2, 1935, page 5.

"Comer's First Wife May Be Brought Here," *The Daily Oklahoman*, December 3, 1935, page 2.

"Comer Victim Hunt Turns to Oil Area," *The Daily Oklahoman*, December 4, 1935, page 2.

"Comer Probe Spurred with Word of Visit," *The Daily Oklahoman*, December 5, 1935, page 1.

"Lake Dragged for Bodies of Comer Victims," *The Daily Oklahoman*, December 8, 1935, page B5.

"Shawnee Pays High Tribute to Ray Evans," *The Daily Oklahoman*, December 13, 1935, page 10.

"Discovery of Evans Body Widens Hunt for other Comer Victims," *The Daily Oklahoman*, December 14, 1935, pages 1 and 2.

"Farmer Finds Body of Evans Near Highway," *The Daily Oklahoman*, December 14, 1935, page 2.

"New Search for Simpsons Futile," *The Daily Oklahoman*, December 14, 1935, page 4.

"Identity Test on Body Due," *The Daily Oklahoman*, December 15, 1935, page 1.

"Never a Dull Day for Him, Blanchard Officer Scores Again," *The Daily Oklahoman*, December 15, 1935, page 4A.

"Letter Seen as Important Identity Link," *The Daily Oklahoman*, December 16, 1935, page 5.

"Comer Victim is Identified," *The Daily Oklahoman*, December 17, 1935, page 5.

"Aid Sought in Simpson Hunt," *The Daily Oklahoman*, December 18, 1935, page 8.

"Reward Approved in Comer Search," *The Daily Oklahoman*, December 19, 1935, page 1.

"Simpson Found Slain near Sapulpa; Comer Victim Search at End," *The Daily Oklahoman*, December 24, 1935, page 1.

"Simpson Case Reward Paid," *The Daily Oklahoman*, December 25, 1935, page 14.

"Trail of Mad Chester Comer Victims Remains Mystery as Last Victims are Buried," *The Daily Oklahoman*, December 27, 1935, page 2.

---###---

Chapter Six: The Bizarre Tahlequah Coed Case

"Chinese Youth Shot by Co-Ed at Tahlequah," Associated Press, *Miami Daily-News Record*, Miami, Oklahoma, March 28, 1935, pages 1 and 2.

"Sensational Shooting at Tahlequah, Chinese Student Badly Wounded," Associated Press, *The Ada Evening-News*, Ada, Oklahoma, March 28, 1935, pages 1 and 4.

"Co-Ed Who Shot Student Released on Bail," Associated Press, *The Ada Evening-News*, March 29, 1935, page 1.

"Co-ed Who Shot Young Chinese Student Released on Bond," Associated Press, *Daily Ardmoreite*, Ardmore, Oklahoma, March 29, 1935, page 1.

"Co-Ed Freed Under $2,500 Bond in Tahlequah Campus Shooting; Wounded Chinese Forgives Her, Associated Press, *Miami Daily-News Record*, Miami, Oklahoma, March 29, 1935, pages 1 and 2.

"Co-Ed Pursues Chinese Student and Shoots Him," Associated Press, *Joplin Globe*, Joplin, Missouri, March 29, 1935, page 1.

"Chinese Official Probes Affair," Associated Press, *Daily Ardmoreite*, March 31, 1935, page 1.

"Wounded Chinese Student Improves," Associated Press, *The Ada Evening-News*, March 30, 1935, page 1.

"Chinese Student Wounded by Co-Ed on College Campus," *Tahlequah Citizen*, Tahlequah, Oklahoma, April 4, 1935, page 1 and 2.

"Tahlequah Girl Threatened Again," Associated Press, *The Ada Evening-News*, April 7, 1935, page 2.

"Co-ed's Hearing May be Postponed," Associated Press, *Daily Ardmoreite*, April 25, 1935, page 10.

"Co-ed's Trial Put off Another Time," Associated Press, *The Ada Evening-News*, April 29, 1935, page 1.

"Two Cases are Set for Hearing Next Week: June Term," *Tahlequah Citizen*, May 23, 1935, page 1.

"Campus Shooting Takes Queer Turn," Associated Press, *Joplin Globe*, May 23, 1935, page 1.

"Publicity Stunt Behind Shooting, Officers Report," Associated Press, *Jefferson City Post-Tribune*, Jefferson City, Missouri, May 23, 1935, page 5.

"Delay Prelim of Tahlequah Shooting Case," Associated Press, *The Ada Evening-News*, May 29, 1935, page 2.

"'I Believe Anyone Would Have Done As I Did…' Declaration Made by Lois Thompson Today," *Tahlequah Citizen*, June 13, 1935 pages 1 and 6.

"Thompson Trial Gets Underway," Associated Press, *The Ada Evening-News*, June 17, 1935, page 4.

"Testimony Begins in Trial for Co-ed for Campus Shooting at Tahlequah, Shaw Testifies He Had No Part in Notes Plot," Associated Press, *Miami News-Record*, Miami, Oklahoma, June 17, 1935, page 6.

"Co-ed Says She Shot Chinese After He Threatened to Kill Her," *Joplin Globe*, June 18, 1935, page 7.

"Coed Denies Sister Lelia Wrote Notes," by John Jameson, Associated Press, *The Ada Evening-News*, June 18, 1935, page 1 and 4.

"Cases of Co-ed into Hands of Jury at Noon," by John Jameson, Associated Press, *The Ada Evening-News*, June 19, 1935, page 1.

"Trial of Co-ed Nearing Jury," Associated Press, *San Antonio Express*, San Antonio, Texas, June 19, 1935, page 5.

"Witness Hits Investigators During Co-ed Trial," Associated Press, *Galveston Daily-News*, Galveston, Texas, June 19, 1935, pages 1 and 2.

"Co-Ed Found Guilty by Jury Sentenced 30 Days in County Jail: Deliberate Four Hours," *Tahlequah Citizen*, June 20, 1935, pages 1 and 2.

"Lois Thompson Found Guilty, Given 30 Days," Associated Press, *The Ada Weekly News*, June 20, 1935, page 7.

"Oklahoma Coed Given Jail Term," Associated Press, *Joplin Globe*, June 20, 1935, page 1.

"Co-ed in Jail on 30-Day Sentence," Associated Press, *The Ada Evening-News*, June 24, 1935, page 2.

"So She Went Out and Shot the Chinese Student," by American Weekly Inc., *San Antonio Light*, August 18, 1935, page 73.

"Crooks Terrorized the Wrong Girl– She Shot the Wrong Man," *The Philadelphia Inquirer*, month & day unpublished, 1935.

---###---

Chapter Seven: The Wife Who Lost Her Head

"Sheriff's Clerk Identifies Torso as that of Wife," *Corona Daily Independent*, Corona, California, January 23, 1946, page 1

"Sheriff Suspect in Wife's Slaying," Associated Press, *Bakersfield Californian*, Bakersfield, California, January 23, 1946, page 1.

"Eggers' Identifies Body as Wife's," *Long Beach Independent*, Long Beach, California, January 24, 1946, pages 1 and 4.

"Eggers' Wife Head Sought," *Oakland Tribune*, Oakland, California, January 28, 1946, page 1.

"Check Story told by LA Wife Slayer," *Berkeley Daily Gazette*, Berkeley, California, January 28, 1946, page 1.

"Eggers Tells Killing Story," *San Mateo Times*, San Mateo, California, January 28, 1946, page 2.

"Wife Butcher Called Henpecked, Tells of Quarrel," *Corona Daily Independent*, January 29, 1946, page 2.

"Weapons Found in Headless Murder," *Port Arthur News*, Port Arthur, Texas, February 1, 1946, page 5.

"Crime," *Oakland Tribune*, February 21, 1946, page 3.

"Torso Slaying Trial Opened in Los Angeles," United Press, *Berkeley Daily Gazette*, May 6, 1946, page 1.

"Sadistic Wife Slayer Still Refused to Disclose Where He Hid Head and Arms," International News Service, *Hammond Times*, Hammond, Indiana, May 9, 1946, page 12.

"Home Sanctity Eggers' Defense," *Los Angeles Times*, May 11, 1946, page A8.

"Sheriffs Describe Hunt for Mrs. Eggers Head," *Los Angeles Times*, May 14, 1946, page 6.

"Eggers Says Headless Body Not His Wife's," *Los Angeles Times*, May 22, 1946, page 2.

"Clear Marine in Torso Case," United Press, *Berkeley Daily Gazette*, May 24, 1946, page 2.

"Eggers Case Arguments Underway," *Los Angeles Times*, May 25, 1946, page 4.

"Jury Studies Eggers' Fate," Associated Press, *Reno Evening Gazette*, Reno, Nevada, May 30, 1946, page 5.

"Los Angeles Briefs, Eggers' Death Asked," *Los Angeles Times*, May 28, page A2.

"Eggers Found Guilty of Murdering His Wife," *Los Angeles Times*, May 31, 1946, page A1.

"Eggers Quits Sheriff's Post," *Los Angeles Times*, June 4, 1946, page A2.

"Eggers Says He is Sane," *Los Angeles Times*, June 20, 1946, page A3.

"Jury Deliberates if Eggers Sane," *Los Angeles Times*, June 28, 1946, page A6.

"Death Sentence Given Eggers in Wife Slaying," *Los Angeles Times*, July 11, 1946, page A1.

"Reprieve Stays Slayer's March into Gas Chamber," Associated Press, *Long Beach Press-Telegram*, February 6, 1948 page A2.

"Set for Wife Slayer," *Oakland Tribune*, October 8, 1948, page 42.

"Wife Murderer Loses Supreme Court Plea," *Los Angeles Times*, October 14, 1948.

"Eggers, Slayer of Wife, Executed," Associated Press, *Long Beach Post-Telegram*, October 15, 1948, page 1.

"Human Jawbone Found in Canyon Miles from Skull," *Los Angeles Times*, December 23, 1948, page A3.

"Murderer Wills $258 to Salvation Army," *Daily Independent-Journal*, San Rafael, California, March 4, 1950, page 9.

"Skull Reported Not That of Mrs. Eggers," *Los Angeles Times*, September 14, 1954, page 2.

"The Brunette Lost Her Head," by Edward D. Sullivan, *Master Detective*, November, 1958.

---###---

Chapter Eight: The York Family Massacre

"Doctor is Charged with Four Murders," *The Abilene Reporter-News*, Abilene, Texas, May 26, 1947, page 1.

"Doctor Says He Doesn't Remember," *The San Antonio Light*, May 26, 1947, pages 1 and 7.

"4 of Family Killed, Doctor Held: Willard York Family Shot Near Comal County Ranch; Dr. Ross Charged," *San Antonio Express*, May 26, 1947, pages 1 and 3.

"Hearing of Dr. Ross Postponed," *The San Antonio Light*, May 27, 1947, pages 1 and 5.

"Dr. L.I. Ross Held Without Bond, York's Brokerage Firm Faced Loss of its Dealer License," *San Antonio Express*, May 27, 1947, pages 1 and 2.

"York Child Reported Better," *The San Antonio Light*, May 28, 1947, page 1.

"Ross Hearing Awaits Discovery of Ann York," *San Antonio Express*, June 4, 1947, page 2.

"Court Awaits Wounded Girl," *The San Antonio Light*, June 4, 1947, page 1.

"Trial for Ross, Charged with Slaying of Four, Set July 28," Associated Press, *Abilene Reporter*, July 10, 1947, page 9.

"Crowd on Hand as Ross Trial Opens," Associated Press, *Big Spring Daily Herald*, Big Spring, Texas, July 28, 1947, page 1.

"Dr. Ross Trial to be Resumed on September 9," *Brownsville Herald*, Brownsville, Texas, July 29, 1947, page 9.

"Doctor Goes on Trial for Slaying Four," Associated Press, *The Laredo Times*, Laredo, Texas, September 9, 1947, page 1.

"Judge Orders Change of Venue in Ross Trial," Associated Press, *The Laredo Times*, September 12, 1947, page 5.

"Lone Survivor Tells of Ambush Slaying of Family," Associated Press, *The Laredo Times*, October 17, 1947, page 1.

"Ross Trial is Near End," Associated Press, *The Laredo Times*, October 21, 1947, page 1.

"Jury Decrees Death Penalty for Dr. Ross," Associated Press, *Big Spring Daily Herald*, October 24, 1947, page 1.

"Dr. Lloyd Ross Denied New Trial," Associated Press, *Denton Record-Chronicle*, Denton, Texas, December 16, page 6.

"Ross Case to be Taken to Criminal Appeals Court," United Press, *Mexia Weekly Herald*, Mexia, Texas, December 18, 1947, page 3.

"Dr. Ross is Ordered Transferred to Wharton Jail for Safekeeping," *San Antonio Express*, January 9, 1948, page 1.

"Lawyer Flays Ross Jury: No Evidence of Sanity Given, Claim," *The San Antonio Light*, June 9, 1948, pages 1 and 2.

"Court Scans Dr. Ross Briefs," *The San Antonio Light*, June 10, 1948, page 3.

"Dr. Ross Must Die, High Court Rules," Associated Press, *The Abilene Reporter-News*, November 3, 1948, page 1.

"Dr. Ross Asks for Rehearing," *San Antonio Express*, December 9, 1948, page 1.

"Dr. Ross, Slayer of Four, Must Die, High Court Says," Associated Press, *The Brownsville Herald*, May 11, 1949, pages 1 and 2.

"He Doesn't Care, Says Sheriff," by William Barnard, Associated Press, *The Brownsville Herald*, May 11, 1949, page 1.

"Court Rules Ross Must Die," *The San Antonio Light*, May 11, 1949, page 1.

"Dr. Ross Insanity Trial Slated," *The San Antonio Light*, June 12, 1949, page 1.

"9 Listed in Ross Defense," *The San Antonio Light*, June 13, 1949, page 2.

"Ross Defense Loses Round, Change of Venue Denied," *The San Antonio Light*, June 14, 1949, page 1.

"New Venue Plea for Ross Looms," *The San Antonio Light*, June 15, 1949, pages 1 and 4.

"Killer Taken to Asylum, Held Insane," Associated Press, *The San Antonio Light*, June 17, 1949, pages 1 and 2.

"Testimony in Ross Suit Set to Resume," *The San Antonio Light*, July 12, 1949, Section C, page 23.

"Ross, York Girls' Affection Related," *The San Antonio Light*, July 14, 1949, page 1.

"$39,375 to York Girl," *The San Antonio Light*, July 21, 1949, page 6.

"Lone Survivor of Mass Slaying Gets $39,375," Associated Press, *The Evening Independent*, Massillon, Ohio, July 21, 1949, page 14.

"Murder on the Lord's Day," by Burton Leeds, *True Detective*, January, 1951.

"Surgeon Facing Ironic Situation in Murder Case," Associated Press, *Del Rio News-Herald*, Del Rio, Texas, July 4, 1957, page 2.

"Suit in 4 Deaths Ended," *San Antonio Light*, May 9, 1958, page 1.

Take a Deep Breath: Insight into a Medical Practice, by Elmer E. Cooper, MD, Nortex Press, 1992, pages 1-6.

When Darkness Falls: Tales of San Antonio Ghosts and Hauntings, by Docia Schultz Williams, Taylor Trade Publishing, 1997, pages 265-274.

---###---

Chapter Nine: Blind Man's Bluff

"Blind Man Hitchhiking on Way East," Associated Press, *Walla Walla Union-Bulletin,* Walla Walla, Washington, September 17, 1948, page 17.

"Hard-Ship End for Blind Youth Hitch-Hiking Across Country for Operation On His Eyes," United Press, *Greenville Delta Democrat-Times,* Greenville, Mississippi, September 19, 1948, page 9.

"Blind Man Hitch-Hikes across Nation, Seeks Free Operation to Regain Sight," United Press, *Lowell Sun,* Lowell, Massachusetts, September 20, 1948, page 1.

"Jerk of Head Ends Moment of Sight for Oregon Blind Man," by David C. Whitney, United Press, *Lubbock Morning Avalanche,* Lubbock, Texas, December 14, 1948, page 3.

"Lecture Planned on Seeing Eye Dogs," *Eugene Register-Guard,* Eugene, Oregon, October 18, 1949, page 10.

"Bomb Blast Rocks Portland Store," Associated Press, *Walla Walla Union-Bulletin,* April 16, 1955, page 1.

"Police Close Store after Payoff Fails," Associated Press, *Walla Walla Union-Bulletin,* April 17, 1955, page 1.

"Bombed Portland Store Re-Opened under Police Guard," Associated Press, *Walla Walla Union-Bulletin,* April 18, 1955, page 1.

"Portland Lawyer is Killed by Auto Bomb," Associated Press, *The Daily Chronicle,* Centralia, Washington, April 22, 1955, page 1.

"Woman Calm When Facing Her Accuser," Associated Press, *The Daily Chronicle,* April 25, 1955, page 1.

"Theatre Has Bomb Threat," Associated Press, *The Daily Chronicle,* May 1, 1955, page 1.

"Boy Chemist Arrested for Bomb Threat," Associated Press, *Walla Walla Union-Bulletin*, June 1, 1955, page 13.

"Spokane Inn Gets Threat," Associated Press, *The Daily Chronicle*, May 25, 1955, page 1.

"Policeman to Cheer Blind Man's Family," Associated Press, *Eugene Register- Guard*, December 25, 1955, page 2.

"Bomb Suspect to Face Exams," United Press, *Spokane Daily Chronicle*, Spokane, Washington, January 4, 1956, page 36.

"Defendant's Plea Surprises Court and His Attorney," Associated Press, *Eugene Register-Guard*, January 18, 1956, page 33.

"Blind Man's Bluff," by Don Whitcomb, *Front Page Detective*, April, 1956.

"Peddicord to Serve 20 Years," *The Oregonian*, April 21, 1956, page 1.

"A Bigger Bomb Tomorrow," by Stuart Whitehouse, *Master Detective*, May, 1956.

"Peddicord Tries Suicide," Associated Press, *Eugene Register-Guard*, May 15, 1956, page 5.

"Store Bomber Changes Tune," Associated Press, *Walla Walla Union-Bulletin*, May 16, 1956, page 15.

"Woman Cleared of Extortion Plot," Associated Press, *Eugene Register-Guard*, May 23, 1956, page 1.

"Oregon News Wire: Woman Freed on Bail," Associated Press, *Walla Walla Union-Bulletin*, July 23, 1956, page 15.

"Mrs. Peddicord Indicted on Mail Fraud Charges," Associated Press, *Eugene Register-Guard*, October 10, 1956, page 7.

"Reward Dispute Still Unsettled," Associated Press, *Eugene Register-Guard*, March 5, 1958, page 22.

"6 Guilty of Mail Fraud," Associated Press, *San Mateo Times*, San Mateo, California, June 2, 1958, page 19.

"Peddicord Gets Five Year Term," United Press International, *The Bend Bulletin*, Bend, Oregon, August 13, 1958.

"Dorothy May McCourtney Brambora," Findagrave.com, Retrieved October 11, 2014.

"William Clarence Peddicord," Findagrave.com, Retrieved October 11, 2014.

Peddicord's parole date – reply to email inquiry to Offender Records Information office, Oregon Department of Corrections, November 6, 2014.

---###---

Chapter Ten: The Orphan Maker of Route 66

1961

"Parents of 4 Murdered on Route 66," Associated Press, *Tucson Daily Citizen*, June 9, 1961, page 1.

"Tourist Couple Slain on U.S. 66, Sons Find Bodies near Seligman," *Arizona Daily Sun*, June 9, 1961, page 1.

"Mom, Dad of 4 Murdered near Seligman, Couple Shot as Sons Slept in Tent Nearby" *Prescott Evening-Courier*, June 9, 1961, page 1.

"Hot Lead Spur Hunt for Arizona Slayers of Spencer Couple," *The Daily Oklahoman*, June 10, 1961, pages 1 and 2.

"Double Murder Shocks Friends," by Bob Hayes, *The Daily Oklahoman*, June 10, 1961, pages 1 and 2.

"Parents Slain in Auto while Four Sons Sleep, Killings Discovered Outside Seligman," *Arizona Republic*, June 10, 1961, pages 1 and 16.

"Seven Shots Fired to Kill Two in Car," *Arizona Republic*, June 11, 1961, pages 1 and 12.

"Roadside Camping Can be Dangerous," Associated Press, *Arizona Republic*, June 11, 1961, page 12.

"Officers Link Pair to Five Murders," Associated Press, *Arizona Republic*, June 11, 1961, page 12.

"Traffic Not Only Danger on Busy Route 66," Associated Press, *Miami Daily News-Record*, Miami, Oklahoma, June 11, 1961, pages 1 and 3.

"Arizona Police Study Autopsy for Death Clue," *The Daily Oklahoman*, June 11, 1961, page 1.

"Sons of Slain County Couple on Way Home," *The Daily Oklahoman*, June 11, 1961, page 1.

"Cyclist Caught in Tucumcari Cleared in Couple's Murders," United Press International, *Scottsdale Daily Progress*, June 12, 1961, page 3.

"Couple's Murders Still a Mystery, US 66 Search Turns up Nothing," *Prescott Evening-Courier*, June 12, 1961, page 1.

"Search for Double Slayer(s) Intensified; Boys Can't Realize Parents Really Dead," *Prescott Evening-Courier*, June 12, 1961, page 8.

"Two AWOL Soldiers Leave Trail of Robbery, Death across Nation," *Prescott Evening-Courier*, June 12, 1961, page 8.

"Boys Home after Tragic Trip Ends," by Katherine Hatch, *The Daily Oklahoman*, June 12, 1961, page 1.

"Cigarettes, Gun Murder Clues," *The Daily Oklahoman*, June 12, 1961, pages 1 and 2.

"Officers Hold Motorcyclist for Slayings," Associated Press, *Ada Evening News*, June 12, 1961, page 3.

"Youths Kill Seven in Rob-Run Attacks, Death Trail from Colorado to Florida," United Press International, *Tucson Daily Citizen*, June 12, 1961, page 1.

"Leads Fizzle Out in Pair's Death," Associated Press, *The Lawton Constitution*, Lawton, Oklahoma, June 12, 1961, page 1.

"Tuesday Rites Set for Slain Couple," United Press International, *The Lawton Constitution*, June 12, 1961, page 11.

"Bloody Trail of 7 Murders Traced by 2 AWOL Soldiers," United Press International, *The Lawton Constitution*, June 12, 1961, page 11.

"Sheriff Seeking New Leads in Seligman Murders," United Press International, *Yuma Daily Sun*, June 12, 1961, page 1.

"Double Slaying Leads Pour In, None Pan Out," *The Daily Oklahoman*, June 13, 1961, page 2.

"Murder Probe Hits Dead End; Leads Checked," *Prescott Evening-Courier*, June 14, 1961, page 1.

"Murdered Couple Buried at Westville," by Mrs. W.F. Langley, *Stilwell Democrat Journal*, Stilwell, Oklahoma, June 15, 1961, page 1.

"Kin Looking after Four Welch Boys," *The Daily Oklahoman*, June 16, 1961, page 16.

"Youths Killed Together, 'So We Expect to Die Together,'" by Preston McGraw, *The Daily Oklahoman*, June 16, 1961, page 6.

"Kidnapping Arrest May be Break in Seligman Probe," *Prescott Evening-Courier*, June 23, 1961, page 1.

"Gilbert Man is Being Quizzed in Seligman Murders," United Press International, *Scottsdale Daily Progress*, June 23, 1961, page 1.

"Police Seek Gilbert Man in Kidnapping," Associated Press, *Tucson Daily Citizen*, June 23, 1961, page 12.

"Californian Sought in Kidnapping," Associated Press, *Pasadena Star-News*, June 24, 1961, page 1.

"Police Issue Bulletin for Wanted Man," Associated Press, *Arizona Daily Sun*, June 24, 1961, page 1.

"23-Year-Old Kidnapper Labeled Arizona's Most Wanted Fugitive," *Arizona Republic*, June 24, 1961, page 22.

"Seligman, Ariz. Murder Suspects Held in Tulsa," United Press International, *Yuma Daily Sun*, June 29, 1961, page 12.

"Fugitive's Attempt at Suicide Fails, Cell Mate Prevents 3rd and 4th Tries by Man Held Here," *The Fort Scott Tribune*, June 30, 1961, page 1.

"Suspect in Seligman Murder Starts Hunger Strike after Suicide Foiled," *Prescott Evening Courier*, June 30, 1961, page 1.

"All the Leads—Except One—In Murder Mystery Here Dead," *Prescott Evening Courier*, June 30, 1961, page 5.

"Fresno Officers Claim Solving of Murder Case," United Press International, *Scottsdale Daily Progress*, June 30, 1961, page 2.

"Bentley's Wife and Mother Say He Did Not Kill Couple," *The Fort Scott Tribune*, July 1, 1961, page 1.

"Utah Kidnap-Killer Hunted Over Far West, Link Seen to US 66 Murder," United Press International, *Arizona Republic*, July 6, 1961, pages 1 and 3.

"2 Gilbert Men Face California Murder Trial," by Jack Karie, *Arizona Republic*, July 7, 1961, page 5.

"Search Continues for Missing Teen-Ager Kidnapped during Tragic Vacation," *Prescott Evening-Courier*, July 10, 1961, page 1.

"Aragon Not Linked with Welch Deaths," *Prescott Evening-Courier*, July 10, 1961, page 1.

"Survivor of Kidnap-Killing Says Goodbye to Hospital, Utah Vacation Nightmare," by Don Beck, *The Deseret News and Telegram*, Salt Lake City, Utah, July 26, 1961, page 18A.

"Wallet of Slain Man Found East of Seligman," United Press International, *Yuma Daily Sun*, August 23, 1961, page 3.

"Arizona Sheriff Says Killer of Vacationing State Pair Identified – Jail Inmates Tip on Slayer Breaks Case," *The Daily Oklahoman*, June 10, 1962, pages 1 and 2.

"Arizona Slaying Mystery Solved?" by Jim Kendall, *The Daily Oklahoman*, June 11, 1962, pages 1 and 2.

"Condemned Killer May Face State Murder Count," Associated Press, *Tucson Daily Citizen*, June 11, 1962, page 22.

"Bentley Charged with Twin Killing," United Press International, *Scottsdale Daily Progress*, June 12, 1962, page 3.

"The Highway of Human Wolves," by Paul McClung, *Front Page Detective*, October, 1962.

"Family Murder on Route 66," by D.L. Champion, *True Detective*, November, 1962.

"Governor Mulls Fate of Convicted Murderer, Associated Press, *Pasadena Star-News*, Pasadena, California, January 17, 1963, page 5.

"Clemency for Murderer Considered," Associated Press, *Eureka Humboldt Times*, Humboldt, California, January 17, 1963, page 5.

"No Reprieve for Killers, Brown Says," United Press International, *Eureka Humboldt Standard*, January 18, 1963, page 15.

"Slayer of Fresno Store Clerk Dies in Gas Chamber," United Press International, *The Bakersfield Californian*, January 23, 1963, page 2.

"Modesto Slayer Executed," Associated Press, *Pasadena Star-News*, January 23, 1963, page 1.

About the Author

Jason Lucky Morrow is a Gulf War veteran and award winning newspaper reporter who now researches and writes vintage true crime stories for his blog, HistoricalCrimeDetective.com. His focus is on obscure but significant criminal cases that are nearly forgotten and have not been adequately explored in decades. Mr. Morrow has lived and worked in Nebraska, Texas, Alabama, Romania, and Oklahoma where he currently resides in the Tulsa area with his wife, Alina.

Visit HistoricalCrimeDetective.com for more vintage true crime stories and follow along for new story updates on our Facebook page.